Workbook/Study Guide

for use with

Managerial Accounting

Eleventh Edition

Ray H. Garrison
Professor Emeritus, Brigham Young University

Eric W. Noreen
Professor Emeritus, University of Washington

Peter C. Brewer
Miami University

 McGraw-Hill Irwin

Boston   Burr Ridge, IL   Dubuque, IA   Madison, WI   New York   San Francisco   St. Louis
Bangkok   Bogotá   Caracas   Kuala Lumpur   Lisbon   London   Madrid   Mexico City
Milan   Montreal   New Delhi   Santiago   Seoul   Singapore   Sydney   Taipei   Toronto

Workbook/Study Guide for use with
MANAGERIAL ACCOUNTING
Ray H. Garrison, Eric W. Noreen, Peter C. Brewer

Published by McGraw-Hill/Irwin, an imprint of The McGraw-Hill Companies, Inc., 1221 Avenue of the Americas, New York, NY 10020. Copyright © 2006, 2003, 2000, 1997, 1994, 1991, 1988, 1985, 1982, 1979, 1976 by The McGraw-Hill Companies, Inc. All rights reserved.

1 2 3 4 5 6 7 8 9 0 QPD/QPD 0 9 8 7 6 5 4

ISBN 0-07-298613-1

www.mhhe.com

The McGraw-Hill Companies

Preface

To The Student

This study guide supplements the eleventh edition of *Managerial Accounting* by Ray Garrison, Eric Noreen, and Peter Brewer. Each chapter of the study guide contains three major sections:

1. The *Chapter Study Suggestions* help you study more efficiently.
2. *Chapter Highlights* summarize in outline form the essential points in a chapter.
3. *Review and Self Test* questions and exercises test your knowledge of the material in the chapter. Solutions are provided. *Caution:* If you want to score well on exams, you *must* work out each solution on your own and *then* check to see whether your solution is correct by comparing it to the solution in the study guide. You cannot learn the material by simply reading the solution provided in the study guide. This does not work.

This study guide can be used as an integral part of the process of learning the material in a chapter. When used for this purpose, we recommend that you follow the steps below:

1. Read the *Chapter Study Suggestions* in this study guide.
2. Read the textbook chapter.
3. Read the outline in the *Chapter Highlights* section of the study guide. If you run across anything in the outline you don't understand, refer back to the textbook for a more detailed discussion.
4. Work the questions and exercises in the study guide and then compare your answers to those given in the study guide. If you find something you don't understand, refer to the textbook for help.
5. Work the homework problems assigned by your instructor.

Alternatively, the study guide can also be used as a very effective way to study for exams. Before reading the chapter in your textbook, read the *Chapter Study Suggestions* in this study guide. Then lay the study guide aside until it is time to prepare for an exam. The *Chapter Highlights* section of the study guide can then be used to review the essential material covered in the chapter. The *Review and Self Test* questions and exercises are excellent practice for exams. The questions and exercises in the study guide are particularly effective used in this way since they are likely to be similar to the questions and exercises your instructor will ask on an exam.

Remember, the study guide is not a substitute for the textbook. Rather, its purpose is to *supplement* the textbook by helping you to learn the material.

Ray H. Garrison
Eric W. Noreen
Peter C. Brewer

Contents

Chapter 1

Managerial Accounting and the Business Environment

Chapter Study Suggestions

This chapter describes the work that managers do and the kinds of information they need in order to do this work effectively. The chapter also describes important aspects of the contemporary business environment. The chapter is unusual in that there is no number-crunching. However, many new terms and concepts must be learned.

CHAPTER HIGHLIGHTS

A.   An organization is a group of people united for a common purpose. Organizations are run by managers who carry out three major activities: planning, directing and motivating, and controlling. All three of these activities involve decision-making.

   1.   *Planning* involves identifying alternatives and selecting the alternative that best furthers the organization's objectives.

   2.   *Directing and motivating* involves mobilizing people to carry out plans and overseeing day-to-day activities.

   3.   *Controlling* involves obtaining feedback to ensure that all parts of the organization are following the plan.

B.   Financial and managerial accounting differ in a number of ways. In contrast to financial accounting, managerial accounting:

   1.   Focuses on providing data for internal uses.

   2.   Places more emphasis on the future.

   3.   Emphasizes relevance and flexibility rather than precision.

   4.   Emphasizes the segments of an organization, rather than just looking at the organization as a whole.

   5.   Is not governed by Generally Acceptable Accounting Practices.

   6.   Is not mandatory.

C.   In many industries, a company that does not continually improve will find itself quickly overtaken by competitors. The text discusses four major approaches to improvement—Just-In-Time (JIT), Total Quality Management (TQM), Process Reengineering, and the Theory of Constraints (TOC). These approaches can be combined.

D.   The Just-In-Time (JIT) approach is based on the insight that reducing inventories—particularly work in process inventories—can be the key to improving operations. Companies maintain work in process inventories to protect against disruptions in the production process and as a consequence of using large batch sizes. However, work in process inventories create a number of problems:

   1.   Work in process inventories tie up funds and take up space.

   2.   Work in process inventories increase the *throughput time*, which is the amount of time required

to make a product. If there is an average of two weeks of work in process inventories, then it takes two weeks longer to complete a unit than if there were no work in process inventories. Long throughput time makes it difficult to respond quickly to customers and can be a major competitive disadvantage.

   3.   When work in process inventories are large, partially completed products are stored for long periods of time before being passed to the next workstation. Therefore, defects introduced at a workstation may not be noticed for quite some time. If a machine is out of calibration or incorrect procedures are being followed, many defective units will be produced before the problem is discovered. And when the defects are finally discovered, it may be very difficult to track down the source of the problem.

   4.   Because of long throughput time, units may be obsolete or out of fashion by the time they are finally completed.

   5.   Large work in process inventories encourage sloppy procedures and mask inefficiencies and problems in the production process. When inventories are reduced, these problems are uncovered and can be identified and dealt with.

E.   *Just-In-Time (JIT)* seeks improvement by reducing inventories to the absolute minimum levels possible. "Just in time" means that raw materials are received just in time to go into production, subassemblies are completed just in time to be assembled into products, and products are completed just in time to be shipped to customers.

F.   A successful JIT system involves some key elements.

   1.   Suppliers must be able to deliver defect-free raw materials and parts in the right quantities at the right time.

   2.   In the JIT approach, a company often sets up a *manufacturing cell* for each product in which all the machines needed to make the product are brought together in one location. This is in contrast to a conventional, "functional plant layout" in which similar machines are grouped together in one location. When a functional plant layout is used, products must be moved long distances between work centers.

   3.   A JIT company must reduce the setup time that is required between batches. A *batch* is consists of a number of units of the same product that are produced together. *Setups* consist of the activities that must be performed whenever production is switched

from making one type of unit to another. For example, if a plastic toy is being made in several different colors, each time the color changes from one batch to another, the vats containing the colored plastic must be emptied and thoroughly cleaned.

4. A JIT company should strive for zero defects. If any units in an order are defective, the whole production process would have to be restarted in order to replace the defective units. This would make it impossible to deliver the order on time.

G. Many benefits result from a JIT system. The most important are:

1. Working capital is increased by recovering funds that were tied up in inventories.

2. Usable space is increased. Areas previously used to store inventories are made available for other, more productive uses.

3. Throughput time is reduced, resulting in greater potential output and quicker response to customer needs.

4. Defect rates are reduced, resulting in less waste and greater customer satisfaction.

H. *Total Quality Management (TQM)* is an approach to continuous improvement that focuses on the customer and that involves systematic problem-solving using teams of front-line workers. A variety of specific tools are available in TQM including benchmarking.

1. *Benchmarking* involves studying how a successful "world-class" company runs a particular operation. For example, a company trying to improve its customer service might study how Disney trains its employees.

2. Perhaps the most important characteristics of TQM are that it empowers front-line workers to solve problems and it focuses attention on solving problems rather than on finger-pointing.

I. *Process Reengineering* is a more radical approach to improvement than TQM. It involves completely redesigning business processes and it is often implemented by outside consultants.

1. In Process Reengineering, all of the steps in a business process are displayed as a flowchart. Ordinarily, many of the steps are unnecessary and are called *non-value-added activities*.

2. The process is then completely redesigned, eliminating non-value-added activities.

3. Process Reengineering should result in a streamlined process that uses fewer resources, takes less time, and generates fewer errors.

4. However, some managers fall into a trap. If Process Reengineering results in laying off workers who are no longer needed, morale will suffer and employees will resist further Process Reengineering efforts.

J. The *Theory of Constraints (TOC)* is based on the idea that every organization has at least one constraint that prevents it from obtaining more of its objective. For example, a machine that is slower than other machines on an assembly line will prevent the company from increasing its rate of output. To improve (in other words, increase its rate of output), the company must focus its improvement efforts on the constraint. Improvement efforts will be largely wasted if focused on machines that are not constraints.

K. *Organizational Structure.*

1. Almost all organizations are decentralized to some degree. *Decentralization* involves delegating decision-making authority to lower levels in the organization.

2. An *organization chart* shows the levels of responsibility and formal channels of communication in an organization. It shows who reports to whom in the organization. Exhibit 1-3 in the text provides an example of an organization chart.

3. A manager may occupy either a line position or a staff position.

    a. *Line positions* are directly related to achieving the basic objectives of the organization.

    b. *Staff positions* provide service, assistance, and specialized support to the line positions. They do not have direct authority over line positions. Accounting is a staff position.

4. The *controller* is the manager of the accounting department.

5. The *Chief Financial Officer (CFO)* is the member of the top management team who is responsible for providing timely and relevant data to support planning and control activities and for preparing financial statements for external users.

L.   Ethics plays a vital role in an advanced market economy.

   1.   If people were generally dishonest, it would become more difficult for companies to raise investment funds, the quality of goods and services would decline, fewer goods and services would be available for sale, and prices would be higher.

   2.   The Institute of Management Accountants has issued Standards of Ethical Conduct for Practitioners of Management Accounting and Financial Management. This is a useful, practical guide for general managers as well as management accountants. The Standards for Ethical Conduct are reproduced in Exhibit 1-5 in the text.

REVIEW AND SELF-TEST
Questions and Exercises

True or False

Enter a T or an F in the blank to indicate whether the statement is true or false.

____ 1. Managerial accounting is as concerned with providing information to stockholders as it is with providing information to managers.

____ 2. When carrying out their control function, managers obtain feedback to ensure that each part of the organization is following the plan.

____ 3. When carrying out their planning function, managers mobilize the organization's resources and oversee day-to-day operations.

____ 4. Managerial accounting focuses more on the segments of an organization than on the organization as a whole.

____ 5. Managerial accounting need not follow Generally Accepted Accounting Principles.

____ 6. An objective of a JIT system is to complete products just in time to ship to customers.

____ 7. The maintenance of large work in process inventories helps reduce the number of defective units that are produced.

____ 8. For JIT to operate successfully, all similar pieces of equipment (such as lathes or drill presses) must be grouped together.

____ 9. Total Quality Management involves a focus on serving the customer and systematic problem-solving using teams made up of front-line workers.

____ 10. Process Reengineering is less likely to result in employee resistance than Total Quality Management.

____ 11. Non-value-added activities are the constraints in the system.

____ 12. Efforts that are designed to improve the rate of output of a workstation should generally be focused on the constraint.

Multiple Choice

Choose the best answer or response by placing the identifying letter in the space provided.

____ 1. Staff positions: a) are not shown on the organization chart; b) are superior in authority to line positions; c) are subordinate in authority to line positions; d) none of these.

____ 2. The controller: a) occupies a staff position; b) occupies a line position; c) has little influence in the decision-making process; d) none of these.

____ 3. Managerial accounting: a) is governed by Generally Accepted Accounting Principles; b) places more emphasis on precision of data than does financial accounting; c) is not mandatory; d) is geared primarily to the past rather than to the future.

____ 4. Financial and managerial accounting are similar in that: a) both emphasize reporting the performance of the entire organization rather than segments of the organization; b) both rely on the same accounting database; c) both focus on providing data for internal uses; d) none of these.

____ 5. In a decentralized organization, decisions are made: a) only by top management; b) only by managers occupying staff positions; c) at the lowest managerial level possible in the organization; d) none of these.

____ 6. Under JIT: a) the plant floor is laid out in a functional format with similar machines grouped together; b) focused factories are used; c) the plant floor is laid out in a single flow line through which all products pass; d) work in process inventories are maximized in order to ensure that all work stations have enough work to stay busy.

____ 7. Which of the following involves systematic problem-solving by teams consisting of front-line workers? a) The Theory of Constraints; b) Total Quality Management; c) Process Reengineering; d) Automation.

Answers to Questions and Exercises

True or False

1. F   The central purpose of managerial accounting is to provide information to managers. Stockholders are served by financial accounting.

2. T   This is what is meant by control.

3. F   Planning involves deciding what to do to achieve the organization's objectives; it does not involve overseeing day-to-day activities.

4. T   The primary concern of managerial accounting is with an organization's segments rather than with the organization as a whole.

5. T   Managerial accounting need not conform to GAAP.

6. T   Under JIT, goods are produced and shipped only as needed to satisfy customer orders.

7. F   Large work in process inventories increase defect rates. Because of delays in passing units on to the next workstation, problems are not detected until after many units have been affected by the problem.

8. F   Typically under JIT, all of the different pieces of equipment needed to manufacture a product are placed on a single flow line, thus breaking up groupings of similar equipment.

9. T   These are common characteristics of TQM.

10. F   The reverse is true. Process Reengineering tends to be imposed from above using outside specialists and it may lead to loss of jobs.

11. F   A non-value-added activity is an activity that consumes resources or takes time that adds nothing of value. It may or may not be a constraint.

12. T   The rate of output of the constraint determines the output of the entire system. Therefore, improvement efforts should ordinarily be focused on the constraint.

Multiple Choice

1. d   Staff positions such as accounting do appear on the organization chart, but they are neither superior nor equal in authority to line positions. They serve the needs of line positions by providing essential services.

2. a   The controller occupies a staff position that provides support to other positions within the organization.

3. c   Managerial accounting is not required by any external law or regulation.

4. b   Since it would be a waste of money to have two data collecting systems existing side by side, managerial accounting and financial accounting rely on much the same data.

5. c   The purpose of decentralization is to move all decisions to the lowest managerial level possible in an organization.

6. b   Under JIT, the plant floor is laid out with many product flow lines—one for each family of products.

7. b   Total Quality Management involves systematic problem-solving by teams consisting of front-line workers.

Chapter 2

Cost Terms, Concepts, and Classifications

Chapter Study Suggestions

✳

This chapter introduces cost terms that will be used throughout the book. The chapter also gives a broad overview of the flow of costs in a manufacturing company. (Chapter 3 covers cost flows in more depth.) As you read the chapter, note each new term and be sure you understand its meaning. It is important to keep in mind that costs are classified in many ways, depending on how the costs will be used. This is the reason for so many different cost terms. To fit the cost terms into a framework, you should frequently refer to Exhibit 2-7 as you go through the chapter.

Exhibit 2-4 presents the *schedule of cost of goods manufactured*. You should memorize the format of this schedule, as well as the material in Exhibit 2-5. Learning this material will help you in Chapter 3 and will also lay a foundation for many chapters that follow.

CHAPTER HIGHLIGHTS

A. *Manufacturing costs* are the costs involved in making a product. Manufacturing costs can be divided into three basic elements: direct materials, direct labor, and manufacturing overhead.

1. *Direct materials* are those materials that become an integral part of a finished product and whose costs can be conveniently traced to it.

a. An example of direct materials would be the tires on a new Ford.

b. Insignificant materials, such as glue, are classified as *indirect materials* rather than as direct materials. It is too costly and inconvenient to trace such small costs to individual units of output.

2. *Direct labor* consists of those labor costs that can be easily traced to individual units of product. Direct labor is sometimes called touch labor.

a. An example of direct labor would be a worker on a manufacturing assembly line.

b. Other labor costs, such as supervisors and janitors, are considered to be *indirect labor* rather than direct labor. These costs cannot be traced to individual units of product since these individuals do not directly work on the product.

3. *Manufacturing overhead* consists of all manufacturing costs except direct materials and direct labor.

a. Manufacturing overhead includes indirect materials, indirect labor, and other manufacturing costs such as factory rent, factory utilities, and depreciation on factory equipment and facilities.

b. Synonyms for manufacturing overhead include factory overhead and indirect manufacturing costs.

4. The terms prime cost and conversion cost are also used to categorize manufacturing costs.

a. *Prime cost* consists of direct materials plus direct labor.

b. *Conversion cost* consists of direct labor plus manufacturing overhead.

B. *Nonmanufacturing costs* are relate to selling and administrative activities.

1. *Selling, or marketing, costs* include all costs associated with marketing finished products such as sales commissions, costs of delivery equipment, costs of finished goods warehouses, and advertising.

2. *Administrative costs* include all costs associated with the general administration of an organization, including secretarial salaries, depreciation of general administrative facilities and equipment, and executive compensation.

C. For purposes of external financial reports, costs can be classified as product costs or period costs.

1. *Period costs* are expensed on the income statement in the period in which they are incurred. (By incurred, we mean the period in which the cost is accrued, not necessarily when it is paid. Remember from financial accounting that items such as salaries are counted as costs not when they are paid, but when the company incurs the liability to pay them. Continue to use the rules you learned in financial accounting.)

2. *Product costs* are matched with units of product and are recognized as an expense on the income statement only when the units are sold. Until that time, product costs are considered to be assets and are recognized on the balance sheet as inventory.

3. In a manufacturing company, product costs include direct materials, direct labor, and manufacturing overhead. Thus, in a manufacturing company, product costs and manufacturing costs are synonymous.

4. In a manufacturing company, period costs and nonmanufacturing costs are synonymous terms. Thus, the period costs are selling and administrative costs.

5. In a merchandising company such as Macy's or Wal-Mart, product costs consist solely of the costs of products purchased from suppliers for resale to customers. All other costs are period costs.

D. Income statements and balance sheets prepared by manufacturing companies differ from those prepared by merchandising companies.

1. The balance sheet of a manufacturing company contains three inventory accounts: Raw Materials, Work in Process, and Finished Goods. In contrast, the balance sheet of a merchandising company contains only one inventory account—Merchandise Inventory.

a. *Raw Materials* inventory consists of materials on hand in stockrooms that will be used to make products. Raw materials are not necessarily basic, unprocessed materials such as iron ore. Raw materials includes any item that the company purchases from suppliers that goes into the company's final product. For example, the stereo system VW buys from its supplier to install in a car is a raw material as far as VW is concerned.

    b.   *Work in Process* consists of unfinished products.

    c.   *Finished Goods* consists of units of product that are completed and ready for sale.

    2. The income statement of a manufacturing company contains an element termed *cost of goods manufactured*. You should study the schedule of cost of goods manufactured in Exhibit 2-4 in the text very carefully.

E. Manufacturing costs (direct materials, direct labor, and overhead) are also known as *inventoriable costs*.

    1. The term inventoriable costs is used since direct materials, direct labor, and overhead costs are assigned to Work in Process and Finished Goods inventory accounts as they are incurred. If goods are either not completed or not sold at the end of a period, these costs will be included as part of these inventory accounts on the balance sheet.

    2. You should carefully study Exhibit 2-5 in the text. It shows the flow of manufacturing costs through inventory accounts and the way these costs become an expense (cost of goods sold) on the income statement. *This is a key exhibit for Chapter 2.*

    3. We can summarize manufacturing and non-manufacturing cost terms as follows:

Synonymous Terms	*Costs Involved*
• Manufacturing costs • Product costs • Inventoriable costs	• Direct materials, direct labor, and manufacturing overhead
• Nonmanufacturing costs • Period costs	• Selling and administrative expenses

F. This section describes the computation of cost of goods manufactured, cost of goods sold, and preparation of the income statement.

    1. Computing the cost of goods sold for a manufacturing company involves a number of steps. These steps rely on the following basic model that describes flows into and out of any inventory account.

        Basic inventory flows:
        Beginning balance
        + Additions to inventory
        = Available
        – Ending balance
        = Withdrawals from inventory

    2. To compute the raw materials used in production, this basic model is written as follows:

        Beginning balance raw materials
        + Purchases of raw materials
        = Raw materials available for use
        – Ending balance raw materials
        = Raw materials used in production

The raw materials used in production could include both direct materials and indirect materials. However, unless otherwise stated in a problem, you can assume no indirect materials are involved.

    3. The next step is to compute the total manufacturing cost for the period. This is the sum of direct materials, direct labor, and manufacturing overhead costs:

        Direct materials
        + Direct labor
        + Manufacturing overhead
        = Total manufacturing cost

    4. The next step is to compute the *cost of goods manufactured*. This refers to the cost of the goods that were *finished* during the period. To compute this amount, use the following version of the basic inventory flow model:

        Beginning balance, work in process
        + Total manufacturing cost
        – Ending balance, work in process
        = Cost of goods manufactured

    5. The final step in the computation of cost of goods sold is also based on the inventory flow model:

        Beginning balance, finished goods
        + Cost of goods manufactured
        = Goods available for sale
        – Ending balance, finished goods
        = Cost of goods sold

    6. The income statement in a manufacturing company may or may not show the computation of the cost of goods sold as above. In the summary income statement below, it is assumed that the details of the cost of goods sold computations are shown separately.

        Sales
        – Cost of goods sold
        = Gross margin
        – Selling and administrative expenses
        = Net operating income

G. For purposes of describing how costs behave in response to changes in activity, costs are often classified as variable or fixed. For example, one might be interested in describing how the costs of admitting patients to a hospital respond to changes in the number of patients admitted. Or, one might be interested in how much it would cost for paint in a furniture factory if the output of the factory were increased by 10%.

1. *Variable costs* are those costs that vary, in total, in direct proportion to changes in the volume or level of activity within the relevant range. Exhibit 2-8 illustrates variable cost behavior. Examples of variable costs include direct materials, (usually) direct labor, commissions to salespersons, and cost of goods sold in a merchandising company such as a shoe store.

2. *Fixed costs* remain constant in total within the relevant range. They include, for example, depreciation, supervisory salaries, and rent. Exhibit 2-8 illustrates fixed cost behavior.

3. The *relevant range* is the range of activity within which the assumptions about cost behavior can be considered valid. If there is a big enough change in activity (for example, a ten-fold increase in volume), even the "fixed" costs are likely to change. Such a large increase in volume would be outside the relevant range.

H. For purposes of assigning costs to objects, costs are classified as direct or indirect.

1. Managers often want to know how much something (e.g., a product, a department, or a customer) costs. The item for which a cost is desired is called a *cost object*.

2. A *direct cost* is a cost that can be easily and conveniently traced to a particular cost object. For example, the salaries and commissions of salespersons in a department store's shoe department would be considered direct costs of the shoe department.

3. An *indirect cost* is a cost that cannot be easily and conveniently traced to the cost object. For example, the salary of the manager of a department store would be considered an indirect cost of the shoe department and other departments.

I. For purposes of making decisions, the following cost terms are often used: differential costs, opportunity costs, and sunk costs.

1. Every decision involves choosing from among at least two alternatives. A difference in cost between two alternatives is called a *differential cost*. Only the differential costs are relevant in making a choice between two alternatives. Costs that are the same for the two alternatives are not affected by the decision and should be ignored.

2. An *opportunity cost* is the potential benefit given up by selecting one alternative over another. Opportunity costs are not recorded in accounting re-

cords. They represent a lost benefit rather than an out-of-pocket cost.

3. A *sunk cost* is a cost that has already been incurred and that cannot be changed by any decision made now or in the future. Sunk costs are never differential costs and should always be ignored when making decisions.

Appendix 2A: Further Classification of Labor Costs

A. Labor costs can be broken down into five main categories: direct labor, indirect labor, idle time, overtime premium, and labor fringe benefits.

1. As mentioned earlier, direct labor consists of those factory labor costs that can be easily traced to products.

2. Indirect labor consists of factory labor costs that are supportive or supervisory. These include the costs of supervisors, superintendents, custodians, maintenance persons, and others who do not work directly on the product.

3. *Idle time* represents the costs of direct labor workers who are unable to perform their assignments due to material shortages, power failures, and the like. Idle time is treated as part of manufacturing overhead.

4. *Overtime premium* consists of any amount paid above an employee's base hourly rate.

   a. For example, if the base rate is $6 per hour and an employee is paid time-and-a-half for overtime, then the overtime premium would be $3 per hour. In other words, the total pay would be $9 per hour of overtime.

   b. An overtime premium is ordinarily not charged to specific jobs, but rather is included as part of manufacturing overhead. An exception is when a customer specifically requests a rush job that results in having to work overtime. In such a case, the overtime premium might be charged directly to that job.

5. *Labor fringe benefits* include employment-related costs paid by the employer, such as insurance, retirement plans, etc.

   a. Many companies include all such costs as part of manufacturing overhead.

   b. The preferred method is to include only the labor fringe benefits relating to indirect labor as part of manufacturing overhead and treat the fringe benefits relating to direct labor as added direct labor costs.

Appendix 2B: Cost of Quality

A. The term quality is used in many ways. It can mean a luxurious product with many features or it can mean a product that is free of defects. We use the term quality in the latter sense. *Quality of conformance* is the degree to which a product or service meets its design specifications and is free of defects or other problems that might affect appearance or performance.

B. Defects (i.e., poor quality of conformance) result in costs that can be classified as prevention costs, appraisal costs, internal failure costs, and external failure costs.

1. Internal failure costs and external failure costs result from defects that occur in products.

a. *Internal failure costs* result from correcting defects in products before they are shipped to customers. Internal failure costs include scrap, reworking of defective units, and downtime.

b. *External failure costs* result when a defective product is delivered to a customer. These costs include warranty repairs, exchanges, returns, and loss of future sales. It is generally best to spot defective goods before they get into the hands of customers. A dissatisfied customer will not buy from the company in the future and is likely to tell others of his or her dissatisfaction.

2. Prevention costs and appraisal costs are incurred to prevent defects and reduce the likelihood of external failures.

a. *Prevention costs* are incurred to reduce or eliminate defects. Prevention is often simple and inexpensive. For example, a simple metal shield can prevent drilling a hole in the wrong place. Prevention costs include the costs of quality engineering and quality improvement projects.

b. *Appraisal costs* are incurred to identify defective products prior to shipping them to customers. These costs include wages of inspection workers and the costs of testing equipment.

C. In most companies, the total cost of quality (the sum of prevention costs, appraisal costs, internal failure costs, and external failure costs) decreases as the defect rate improves—at least until very low levels of defect rates occur. (A higher quality of conformance means a lower defect rate.) Exhibit 2B-2 illustrates this relation between total cost of quality and defect rates.

1. Reducing the defect rate (e.g., defects per million parts) involves spending more on prevention and appraisal. However, this additional spending is usually more than offset by reductions in the costs of internal and external failures caused by defects.

2. Most companies would benefit from putting more effort into prevention. This reduces the need for appraisal and decreases the incidence of internal and external failures.

D. Quality costs are summarized for management on a *quality cost report* such as in Exhibit 2B-3.

1. The report classifies the costs of quality into the four categories discussed above.

2. The report should summarize costs associated with defective products and services throughout the organization—all the way from research and development through customer service. The report should not be limited to just manufacturing costs.

3. Such a report helps managers see the financial significance of defects and it aids managers in diagnosing whether their quality costs are poorly distributed (e.g., too much external failure cost relative to prevention cost).

REVIEW AND SELF-TEST
Questions and Exercises

True or False

Enter a T or an F in the blank to indicate whether the statement is true or false.

____ 1. Raw materials consist of basic natural resources, such as crude oil.

____ 2. A supervisor's salary would be considered direct labor.

____ 3. Nonmanufacturing costs consist of selling costs and administrative costs.

____ 4. All selling and administrative costs are period costs.

____ 5. The terms product cost and manufacturing cost are synonymous.

____ 6. The cost of goods manufactured is an expense in a manufacturing company.

____ 7. A cost such as factory depreciation may be on the balance sheet as an asset if goods are uncompleted or unsold at the end of a period.

____ 8. Inventoriable costs and product costs are synonymous terms in a manufacturing company.

____ 9. Total variable cost will change in proportion to changes in the level of activity.

____ 10. A fixed cost is constant per unit of product.

____ 11. Manufacturing overhead is an indirect cost with respect to units of product.

____ 12. Sunk costs can be either variable or fixed.

____ 13. Property taxes and insurance on a factory building are examples of manufacturing overhead.

____ 14. (Appendix 2A) An overtime premium is ordinarily charged to the specific jobs worked on during overtime periods.

____ 15. (Appendix 2B) A product containing defects has a poor quality of conformance.

____ 16. (Appendix 2B) The best quality systems are those that put their emphasis on appraisal costs

____ 17. (Appendix 2B) It is usually better to incur internal than external failure costs.

Multiple Choice

Choose the best answer or response by placing the identifying letter in the space provided.

____ 1. If the activity level increases, one would expect the fixed cost per unit to: a) increase; b) decrease; c) remain unchanged; d) none of these.

____ 2. Which of the following costs would not be a period cost? a) indirect materials; b) advertising; c) administrative salaries; d) shipping costs; e) sales commissions.

____ 3. The term used to describe the cost of goods transferred from work in process inventory to finished goods inventory is: a) cost of goods sold; b) raw materials; c) period cost; d) cost of goods manufactured.

____ 4. Manufacturing cost is synonymous with all of the following terms except: a) product cost; b) inventoriable cost; c) period cost.

____ 5. If the activity level drops by 5%, one would expect the variable costs: a) to increase per unit of product; b) to drop in total by 5%; c) to remain constant in total; d) to decrease per unit of product.

____ 6. All of the following are considered to be product costs for financial reporting except: a) indirect materials; b) advertising; c) rent on factory space; d) idle time.

____ 7. Walston Manufacturing Company has provided the following data concerning its raw materials inventories last month:

Beginning raw materials inventory	$80,000
Purchases of raw materials	$420,000
Ending raw materials inventory	$50,000

The cost of the raw materials used in production for the month was: a) $500,000; b) $450,000; c) $390,000; d) $470,000.

____ 8. Juniper Company has provided the following data concerning its manufacturing costs and work in process inventories last month:

Raw materials used in production	$270,000
Direct labor	$140,000
Manufacturing overhead	$190,000
Beginning work in process inventory	$50,000
Ending work in process inventory	$80,000

The cost of goods manufactured for the month was: a) $730,000; b) $630,000; c) $600,000; d) $570,000.

___ 9. Vonder Inc. has provided the following data concerning its finished goods inventories last month:

Beginning finished goods inventory $110,000
Cost of goods manufactured $760,000
Ending finished goods inventory $70,000

The cost of goods sold for the month was: a) $800,000; b) $720,000; c) $950,000; d) $280,000.

___ 10. (Appendix 2A) A machinist earns $10 per hour. During a given week he works 40 hours, of which he is idle 5 hours. For the week: a) $400 cost should be charged to direct labor, b) $50 cost should be charged to overtime premium; c) $50 cost should be charged to overhead; d) $425 cost should be charged to direct labor, and $25 cost should be charged to overhead.

___ 11. (Appendix 2B) The cost of quality training is an example of a(n): a) prevention cost; b) appraisal cost; c) internal failure cost; d) external failure cost.

___ 12. (Appendix 2B) The cost of warranty repairs is an example of a(n): a) prevention cost; b) appraisal cost; c) internal failure cost; d) external failure cost.

___ 13. (Appendix 2B) The cost of rework labor is an example of a(n): a) prevention cost; b) appraisal cost; c) internal failure cost; d) external failure cost.

___ 14. (Appendix 2B) The cost of supplies used in testing and inspection is an example of a(n): a) prevention cost; b) appraisal cost; c) internal failure cost; d) external failure cost.

___ 15. (Appendix 2B) The cost of lost sales due to a reputation for poor quality is an example of a(n): a) prevention cost; b) appraisal cost; c) internal failure cost; d) external failure cost.

Exercises

2-1. Classify each of the following costs as either period costs or product costs. Also indicate whether the cost is fixed or variable with respect to changes in the amount of output produced and sold.

		Period Cost	Product Cost	Variable Cost	Fixed Cost
-	Example: Rent on a sales office	X	___	___	X
-	Example: Direct materials	___	X	X	___
a.	Sales commissions......................................	___	___	___	___
b.	Rent on a factory building	___	___	___	___
c.	Headquarters secretarial salaries	___	___	___	___
d.	Assembly line workers	___	___	___	___
e.	Product advertising	___	___	___	___
f.	Cherries in a cannery	___	___	___	___
g.	Top management salaries	___	___	___	___
h.	Lubricants for machines	___	___	___	___
i.	Shipping costs via express service	___	___	___	___
j.	Executive training program	___	___	___	___
k.	Factory supervisory salaries	___	___	___	___

2-2.   Using the following data and the form that appears below, prepare a schedule of cost of goods manufactured.

Lubricants for machines	$4,500
Rent, factory building	$16,000
Direct labor	$90,000
Indirect materials	$2,000
Sales commissions	$24,600
Factory utilities	$5,800
Insurance, factory	$2,000
Purchases of raw materials	$120,000
Work in process, beginning	$16,000
Work in process, ending	$11,500
Raw materials, beginning	$15,000
Raw materials, ending	$5,000
Depreciation of office equipment	$4,000

Schedule of Cost of Goods Manufactured

(See Exhibit 2-4 in the text for the proper format)

Direct materials:

_____.......................... $_____

_____..........................   _____

_____..........................   _____

_____..........................   _____

_____..........................   _____

Direct labor...   _____

Manufacturing overhead:

_____..........................   _____

_____..........................   _____

_____..........................   _____

_____..........................   _____

_____..........................   _____

_____..........................   _____

_____..........................   _____

_____..........................   _____

_____..........................   _____

Cost of Goods Manufactured....................................... $_____

2-3.   Harry is considering whether to produce and sell classic wooden surfboards in his spare time. His garage was constructed at a cost of $12,000 several years ago and could be used for production purposes. The garage would be depreciated over a 20-year life. Harry has determined that each surfboard will require $30 of wood. He would hire students to do most of the work and would pay them $35 for each surfboard completed. He would rent tools at a cost of $400 per month. Harry can draw money out of savings to provide the capital needed to get the operation going. The savings are earning interest at 6% annually. An ad agency would handle advertising at a cost of $500 per month. Harry would hire students to sell the surfboards and pay a commission of $20 per board.

Required:

From the foregoing information, identify all the examples you can of the following types of costs (a single item may be identified as many types of costs). A cost should be classified as variable in this case if it is variable with respect to the number of surfboards produced and sold. A cost should be classified as a differential cost if it differs between the alternatives of producing or not producing the surfboards.

	Variable cost	Fixed cost	Selling & admin. cost	Product cost	Manuf. ovhd. cost	Sunk cost	Opportunity cost	Differential cost
Original cost of garage	____	____	____	____	____	____	____	____
Depreciation on the garage............	____	____	____	____	____	____	____	____
Wood for each surfboard...............	____	____	____	____	____	____	____	____
Student workers............................	____	____	____	____	____	____	____	____
Tool rental....................................	____	____	____	____	____	____	____	____
Interest on savings.........................	____	____	____	____	____	____	____	____
Advertising costs	____	____	____	____	____	____	____	____
Sales commissions.........................	____	____	____	____	____	____	____	____

2-4.   (Appendix 2A) Sally Anderson worked 47 hours last week. She was idle 3 hours and spent the remaining 44 hours working directly on the manufacture of finished products. Sally is paid $8 per hour and time-and-a-half for work in excess of 40 hours per week. Allocate her week's wages between direct labor and manufacturing overhead using the form that appears below.

Direct labor		$_____
Manufacturing overhead:		
Idle time..	$_____	
Overtime premium	_____	_____
Total earnings		$_____

2-5.   (Appendix 2B) The management of Jehrol Fantasy Products would like for you to compile a quality cost report for the company using the following data.

Net cost of scrap	$90,000
Disposal of defective products	$17,000
Maintenance of test equipment	$61,000
Rework labor and overhead	$69,000
Depreciation of test equipment	$28,000
Systems development	$40,000
Quality training	$82,000
Warranty repairs and replacements	$89,000
Liability arising from defective products	$61,000

The company's total sales for the year was $10,000,000.
    Prepare the company's quality cost of report using the form below:

JEHROL FANTASY PRODUCTS
Quality Cost Report

	Amount	Percent of Sales
Prevention costs:		
_____	$_____	
_____	_____	_____
Total prevention cost	_____	_____
Appraisal costs:		
_____		
_____	_____	_____
Total appraisal cost	_____	_____
Internal failure costs:		
_____		
_____		
_____	_____	_____
Total internal failure cost	_____	_____
External failure costs:		
_____		
_____	_____	_____
Total external failure cost	_____	_____
Total quality cost	$_____	_____

Answers to Questions and Exercises

True or False

1. F Raw materials consist of any materials used to make a product. The finished goods of one company can be the raw materials of another company.

2. F Supervisors do not work directly on products and therefore are not direct labor.

3. T Nonmanufacturing cost is synonymous with selling and administrative costs.

4. T Selling and administrative costs are period costs because they are charged against income in the period in which they are incurred, rather than being added to the cost of manufactured or purchased goods.

5. T These two terms are synonymous.

6. F Cost of goods manufactured is not an expense. It is the amount transferred from work in process to finished goods inventory when goods are completed. This is a subtle, but important, point.

7. T Manufacturing costs are assigned to units during production. If these units are not complete or not sold at the end of a period, then the manufacturing costs incurred to date are included as part of Work in Process or Finished Goods inventories which are assets on the balance sheet.

8. T These two terms are synonymous.

9. T Since a variable cost is constant per unit, it will change in total in proportion to changes in the level of activity. If activity increases by 5%, then the total variable cost should also increase by 5%.

10. F A fixed cost is constant in total amount; on a per unit basis, it varies inversely with changes in the level of activity.

11. T Manufacturing overhead cost is an indirect cost; only direct materials and direct labor are direct manufacturing costs.

12. T A sunk cost is a cost that has already been incurred and can be variable or fixed. If obsolete materials have already been purchased, for example, then the cost of the materials is a sunk cost.

13. T Manufacturing overhead consists of all production costs except direct materials and direct labor.

14. F Overtime premium is ordinarily added to manufacturing overhead cost and spread over all jobs worked on during the period.

15. T Quality of conformance indicates how well a product meets its design specifications and is free of defects and other problems.

16. F The best quality systems put their emphasis on prevention costs.

17. T Internal failure costs keep defective products from being shipped to customers, which can have a devastating effect on the company's reputation.

Multiple Choice

1. b The fixed cost per unit should drop since a constant amount is spread over more units.

2. a Indirect materials would be part of manufacturing overhead, and thus it would be a product cost.

3. d Goods that are completed and ready for sale move out of work in process and into finished goods. The cost of such goods is termed cost of goods manufactured.

4. c A period cost represents a cost charged against the period in which the cost is incurred; it has nothing to do with the manufacture of a product.

5. b By definition, total variable cost changes in proportion to changes in the activity level.

6. b Advertising is a period cost, rather than a product cost.

7. b The computations are as follows:

Beginning raw materials inventory .... $ 80,000
Add: Purchases of raw materials 420,000
Raw materials available for use 500,000
Deduct: Ending raw materials inventory ... 50,000
Raw materials used in production $450,000

8. d   The computations are as follows:

Raw materials used in production	$270,000
Direct labor	140,000
Manufacturing overhead	190,000
Total manufacturing costs	600,000
Add: Beginning work in	
process inventory	50,000
	650,000
Deduct: Ending work in	
process inventory	80,000
Cost of goods manufactured	$570,000

9. a   The cost of goods sold is computed as follows:

Beginning finished goods inventory	$110,000
Add: Cost of goods manufactured	760,000
Goods available for sale	870,000
Deduct: Ending finished	
goods inventory	70,000
Cost of goods sold	$800,000

10. c   All of the cost of idle time is charged to manufacturing overhead. Thus, $10 per hour × 5 hours = $50.

11. a   See Exhibit 2B-1.

12. d   See Exhibit 2B-1.

13. c   See Exhibit 2B-1.

14. b   See Exhibit 2B-1.

15. d   See Exhibit 2B-1.

Exercises

2-1.

		Period Cost	*Product Cost*	*Variable Cost*	*Fixed Cost*
a.	Sales commissions	X		X	
b.	Rent on a factory building		X		X
c.	Headquarters secretarial salaries	X			X
d.	Assembly line workers		X	X	
e.	Product advertising	X			X
f.	Cherries in a cannery		X	X	
g.	Top management salaries	X			X
h.	Lubricants for machines		X	X	
i.	Shipping costs via express service	X		X	
j.	Executive training program	X			X
k.	Factory supervisory salaries		X		X

2-2.   Direct materials:

Raw materials inventory, beginning	$ 15,000	
Add: Purchases of raw materials	120,000	
Raw materials available for use	135,000	
Deduct: Raw materials inventory, ending	5,000	
Raw materials used in production		$130,000
Direct labor		90,000
Manufacturing overhead:		
Lubricants for machines	4,500	
Rent, factory building	16,000	
Indirect materials	2,000	
Factory utilities	5,800	
Insurance, factory	2,000	
Total overhead costs		30,300
Total manufacturing costs		250,300
Add: Work in process, beginning		16,000
		266,300
Deduct: Work in process, ending		11,500
Cost of Goods Manufactured		$254,800

Note: Sales commissions and depreciation on office equipment are not manufacturing costs.

2-3.

	Variable cost	Fixed cost	Selling & admin. cost	Product cost	Manuf. ovhd. cost	Sunk cost	Opportunity cost	Differential cost
Original cost of garage						X		
Depreciation on the garage		X		X	X			(1)
Wood for each surfboard	X			X				X
Student workers	X			X				X
Tool rental		X		X	X			X
Interest on savings							X	(2)
Advertising costs		X	X					X
Sales commissions	X		X					X

(1) This is not a differential cost if the depreciation on the garage is the same regardless of whether it is used to make surfboards or is used conventionally as a residential garage.
(2) This may be considered to be a differential cost, although some would say that it is not since it is a foregone benefit rather than a cost *per se*.

2-4.

Direct labor (44 hours × $8 per hour)		$352
Manufacturing overhead:		
Idle time (3 hours × $8 per hour)	$24	
Overtime premium (7 hours × $4 per hour)	28	52
Total earnings		$404

2-5.

JEHROL FANTASY PRODUCTS
Quality Cost Report

	Amount	Percent of Sales
Prevention costs:		
Systems development	$ 40,000	0.40 %
Quality training	82,000	0.82
Total prevention costs	122,000	1.22
Appraisal costs:		
Depreciation of test equipment	28,000	0.28
Maintenance of test equipment	61,000	0.61
Total appraisal cost	89,000	0.89
Internal failure costs:		
Rework labor and overhead	69,000	0.69
Net cost of scrap	90,000	0.90
Disposal of defective products	17,000	0.17
Total internal failure cost	176,000	1.76
External failure costs:		
Warranty repairs and replacements	89,000	0.89
Liability arising from defective products	61,000	0.61
Total external failure cost.....................................	150,000	1.50
Total quality cost	$537,000	5.37 %

Chapter 3

Systems Design: Job-Order Costing

Chapter Study Suggestions

✳

This chapter expands on the concepts introduced in Chapter 2 and provides more details concerning how product costs are determined. The chapter covers a costing method called *job-order costing*. Exhibit 3-5 provides an overall view of the flow of costs and the documents used in a job-order cost system. Pay particular attention to the section in the chapter titled "Application of Manufacturing Overhead." *Overhead application is a key concept.*

Exhibits 3-6, 3-7, and 3-8 show how direct materials, direct labor, and overhead costs are assigned to jobs. Study these exhibits with particular care—these concepts are likely to show up in homework. Exhibits 3-10 and 3-11 summarize the cost flows and illustrate the statements of cost of goods manufactured and cost of goods sold. Note particularly the difference between the schedule of cost of goods manufactured in Exhibit 3-11 and the schedule of cost of goods manufactured in Chapter 2. Study and then *restudy* the section titled "Underapplied and Overapplied Overhead," paying particular attention to how under- and overapplied overhead is computed.

CHAPTER HIGHLIGHTS

A. Process costing and job-order costing are the two basic costing systems commonly used in manufacturing and in many service organizations.

1. *Process costing* is used in situations where a single homogeneous product such as bricks are produced for long periods of time.

2. *Job-order costing* is used in situations where many different products or services are produced each period. Examples include special-order printing and furniture manufacturing where products are typically produced in small batches. For example, two or three sofas of a particular design and fabric covering might be made in one batch. Each batch is called a "job." In a consulting company, a job would be a particular consulting project.

B. We begin our discussion of job-order costing with raw materials. When materials are purchased, their costs are recorded in the Raw Materials inventory account, which is an asset. If the materials are paid for with cash, the journal entry would look like this:

Raw Materials	XXX	
Cash		XXX

1. When a job is started, materials are withdrawn from storage. The document that authorizes this withdrawal is called a *materials requisition form*. This form lists all the materials required to complete a specific job. The journal entry to record withdrawal of raw materials from the storeroom for use in production is:

Work in Process (direct materials)	XXX	
Manuf. Ovhd. (indirect materials)	XXX	
Raw Materials		XXX

Materials that are traced directly to jobs are classified as *direct materials* and are debited to Work in Process. Any materials that are not directly traced to jobs are classified as *indirect materials* and are debited to a special control account called *Manufacturing Overhead*.

2. When materials are placed into production, they are also recorded on a *job cost sheet*, which summarizes all production costs assigned to a particular job. Exhibit 3-2 in the text illustrates a job cost sheet.

C. Labor costs are recorded on *time tickets* or *time sheets* that are filled out by employees. These documents list the amount of time each employee works on specific jobs and tasks.

1. Labor time spent working directly on specific jobs is termed *direct labor*. Labor time spent working on supportive tasks (e.g., supervision, maintenance, janitorial) is termed *indirect labor*. The entry to record labor costs is:

Work in Process (direct labor)	XXX	
Manuf. Ovhd. (indirect labor)	XXX	
Salaries and Wages Payable		XXX

2. Direct labor costs are added to the individual job cost sheets at the same time they are recorded in the formal accounts.

D. As explained in Chapter 2, manufacturing overhead consists of *indirect* costs that cannot be easily traced to individual products or jobs. Rather than attempting to trace these costs to jobs (which may be impossible), overhead costs are commonly assigned to jobs using a *predetermined overhead rate*.

1. The predetermined overhead rate is computed *before* the year begins and is based entirely on estimated data. Ordinarily, the rate is computed for an entire year to eliminate seasonal fluctuations. The formula is:

$$\text{Predetermined overhead rate} = \frac{\text{Estimated total manufacturing overhead cost}}{\text{Estimated total amount of the allocation base}}$$

An *allocation base* is a measure of activity, such as direct labor-hours, direct labor cost, or machine-hours. The allocation base is something that all jobs have in common—for example, all of the jobs may require direct labor-hours. Ideally, the allocation base should actually cause variations in manufacturing overhead costs, but in practice this ideal is often ignored.

2. Suppose direct labor-hours is used as the allocation base; the estimated total manufacturing overhead cost for next year is $400,000; and, the estimated total number of direct labor-hours for next year is 10,000. Then the predetermined overhead rate would be $40 per direct labor-hour ($400,000 ÷ 10,000 direct labor-hours).

3. To assign overhead costs to a job, the predetermined overhead rate is multiplied by the amount of the allocation base incurred by the job. For example, suppose that a particular job incurs 20 direct labor-hours and the predetermined overhead rate is $40 per direct labor-hour. Then $800 (20 direct labor-hours × $40 per direct labor-hour) of overhead cost would be *applied* to that job. This $800 is called the *overhead applied*. Note that this is not actual overhead spending

on the job. The $800 may have little to do with any overhead that is actually caused by the job. It is simply a way of distributing the overhead costs that were estimated at the beginning of the year among the jobs worked on during the year.

4. The overhead that is applied to a job is entered on its job cost sheet and is recorded in the company's formal accounts with the following journal entry:

| Work in Process | XXX | |
| Manufacturing Overhead | | XXX |

5. Turn to Exhibit 3-8 in the text to see how overhead costs flow through the accounts and onto the job cost sheets. Notice from the exhibit that applying overhead to jobs and recording actual overhead costs represent two separate and distinct processes. *This is a key concept that you must understand.*

6. Actual overhead costs are *not* charged to Work in Process. Instead, they are charged to the Manufacturing Overhead control account as we saw in the entries for indirect labor and indirect materials above. Note that *actual overhead costs all appear as debits to Manufacturing Overhead.*

E. When jobs are completed, their costs are transferred from Work in Process to Finished Goods. The journal entry is:

| Finished Goods | XXX | |
| Work in Process | | XXX |

When completed products are sold, their costs are transferred from Finished Goods to Cost of Goods Sold. The journal entry is:

| Cost of Goods Sold | XXX | |
| Finished Goods | | XXX |

F. Exhibits 3-10, 3-11 and 3-12 are key exhibits that summarize much of the material in the chapter. Study these exhibits with care. Note particularly how the manufacturing overhead costs are handled.

G. Generally, the amount of overhead cost *applied* to Work in Process will differ from the amount of *actual* overhead cost incurred. This difference will be reflected in a debit or credit balance in the Manufacturing Overhead account.

1. If overhead applied is less than the actual overhead costs incurred, then overhead has been *underapplied.* In this case, the Manufacturing Overhead account will have a debit balance.

2. If overhead applied to Work in Process exceeds the amount of overhead cost actually incurred, then overhead has been *overapplied.* In this case the Manufacturing Overhead account will have a credit balance.

3. In addition to observing the balance in the Manufacturing Overhead account, under- or overapplied overhead can be computed as follows:

Actual overhead costs	$XXX
Less: Overhead costs applied to Work in Process*	XXX
Underapplied (overapplied) overhead	$XXX

* Predetermined overhead rate × Actual amount of the allocation base incurred during the period.

4. At the end of a period, under- or overapplied overhead may be closed out to Cost of Goods Sold or it may be allocated among Work in Process, Finished Goods, and Cost of Goods Sold.

a.   Closing out any balance to Cost of Goods Sold is simpler than the other method. If overhead has been underapplied, the entry would be:

| Cost of Goods Sold | XXX | |
| Manufacturing Overhead | | XXX |

This entry increases Cost of Goods Sold. If overhead has been underapplied, not enough overhead cost was applied to jobs during the period and therefore costs are understated in the accounts. The journal entry above adjusts Cost of Goods Sold so that it is no longer understated.

If overhead has been overapplied, the journal entry would be:

| Manufacturing Overhead | XXX | |
| Cost of Goods Sold | | XXX |

This entry decreases Cost of Goods Sold. If overhead has been overapplied, too much overhead cost was applied to jobs during the period and therefore costs are overstated in the accounts. The journal entry above adjusts Cost of Goods Sold so that it is no longer overstated.

b.   Allocating any under- or overapplied overhead among inventory accounts and Cost of Goods Sold is more complex, but is considered to be more accurate. The allocation is based on the amount of the overhead applied from the current period that remain in the ending balances of the Work in Process, Finished Goods, and Cost of Goods Sold accounts. Assuming that overhead is underapplied, the entry would be:

Work in Process	XXX
Finished Goods	XXX
Cost of Goods Sold	XXX
Manufacturing Overhead	XXX

H.   Largely for simplicity, the chapter assumes that a single "plant-wide" overhead rate is used. Many companies use *multiple overhead rates* rather than a single plant wide rate. In such a system, each processing department, work center, or business activity has its own predetermined overhead rate. These more complex systems will be investigated in a later chapter.

Appendix 3A: The Predetermined Overhead Rate and Capacity

A.   Traditionally, the denominator in the predetermined overhead rate is the *estimated* total amount of the allocation base for the next year.

$$\text{Predetermined overhead rate} = \frac{\text{Estimated total manufacturing overhead cost}}{\text{Estimated total amount of the allocation base}}$$

This traditional approach can lead to some potential problems.

   1.   If demand falls due to a recession or other reason, the estimated total amount of the allocation base is likely to fall. For example, in a recession total sales are likely to fall and the company may use less overtime or lay off workers so that the total amount of direct labor-hours declines as well. Since manufacturing overhead cost tends to be relatively fixed, the predetermined overhead rate will rise as the general level of activity falls. This will result in higher product costs and may lead managers to attempt to increase prices—which would be unwise in a recession.

   2.   Under the traditional method, products and services are charged for the resources they *don't* use as well as the resources they do use. Suppose, for example, that a particular product uses 10% of the capacity of a machine. Under the traditional method, if the machine is expected to be idle 50% of the time, the product will be charged for 20% of the cost of the machine. In effect, the product will be charged 10% of the total cost of the machine for the time it uses and 10% of the total cost of the machine for the idle capacity it does not use.

B.   An alternative to the traditional method is to base the predetermined overhead rate on the total amount of the allocation base at capacity. For example, suppose that the estimated amount of machine-hours for the upcoming year is 80,000 hours even though the plant has capacity for 100,000 hours. Under this approach, the predetermined overhead rate would be based on the capacity of 100,000 hours rather than on the expected usage of 80,000 hours. This method has a number of advantages:

   1.   Product costs are stable and do not increase as the level of activity declines and decrease as the level of activity rises.

   2.   Products are charged only for their share of the costs of the resources they actually use.

C.   When the predetermined overhead rate is based on the total amount of the allocation base at capacity, overhead will ordinarily be underapplied. This is because of idle capacity. Rather than closing out this underapplied overhead to Cost of Goods Sold or allocating it among inventories and Cost of Goods Sold, the underapplied overhead is treated as a period expense and is separately disclosed as "Cost of Unused Capacity." This treatment makes the costs of idle capacity much more visible than under the conventional approach.

REVIEW AND SELF-TEST
Questions and Exercises

True or False

Enter a T or an F in the blank to indicate whether the statement is true or false.

___ 1. A company producing many different kinds of furniture would probably use a job-order cost system.

___ 2. Process costing systems are used in situations where output is homogeneous—the company makes a single product for long periods of time.

___ 3. Most factory overhead costs are direct costs and can be easily traced to specific jobs.

___ 4. The predetermined overhead rate is computed using estimates of overhead cost and the amount of the allocation base.

___ 5. The predetermined overhead rate is generally computed on a monthly basis rather than on an annual basis to increase the accuracy of unit costs.

___ 6. The cost of indirect materials used in production is added to the Manufacturing Overhead account rather than added directly to Work in Process.

___ 7. The job cost sheet is used to accumulate the costs charged to a particular job.

___ 8. Actual manufacturing overhead costs are charged directly to the Work in Process account as the costs are incurred.

___ 9. Selling and administrative expenses are charged to the Manufacturing Overhead account.

___ 10. If more overhead is applied to Work in Process than is actually incurred, then overhead cost will be overapplied.

___ 11. A debit balance in the Manufacturing Overhead account at the end of a period would mean that overhead was underapplied for the period.

___ 12. Any balance in the Work in Process account at the end of a period should be closed to Cost of Goods Sold.

___ 13. Under- or overapplied overhead is computed by finding the difference between actual overhead costs and the amount of overhead cost applied to Work in Process.

Multiple Choice

Choose the best answer or response by placing the identifying letter in the space provided.

___ 1. In a job-order costing system, the basic document for accumulating costs for a specific job is: a) the materials requisition form; b) the job cost sheet; c) the Work in Process inventory account; d) the labor time ticket.

___ 2. Suppose $30,000 of raw materials are purchased. What account is debited? a) Work in Process inventory; b) Raw Materials inventory; c) Cost of Goods Sold; d) Manufacturing Overhead.

___ 3. Suppose $20,000 of raw materials are withdrawn from the storeroom to be used in production. Of this amount, $15,000 consists of direct materials and $5,000 consists of indirect materials. What account or accounts will be debited? a) Work in Process $15,000 and Raw Materials $5,000; b) Raw Materials $15,000 and Manufacturing Overhead $5,000; c) Manufacturing Overhead $15,000 and Work in Process $5,000; d) Work in Process $15,000 and Manufacturing Overhead $5,000.

___ 4. Suppose $70,000 of wages and salaries are earned by employees. Of this amount, $20,000 consists of direct labor; $10,000 consists of indirect labor; and $40,000 consists of administrative salaries. What account or accounts will be debited? a) Work in Process $20,000 and Manufacturing Overhead $10,000 and Administrative Salary Expense $40,000; b) Direct Labor $20,000 and Indirect Labor $10,000 and Administrative Salary Expense $40,000; c) Work in Process $20,000 and Manufacturing Overhead $50,000; d) Direct Labor $20,000 and Manufacturing Overhead $50,000.

___ 5. Suppose jobs are completed whose job cost sheets total to $120,000. What account will be debited? a) Manufacturing Overhead $120,000; b) Cost of Goods Sold $120,000; c) Work in Process $120,000; d) Finished Goods $120,000.

___ 6. Suppose a total of $30,000 of overhead is applied to jobs. What account will be debited? a) Manufacturing Overhead $30,000; b) Cost of Goods Sold $30,000; c) Work in Process $30,000; d) Finished Goods $30,000.

_____ 7. Last year, a company reported estimated overhead, $100,000; actual overhead, $90,000; and applied overhead, $92,000. The company's overhead cost for the year would be: a) underapplied, $10,000; b) underapplied, $8,000; c) overapplied, $2,000; d) overapplied, $10,000.

_____ 8. Jurden Company bases its predetermined overhead rates on machine-hours. At the beginning of the year, the company estimated its manufacturing overhead for the year would be $60,000 and there would be a total of 40,000 machine-hours. Actual manufacturing overhead for year amounted to $65,100 and the actual machine-hours totaled 42,000. Manufacturing overhead for the year would be: a) underapplied by $2,100; b) overapplied by $3,000; c) underapplied by $3,000; d) overapplied by $5,100.

_____ 9. On January 1, Hessler Company's Work in Process account had a balance of $18,000. During the year, direct materials costing $35,000 were placed into production. Direct labor cost for the year was $60,000. The predetermined overhead rate for the year was set at 150% of direct labor cost. Actual overhead costs for the year totaled $92,000. Jobs costing $190,000 to manufacture according to their job cost sheets were completed during the year. On December 31, the balance in the Work in Process inventory account would be: a) $13,000; b) $18,000; c) $15,000; d) $8,000.

_____ 10. The Cost of Goods Manufactured represents: a) the amount of cost charged to Work in Process during the period; b) the amount transferred from Work in Process to Finished Goods during the period; c) the amount of cost placed into production during the period; d) none of these.

_____ 11. If overhead is overapplied for a period, it means that: a) the predetermined overhead rate used to apply overhead cost to Work in Process was too low; b) the company incurred more overhead cost than it charged to Work in Process; c) too much cost has been assigned to jobs; d) none of these.

_____ 12. Malt Company's Manufacturing Overhead account showed a $10,000 underapplied overhead balance on December 31. Other accounts showed the following amounts of overhead applied from the current period in their ending balances:

Work in Process..............	$40,000
Finished Goods	$60,000
Cost of Goods Sold.........	$100,000

If the company allocates the underapplied overhead among Cost of Goods Sold, Work in Process, and Finished Goods, the amount allocated to Work in Process would be: a) $2,000; b) $4,000; c) $1,600; d) $1,800.

Exercises

3-1.   Bartle Company uses a job-order cost system and applies overhead with a predetermined overhead rate based on direct labor-hours. At the beginning of the year the estimated total manufacturing overhead for the year was $150,000 and the estimated level of activity was 100,000 direct labor-hours. At the end of the year, cost records revealed that actual overhead costs of $160,000 had been incurred and that 105,000 direct labor-hours had been worked.

 a. The predetermined overhead rate for the year was $_____

 b. Manufacturing overhead cost applied to work in process during the year was $_____

 c. The amount of underapplied or overapplied overhead cost for the year was $_____

3-2. The following selected account balances are taken from the books of Pardoe Company as of January 1 of the most recent year:

Cash	*Work in Process*	*Accounts Payable*	*Sales*
12,000	40,000	75,000	

Accounts Receivable	*Finished Goods*	*Salaries and Wages Payable*	*Cost of Goods Sold*
48,000	100,000	12,000	

Prepaid Insurance	*Accumulated Depreciation*		
8,000	120,000		

Raw Materials	*Manufacturing Overhead*		
30,000			

The following data relate to the activities of Pardoe Company during the year:

1. Raw materials purchased on account, $150,000.
2. Raw materials issued to production, $145,000 (all direct materials).
3. Advertising cost incurred for the year, $50,000 (credit accounts payable).
4. Utilities cost incurred for the factory, $35,000 (credit accounts payable).
5. Salaries and wages costs incurred: direct labor, $250,000 (30,000 hours); indirect labor, $75,000; selling and administrative, $140,000.
6. Depreciation recorded for the year, $20,000, of which 75% related to the factory and 25% related to selling and administrative functions.
7. Other factory overhead costs incurred for the year, $30,000 (credit accounts payable).
8. Other selling and administrative expenses incurred for the year, $25,000 (credit accounts payable).
9. Prepaid insurance of $4,000 expired during the year; all of this is related to the factory.
10. The company applies overhead on the basis of direct labor-hours at $5.50 per hour.
11. The cost of goods manufactured for the year totaled $550,000.
12. Goods that cost $540,000 according to their job cost sheets were sold on account for $800,000.
13. Collections on account from customers during the year totaled $790,000.
14. Cash disbursed during the year: on accounts payable, $300,000; for salaries and wages, $460,000.

Required:

a. Post the above entries directly to Pardoe Company's T-accounts on the previous page. Key your entries with the numbers 1-14.

b. Compute the ending balance in each T-account.

c. Is overhead underapplied or overapplied for the year? Close the balance to Cost of Goods Sold. (Key the entry as #15.)

d. Prepare an income statement for the year using the form that appears below.

PARDOE COMPANY
Income Statement

Sales	$_____
Less cost of goods sold...	_____
Gross margin	_____
Less operating expenses:	
_____..............................	$_____
_____..............................	_____
_____..............................	_____
_____..............................	_____ _____
Net operating income	$_____

Chapter 3

3-3.   The following data were taken from the Precision Milling Machine, Inc., cost records for the current year. Compute the amount of raw materials used in production during the year:

Raw materials inventory, beginning	$10,000
Raw materials inventory, ending	$15,000
Purchases of raw materials	$145,000

_____

_____

_____

_____

_____

_____

_____

_____

3-4.   Suppose all of the raw materials used in production by Precision Milling Machine in the preceding exercise were direct materials. The company has supplied the following additional information:

Direct labor cost	$240,000
Manufacturing overhead applied	$90,000
Work in process inventory, beginning	$60,000
Work in process inventory, ending	$75,000

Compute the cost of goods manufactured for the year.

_____

_____

_____

_____

_____

_____

_____

_____

3-5.   Precision Milling Machine Company has supplied the following additional information. Use this data together with your answer to exercise 3-4 above to compute the (adjusted) Cost of Goods Sold for the company. Close out any balance in Manufacturing Overhead to Cost of Goods Sold.

Actual manufacturing overhead incurred	$88,000
Finished goods inventory, beginning	$120,000
Finished goods inventory, ending	$145,000

3-6.   **Critical thought writing exercise:** Quality Foods, Inc., is a major producer of canned vegetables, fruits, and other goods. This year the company planned a normal year of producing canned goods and set its predetermined overhead rate the same as in other years. However, during the year a major freeze in key growing areas wiped out much of the expected fruit crop and the company was able to do little canning of fruit. A large amount of the manufacturing overhead cost associated with producing canned goods consists of depreciation and other fixed costs. Would you expect Quality Foods, Inc., to have underapplied or overapplied manufacturing overhead cost this year? Explain.

Answers to Questions and Exercises

True or False

1. T Job-order costing is used when many different kinds of products are made.

2. T Process costing is generally used when output is homogeneous.

3. F Only direct materials and direct labor are direct costs; manufacturing overhead cannot be easily traced to specific jobs.

4. T Estimates are used since a rate must be developed before the period begins.

5. F The predetermined overhead rate is usually computed on an annual basis to smooth out month-to-month variations in cost and activity.

6. T Indirect costs are charged to the Manufacturing Overhead account.

7. T A separate job cost sheet is prepared for each job, and is used to accumulate costs as they are charged to the job.

8. F Actual manufacturing overhead costs are charged to the Manufacturing Overhead account—not to Work in Process.

9. F Selling and administrative expenses are period costs, not product costs; thus, they are deducted as expenses on the income statement in the period they are incurred.

10. T This is true by definition.

11. T A debit balance in Manufacturing Overhead would mean that more overhead cost was incurred than was applied to Work in Process. Thus, manufacturing overhead would be underapplied.

12. F Any balance in the Manufacturing Overhead account (not Work in Process) should be closed to Cost of Goods Sold or allocated among ending inventories and Cost of Goods Sold. Work in Process is an inventory account that appears on the balance sheet.

13. T By definition, this is how under- or overapplied overhead cost is computed.

Multiple Choice

1. b The job cost sheet is used to accumulate direct materials, direct labor, and overhead costs.

2. b The journal entry would be:

Raw Materials	30,000	
Cash or Accounts Payable		30,000

3. d The journal entry would be:

Work in Process	15,000	
Manufacturing Overhead	5,000	
Raw Materials		20,000

4. a The journal entry would be:

Work in Process	20,000	
Manufacturing Overhead	10,000	
Administrative Salaries Expense	40,000	
Wages and Salaries Payable		70,000

5. d The journal entry would be:

Finished Goods	120,000	
Work in Process		120,000

6. c The journal entry would be:

Work in Process	30,000	
Manufacturing Overhead		30,000

7. c Under- or overapplied overhead represents the difference between actual overhead cost and applied overhead cost. The computation in this case would be:

Actual overhead cost	$90,000
Applied overhead cost	92,000
Overapplied overhead cost	$(2,000)

8. a The predetermined overhead rate is $60,000 ÷ 40,000 hours = $1.50 per hour.

Actual overhead cost	$65,100
Applied overhead cost ($1.50 × 42,000 hours)	63,000
Underapplied overhead cost	$ 2,100

Chapter 3

9. a The solution would be:

Work in Process

Balance	18,000	190,000	Finished
Direct materials	35,000		
Direct labor	60,000		
Overhead applied*	90,000		
Balance	13,000		

*$60,000 \times 150\% = \$90,000$

10. b The cost of goods manufactured represents the costs of goods completed during a period; thus, it is the amount transferred from Work in Process to Finished Goods.

11. c If overhead is overapplied, then more overhead cost has been added to jobs than has been incurred. Therefore, too much overhead cost will have been assigned to jobs.

12. a The computations would be:

Work in Process	$ 40,000	20%
Finished Goods	60,000	30
Cost of Goods Sold	100,000	50
Total cost	$200,000	100%

$20\% \times \$10,000 = \$2,000.$

Exercises

3-1. a. $\dfrac{\$150,000}{100,000 \text{ DLHs}} = \$1.50 \text{ per DLH}$

b. 105,000 DLHS $\times$ $1.50 per DLH = $157,500 applied

c.
Actual overhead cost	$160,000
Applied overhead cost	157,500
Underapplied overhead cost	$ 2,500

3-2. The answers to parts (a) and (b) are on the following page.

c. Overhead is overapplied by $6,000.

d.

PARDOE COMPANY
Income Statement

Sales		$800,000
Less cost of goods sold ($540,000 – $6,000)		534,000
Gross margin		266,000
Less operating expenses:		
Advertising expense	$ 50,000	
Salaries expense	140,000	
Depreciation expense	5,000	
Other expenses	25,000	220,000
Net operating income		$ 46,000

3-2.   a. & b.

Cash		Accumulated Depreciation		Sales	
Bal. 12,000	760,000 (14)		120,000 Bal.		800,000 (12a)
(13) 790,000			20,000 (6)		
42,000			140,000		

Accounts Receivable		Manufacturing Overhead		Cost of Goods Sold	
Bal. 48,000	790,000 (13)	(4) 35,000	165,000 (10)	(12b) 540,000	6,000 (15)
(12a) 800,000		(5) 75,000		534,000	
58,000		(6) 15,000			
		(7) 30,000			

Prepaid insurance		(9) 4,000		Salaries Expense	
Bal. 8,000	4,000 (9)	(15) 6,000	6,000	(5) 140,000	
4,000					

Raw Materials		Accounts Payable		Advertising Expense	
Bal. 30,000	145,000 (2)	(14) 300,000	75,000 Bal.	(3) 50,000	
(1) 150,000			150,000 (1)		
35,000			50,000 (3)		
			35,000 (4)		

Work in Process			30,000 (7)	Depreciation Expense	
Bal. 40,000	550,000 (11)		25,000 (8)	(6) 5,000	
(2) 145,000			65,000		
(5) 250,000					
(10) 165,000					
50,000					

				Other Selling and Administrative Expenses	
Finished Goods		Salaries and Wages Payable		(8) 25,000	
Bal. 100,000	540,000 (12b)	(14) 460,000	12,000 Bal.		
(11) 550,000			465,000 (5)		
110,000			17,000		

3-3.	Raw materials inventory, beginning	$ 10,000
	Add: Purchases of raw materials	145,000
	Total	155,000
	Deduct: Raw materials inventory, ending	15,000
	Raw materials used in production	$140,000

3-4.	Direct materials	$140,000
	Direct labor	240,000
	Manufacturing overhead applied	90,000
	Total manufacturing cost	470,000
	Add: Beginning work in process inventory	60,000
		530,000
	Deduct: Ending work in process inventory	75,000
	Cost of goods manufactured	$455,000

3-5.	Finished goods inventory, beginning	$120,000
	Add: Cost of goods manufactured	455,000
	Goods available for sale	575,000
	Deduct: Finished goods, ending	145,000
	Unadjusted cost of goods sold	430,000
	Deduct: Overapplied overhead (see below)	2,000
	Adjusted cost of goods sold	$428,000
	Actual manufacturing overhead cost incurred	$88,000
	Applied manufacturing overhead cost	90,000
	Overapplied overhead cost	($ 2,000)

3-6.   Quality Foods, Inc. would probably have underapplied manufacturing overhead cost for the year. Since a large amount of the manufacturing overhead cost associated with producing canned goods is fixed, the company's *actual* manufacturing overhead costs would be about as planned. However, the company's *applied* manufacturing overhead costs would be less than planned since less productive activity would take place in the plant due to the loss of the fruit crop. Thus, with a large amount of *actual* overhead cost and less than planned *applied* overhead cost, the company would end the year with an underapplied balance in its Manufacturing Overhead account.

Chapter 4

Systems Design: Process Costing

Chapter Study Suggestions

✳

The chapter is divided into five main parts. The first part compares job-order and process costing. Exhibit 4-1, which outlines the differences between the two costing methods, is the key to understanding this part. The second part of the chapter describes cost flows in a process costing system. Study Exhibit 4-3 carefully, as well as the journal entries that follow. The third part of the chapter deals with a concept known as equivalent units of production. Pay particular attention to the computations in Exhibits 4-5 and 4-6.

The fourth part of the chapter illustrates preparing a production report using the weighted-average method. The production report is complex and you will need to take the time required to learn how it is constructed. Exhibit 4-9 provides a detailed example of a production report.

Appendix 4A covers the FIFO method. If your instructor assigns this appendix, pay particular attention to Exhibit 4A-3, which shows the format of a FIFO production report, and Exhibit 4A-4, which compares the weighted-average and FIFO methods.

CHAPTER HIGHLIGHTS

A. Process costing is used in industries that produce homogeneous products such as bricks, flour, and cement. It is also used in some assembly-type operations, as well as in utilities producing gas, water, and electricity.

B. Process costing is similar to job-order costing in three ways:

1. Both systems have the same basic purposes, which are to assign material, labor, and overhead costs to products and to provide a mechanism for computing unit costs.

2. Both systems use the same basic manufacturing accounts: Manufacturing Overhead, Raw Materials, Work in Process, and Finished Goods.

3. Costs flow through these accounts in basically the same way in both systems.

C. Process costing differs from job-order costing in four ways:

1. A single product is produced on a continuous basis, and each unit is essentially the same.

2. Costs are accumulated by department, rather than by job.

3. The department production report (rather than the job cost sheet) is the key document showing the accumulation and disposition of costs.

4. Unit costs are computed by department (rather than by job).

D. A *processing department* is any work center where work is performed on a product and where materials, labor, or overhead costs are added. Processing departments in a process costing system have two common features. First, the activity carried out in the department is performed uniformly on all units passing through it. Second, the output of the department is basically homogeneous.

E. Less effort is usually required to use a process costing system than a job-order costing system; costs only need to be traced to a few processing departments rather than to many individual jobs.

F. Exhibit 4-3 provides a T-account model of cost flows in a process costing system. A separate work in process account is maintained for each processing department. Materials, labor, and overhead costs are entered directly into each processing department's work in process account.

G. Once costs have been totaled for a department, the department's output must be determined so that unit costs can be computed. Units that have only been partially completed pose a problem. A unit that is only 10% complete should not count as much as a unit that has been completed and transferred on to the next department.

1. *Equivalent units* are the number of whole, complete units one could obtain from the materials and effort contained in partially completed units. Equivalent units are computed using the following formula:

$$\text{Equivalent units} = \frac{\text{Number of}}{\text{partially completed}} \times \frac{\text{Percentage}}{\text{completion}}$$
$$\text{units}$$

2. *Equivalent units of production* is used to compute the cost per equivalent unit. Under the weighted-average method, the equivalent units of production are determined as follows:

Units completed and transferred out	XXX
+ Equivalent units of ending inventory	XXX
= Equivalent units of production	XXX

H. A separate cost per equivalent unit amount is computed within each processing department for each cost category. The cost categories may include:

1. Costs of prior departments associated with units transferred into the department.

2. Materials costs added in the department.

3. Direct labor costs added in the department.

4. Manufacturing overhead costs applied in the department.

In process costing, direct labor costs and manufacturing overhead costs are often combined into one cost category called *conversion costs*.

I. Note the following points concerning process costing.

1. The equivalent units of production and the cost per equivalent unit must be computed separately for each cost category.

2. Units transferred out of the department to the next department—or, in the case of the last department, to finished goods—are always considered to be 100% complete with respect to the work done by the transferring department.

3. The first processing department will not have a cost category for the costs of units transferred in, but

subsequent departments will have such a cost category. Units in process in a department are considered to be 100% complete with respect to the costs of the prior department.

J. The purpose of the *production report* is to summarize all of the activity that takes place in a department for a period. A production report has three parts:

1. A *quantity schedule*, which shows the flow of units through the department, and the computation of equivalent units for each cost category for the period.

2. A statement showing computation of the *cost per equivalent unit* for each cost category for the period.

3. A *reconciliation* of all cost flows into and out of the department during the period.

Refer to Exhibit 4-9 in the text as you go through the explanation of the production report below.

K. The purpose of the *quantity schedule* on the production report is to show the flow of units through a department. The schedule shows the number of units to be accounted for in a department and it shows how those units have been accounted for.

1. The format of the quantity schedule under the weighted-average method is:

Units to be accounted for:
    Work in process, beginning   XXX
    Started into production   XXX
  Total units to be accounted for   XXX

Units accounted for as follows:
    Transferred out to the next
      department or to finished goods   XXX
    Work in process, ending   XXX
  Total units accounted for   XXX

2. The equivalent units for the units transferred out and for the ending work in process inventory are listed next to the quantity schedule on the production report.

L. The second step in preparing a production report is to compute the *cost per equivalent unit* for each cost category. Under the weighted-average method, this involves summing the costs from the beginning inventory with any costs added during the period. This total cost is then divided by the equivalent units of production for the cost category to determine the cost per equivalent unit.

M. The final step in a production report is to prepare a *reconciliation* of all costs. Costs are accounted for as either transferred out during the period or assigned to

the ending work in process inventory. Costs are determined as follows:

1. Units transferred out. These units are presumed to be 100% complete. (If they were not complete with respect to the work done in the department, they would not be transferred out.) The costs of units transferred out are computed by multiplying the number of units transferred out by the cost per equivalent unit for each cost category. These costs are then summed.

2. Units in ending work in process inventory. Within each cost category, the number of equivalent units is multiplied by the cost per equivalent unit for that cost category. These costs are then summed.

N. Study Exhibit 4-9 carefully; it shows how the weighted-average method works. Note that this method combines costs from the beginning inventory with costs from the current period. It is called the weighted-average method because it averages together costs from the prior period with costs of the current period.

O. *Operation costing* is a hybrid system containing elements of both job-order and process costing. It is most commonly used when products use different materials but follow the same basic processing steps. For example, a factory that assembles personal computers might make many different models that use different components. However, all of the models go through the assembly department, testing department, and packing and shipping department.

1. In operation costing, products are handled in batches and each batch is charged with its own specific materials. In this sense, operation costing is similar to job-order costing.

2. Labor and overhead costs are accumulated by department and these costs are assigned to the batches on an average per unit basis as in process costing.

Appendix 4A: FIFO Method

A. The *FIFO method* is more complex than the weighted-average method, but is considered to be more accurate. The FIFO method keeps units and costs from the prior period separate from the units and costs of the current period.

B. The production report under the FIFO method is similar to the production report under the weighted-average method. However, important differences in the reports are easy to overlook. Refer to Exhibit 4A-3 as you read the explanations that follow below.

C. The format of the quantity schedule under the FIFO method follows:

Units to be accounted for:
Work in process, beginning	XXX
Started into production	XXX
Total units to be accounted for	XXX

Units accounted for as follows:
Transferred out:
Units from beginning inventory	XXX
Units started and completed	XXX
Work in process, ending	XXX
Total units accounted for	XXX

D. Under the FIFO method, the equivalent units of production are determined as follows:

Equivalent units to complete the beginning inventory	XXX
+ Units started and completed this period	XXX
+ Equivalent units in ending inventory	XXX
= Equivalent units of production	XXX

The difference between the equivalent units of production under the FIFO method and under the weighted-average method is that the weighted-average method includes the equivalent units in beginning inventory whereas the FIFO method does not. This is most easily seen from the following alternative method of computing the equivalent units of production under the FIFO method:

Units completed this period	XXX
– Equivalent units in beginning inventory	XXX
+ Equivalent units in ending inventory	XXX
= Equivalent units of production	XXX

E. After preparing the quantity schedule and computing the equivalent units, the costs per equivalent unit are computed. Under the FIFO method, these costs are computed using *only* costs added during the current period.

F. The final step in the production report is to prepare a reconciliation of all costs for the period.

1. Costs are accounted for as either transferred out during the period or assigned to the ending work in process inventory.

2. In computing the cost of units transferred out under the FIFO method, the units in beginning work in process inventory are kept separate from the units started and completed during the current period.

G. Comparing the weighted-average and FIFO methods, four points should be noted:

1. In most situations, the two methods will produce unit costs that are nearly the same.

2. From the standpoint of cost control, the FIFO method is superior to the weighted-average method since it separates the costs of the prior period from the costs of the current period.

3. Although the FIFO method is more complex to apply than the weighted-average method, computers can handle this complexity with ease.

4. Any difference in costs reported using the FIFO and weighted-average methods must be due to the existence of beginning work in process inventories. Because work in process inventories are reduced in a JIT program, the differences between the two methods will diminish.

REVIEW AND SELF-TEST
Questions and Exercises

True or False

Enter a T or an F in the blank to indicate whether the statement is true or false.

____ 1. A utility such as a water company would typically use a process costing system.

____ 2. Under process costing it is important to identify the materials, labor, and overhead costs associated with a particular customer's order just as under job-order costing.

____ 3. In a process costing system, the production report replaces the job cost sheet.

____ 4. In a process costing system, a work in process account is maintained for each processing department.

____ 5. Operation costing employs aspects of both job-order and process costing systems.

____ 6. Since costs are accumulated by department in a process costing system, there is no need for a finished goods inventory account.

____ 7. In process costing, costs incurred in a department are not transferred to the next department.

____ 8. If beginning work in process inventory contains 500 units that are 60% complete, then the inventory contains 300 equivalent units.

____ 9. (Appendix 4A) Under the FIFO method, costs in the beginning work in process inventory are kept separate from costs of the current period.

____ 10. (Appendix 4A) Under the FIFO method, units in beginning work in process inventory are treated as if they were completed before any new units are completed.

____ 11. (Appendix 4A) Under the FIFO method, units transferred out are treated in separate blocks— one block consisting of the units in the beginning inventory, and the other block consisting of the units started and completed during the period.

____ 12. (Appendix 4A) The weighted-average and FIFO methods will typically produce significantly different unit costs when beginning work in process inventory is zero.

____ 13. (Appendix 4A) From the standpoint of cost control, the weighted-average method is superior to the FIFO method.

Multiple Choice

Choose the best answer or response by placing the identifying letter in the space provided.

____ 1. The Mixing Department of Deerdon Company started 4,800 units into process during the month. 500 units were in the beginning inventory and 300 units were in the ending inventory. How many units were completed and transferred out during the month? a) 5,000; b) 4,600; c) 5,300; d) 5,100.

____ 2. Last month the Welding Department of Eager Company started 8,000 units into production. The department had 2,000 units in process at the beginning of the month, which were 60% complete with respect to conversion costs, and 3,000 units in process at the end of the month, which were 30% complete with respect to conversion costs. A total of 7,000 units were completed and transferred to the next department during the month. Using the weighted-average method, the equivalent units of production for conversion costs for the month would be: a) 7,900; b) 8,500; c) 9,200; d) 9,500.

____ 3. (Appendix 4A) Refer to the data in question 2 above. Using the FIFO method, the equivalent units of production for conversion costs for the month would be: a) 8,300; b) 7,700; c) 6,700; d) 7,300.

____ 4. At the beginning of the month, 200 units were in process in the Stamping Department and they were 70% complete with respect to materials. During the month 2,000 units were transferred to the next department. At the end of the month, 100 units were still in process and they were 60% complete with respect to materials. The materials cost in the beginning work in process inventory was $2,721 and $39,200 of materials costs were added during the month. Using the weighted-average method, what is the cost per equivalent unit for materials costs? a) $19.06; b) $20.35; c) $20.42; d) $19.60.

____ 5. The Weaving Department of a company had $8,000 of conversion cost in its beginning work in process inventory and added $64,000 of conversion cost during the month. The department completed 37,000 units during the month and had 10,000 units in the ending work in process inventory that were 30% complete with respect to conversion cost. Using the weighted-average method, the amount of cost assigned to the units in ending inventory would be: a) $12,600; b) $4,800; c) $11,200; d) $5,400.

____ 6. The Heat Treatment Department at Northern Pipe is the third department in a sequential process. The work in process account for the department would consist of: a) costs transferred in from the prior department; b) materials costs added in the heat treatment department; c) conversion costs added in the heat treatment department; d) all of the above.

____ 7. (Appendix 4A) Mercer Corp. uses the FIFO method in its process costing system. The Cutting Department had $6,000 of materials cost in its beginning work in process inventory and $75,000 in materials cost was added during the period. The equivalent units of production for materials for the period was 20,000. The cost per equivalent unit for materials would be: a) $3.75; b) $4.05; c) $0.30; d) $3.30.

____ 8. (Appendix 4A) Danmount Corp. uses the FIFO method in its processing costing system. The cost per equivalent unit of conversion cost in the first processing department was $4.00 this month. 1,000 units were in beginning work in process inventory in the department at the beginning of the month. These 1,000 units were 30% complete with respect to conversion cost and had already incurred $1,000 in conversion cost. A total of 10,000 units were transferred to the second processing department during the month. 2,000 units were in the ending work in process inventory at the end of the month and they were 60% complete with respect to conversion cost. How much conversion cost would have been assigned to the units that were transferred to the second processing department during the month? a) $40,000; b) $39,800; c) $38,800; d) $44,600.

Exercises

4-1.   Diebold Company has a process costing system. Data relating to activities in the Mixing Department for March follow:

	Units	Percent Complete Materials	Percent Complete Conversion
Work in process, March 1	5,000	100%	60%
Units started into production	80,000		
Work in process, March 31	2,000	100%	50%

All materials are added at the start of processing in the Mixing Department.
    Using the weighted-average method, fill in the following quantity schedule and a computation of equivalent units for the month:

	Quantity Schedule
Units to be accounted for:	
Work in process, beginning	
(materials 100% complete;	
conversion _____% complete)	_____
Started into production	_____
Total units to be accounted for	_____

	Quantity Schedule	Equivalent Units Materials	Equivalent Units Conversion
Units accounted for as follows:			
Transferred out during the month	_____	_____	_____
Work in process, ending			
(materials 100% complete;			
conversion _____% complete)	_____	_____	_____
Total units accounted for	_____	_____	_____

4-2. Minden Company uses the weighted-average method in its process costing system. Complete the cost reconciliation section of the production report below for the Welding Department, the first processing department in the company.

Production Report, Welding Department

Quantity schedule and equivalent units

	Quantity Schedule
Units to be accounted for:	
Work in process, beginning	
(materials 100% complete; labor	
and overhead 20% complete)	5,000
Started into production	75,000
Total units to be accounted for	80,000

		Equivalent Units		
		Materials	Labor	Overhead
Units accounted for as follows:				
Transferred out	72,000	72,000	72,000	72,000
Work in process, ending				
(materials 100% complete; labor				
and overhead 75% complete)	8,000	8,000	6,000	6,000
Total units accounted for	80,000	80,000	78,000	78,000

Costs per equivalent unit

	Total Cost	Materials	Labor	Overhead	Whole Unit
Cost to be accounted for:					
Work in process, beginning	$ 9,500	$ 4,500	$ 3,000	$ 2,000	
Cost added by the department	460,500	75,500	231,000	154,000	
Total cost (a)	$470,000	$ 80,000	$234,000	$156,000	
Equivalent units (b)		80,000	78,000	78,000	
Cost per equivalent unit (a)÷(b)		$1.00 +	$3.00 +	$2.00 =	$6.00

Cost reconciliation

		Equivalent Units		
		Materials	Labor	Overhead
Cost accounted for as follows:				
Transferred out	$_____	_____	_____	_____
Work in process, ending:				
Materials	_____	_____		
Labor	_____		_____	
Overhead	_____			_____
Total work in process, ending	_____			
Total cost accounted for	$ 470,000			

4-3.　(Appendix 4A) Sinclair Company uses the FIFO method in its process costing system. Complete the cost reconciliation section of the production report for the Cooking Department, the first processing department in the company.

Production Report, Cooking Department

Quantity schedule and equivalent units	*Quantity Schedule*			
Units to be accounted for:				
Work in process, beginning (materials 100% complete; labor and overhead 25% complete)	8,000			
Started into production	62,000			
Total units accounted for	70,000			

		Equivalent Units		
		Materials	*Labor*	*Overhead*
Units accounted for as follows:				
Transferred out:				
Units from the beginning inventory	8,000	—	6,000	6,000
Units started and completed this month	57,000	57,000	57,000	57,000
Work in process, ending (materials 100% complete; labor and overhead 80% complete)	5,000	5,000	4,000	4,000
Total units accounted for	70,000	62,000	67,000	67,000

Costs per equivalent unit	*Total Cost*	*Materials*	*Labor*	*Overhead*	*Whole Unit*
Cost to be accounted for:					
Work in process, beginning	$ 16,800				
Added by the department (a)	260,500	$93,000	$134,000	$33,500	
Total cost to be accounted for	$277,300				
Equivalent units (b)		62,000	67,000	67,000	
Cost per equivalent unit, (a) ÷ (b)		$ 1.50　+	$ 2.00　+	$ 0.50　=	$　4.00

Cost reconciliation		*Equivalent Units*		
		Materials	*Labor*	*Overhead*
Cost accounted for as follows:				
Transferred out:				
From the beginning inventory:				
Cost in the beginning inventory	$_____			
Cost to complete these units:				
Materials	_____	_____		
Labor	_____		_____	
Overhead	_____			_____
Total cost from the beginning inventory	_____			
Units started and completed this month	_____	_____	_____	_____
Total cost transferred out	_____			
Work in process, ending:				
Materials	_____	_____		
Labor	_____		_____	
Overhead	_____			_____
Total work in process, ending	_____			
Total cost accounted for	$___277,300			

Answers to Questions and Exercises

True or False

1. T Process costing is widely used by utilities since their output (water, gas, electricity) is homogeneous.

2. F Since units are indistinguishable from each other, there is no need to identify costs by customer order.

3. T See the discussion in Exhibit 4-1.

4. T In a process costing system a work in process inventory account is maintained for each department. A production report is also prepared for each department.

5. T In operation costing, materials are often handled as in job-order costing while labor and overhead costs are handled as in process costing.

6. F A finished goods inventory account is needed in a process costing system for unsold finished units, just as in a job-order costing system.

7. F As units move from one department to another, the costs that have been incurred to that point are transferred forward with the units.

8. T 500 units × 60% = 300 equivalent units.

9. T Costs in the beginning work in process inventory are kept separate from costs of the current period so that the cost per equivalent unit of units produced during the current period will reflect only current period costs.

10. T The FIFO method assumes that the units that are first in (i.e., in beginning inventory) are the first out (i.e., completed).

11. T This point is illustrated in Exhibit 4A-3.

12. F When there are no beginning inventories, the weighted-average and FIFO methods will produce identical results.

13. F The reverse is true—from a standpoint of cost control, the FIFO method is superior to the weighted-average method.

Multiple Choice

1. a.

Beginning inventory	500
Units started into process	4,800
Total units	5,300
Less ending inventory	300
Completed and transferred	5,000

2. a.

Units completed and transferred	7,000
Work in process, ending:	
3,000 units × 30%	900
Equivalent units of production	7,900

3. c.

Work in process, beginning:	
2,000 units × 40%*	800
Units started and completed**	5,000
Work in process, ending:	
3,000 units × 30%	900
Equivalent units of production	6,700

*100% – 60% = 40%
**7,000 units – 2,000 units = 5,000 units.

4. b.

Cost in beginning work in process	$ 2,721
Cost added during the month	39,200
Total cost (a)	$41,921

Units transferred out	2,000
Equivalent units in ending work in process inventory (100 × 60%)	60
Equivalent units (b)	2,060
Cost per EU (a) ÷ (b)	$20.35

5. d.

Cost in beginning work in process	$ 8,000
Cost added during the year	64,000
Total cost (a)	$72,000

Units transferred out	37,000
Equivalent units in ending work in process inventory (10,000 × 30%)	3,000
Equivalent units (b)	40,000
Cost per EU (a) ÷ (b)	$1.80

3,000 units × $1.80 per unit = $5,400.

6. d Costs in the department's work in process inventory account include costs transferred in from the previous department and any costs added in the department itself—including materials, labor, and overhead. Labor and overhead together equal conversion cost.

7. a $75,000 \div 20,000$ units = $3.75 per unit.

8. b   Transferred to the next department:
         From the beginning inventory:

Cost in the beginning inventory	$ 1,000
Cost to complete these units ($70\% \times 1,000 \times \$4$)	2,800
Units started and completed this month ($9,000* \times \$4$)	36,000
	$39,800

     * 10,000 units transferred –
      1,000 units in beginning inventory

Exercises

4-1.

	Quantity Schedule		
Units to be accounted for:			
Work in process, beginning (materials 100% complete; conversion 60% complete)	5,000		
Started into production	80,000		
Total units to be accounted for	85,000		

		Equivalent Units	
		Materials	*Conversion*
Units accounted for as follows:			
Transferred out during the month	83,000	83,000	83,000
Work in process, ending (materials 100% complete; conversion 50% complete)	2,000	2,000	1,000
Total units accounted for	85,000	85,000	84,000

4-2.

	Total Cost	*Equivalent Units*		
		Materials	*Labor*	*Overhead*
Cost accounted for as follows:				
Transferred out: (72,000 units × $6 per unit)	$432,000	72,000	72,000	72,000
Work in process, ending:				
Materials cost ($ 1 per EU)	8,000	8,000		
Labor cost ($3 per EU)	18,000		6,000	
Overhead cost ($2 per EU)	12,000			6,000
Total work in process, ending	38,000			
Total cost accounted for	$470,000			

4-3.

	Total Cost	Equivalent Units		
		Materials	*Labor*	*Overhead*
Cost accounted for as follows:				
Transferred out:				
From the beginning inventory:				
Cost in the beginning inventory	$ 16,800			
Cost to complete these units:				
Materials ($1.50 per EU)	0	0		
Labor ($2.00 per EU)	12,000		6,000	
Overhead ($0.50 per EU)	3,000			6,000
Total cost from beginning inventory	31,800			
Units started and completed during				
the month: (57,000 × $4.00)	228,000	57,000	57,000	57,000
Total cost transferred out	259,800			
Work in process, ending:				
Materials cost ($1.50 per EU)	7,500	5,000		
Labor cost ($2.00 per EU)	8,000		4,000	
Overhead cost ($0.50 per EU)	2,000			4,000
Total work in process, ending	17,500			
Total cost accounted for	$277,300			

Chapter 5

Cost Behavior: Analysis and Use

Chapter Study Suggestions

✳

Chapter 5 expands on the discussion of fixed and variable costs that was started in Chapter 2. In addition, the chapter introduces a new cost concept—mixed costs—and shows how mixed costs can be broken down into fixed and variable elements. Focus most of your study time on the section titled "The Analysis of Mixed Costs" that is found midway through the chapter. Pay particular attention to how a *cost formula* is derived and how a cost formula is used to predict future costs at various levels. Memorize the cost formula equation $Y = a + bX$. You need to understand this equation to complete most of the homework exercises and problems.

At the end of the chapter, a new format for the income statement is introduced that emphasizes cost behavior. Exhibit 5-14 illustrates the format of the contribution income statement. *This format should be memorized*—you will be using it throughout the rest of the book.

CHAPTER HIGHLIGHTS

A. A *variable cost* is a cost that varies, in total, in proportion to changes in the level of activity. Variable costs are constant on a *per unit* basis.

   1. Activity is often measured in terms of the volume of goods produced or services provided by the organization. However, other measures of activity may be used for specific purposes such as patients admitted to a hospital, number of machinery setups performed, number of sales calls made, and so on.

   2. A variable cost is shown graphically in Exhibit 5-1. Note that a variable cost is a straight line that goes through zero (i.e., the origin) on the graph.

B. A *fixed cost* is a cost that remains constant in total within the relevant range. Fixed cost per unit varies inversely with changes in activity. As activity increases, per unit fixed costs fall.

   1. Fixed costs can be classified into committed and discretionary fixed costs.

      a. *Committed fixed costs* relate to investments in facilities, equipment, and the basic organization of a company. These costs are difficult to adjust.

      b. *Discretionary fixed costs* result from annual decisions by management to spend in certain areas, such as advertising, research, and management development programs. These costs are easier to modify than committed fixed costs.

   2. Even committed fixed costs may change if the change in activity is big enough. Exhibit 5-6 illustrates this idea. However, within the band of activity known as the relevant range, total fixed cost is constant.

C. A *mixed cost* (or semivariable cost) is a cost that contains both variable and fixed cost elements. Exhibit 5-7 illustrates a mixed cost. Note that in the case of a mixed cost, the straight line representing the relation between total cost and activity does not go through zero (i.e., the origin).

   1. Examples of typical mixed costs include electricity, costs of processing bills, costs of admitting patients to a hospital, and maintenance.

   2. The fixed portion of a mixed cost represents the cost of providing capacity. The variable portion represents the additional cost of using the capacity.

D. The relevant range and curvilinear costs.

   1. For simplicity, a strict linear relation between cost and volume is usually assumed. However, many cost relationships are curvilinear, such as illustrated in Exhibit 5-4.

   2. The straight-line assumption is reasonable since any small portion of a curvilinear cost can be approximated by a straight line. The *relevant range* is the range of activity within which a particular straight line is a valid approximation to the curvilinear cost.

E. Cost formula for a mixed cost.

   1. The fixed and variable cost elements of a mixed cost can be expressed in a *cost formula*, which can be used to predict costs at all levels of activity within the relevant range. This formula is expressed as follows:

$$Y = a + bX$$
where:
   Y = *dependent variable* (the total mixed cost)
   a = vertical intercept (the total fixed cost)
   b = slope of the line (the variable cost)
   X = *independent variable* (the activity level)

   2. Each of the methods discussed below can be used to estimate the variable cost per unit, b, and the total fixed cost, a, based on data from prior periods. Then with the use of the cost formula, the expected amount of total cost, Y, can be computed for any expected activity level, X, within the relevant range.

F. The analysis of a mixed cost begins with records of past cost and activity. The first step is to plot the cost and activity data on a *scattergraph*. The cost is represented on the vertical, Y, axis and activity is represented on the horizontal, X, axis.

   1. If the scattergraph plot indicates that the relation between cost and activity is approximately linear (i.e., a straight line), the analysis can proceed to the next stage of estimating the variable cost per unit of activity and the fixed cost per period.

   2. A quick and dirty way to estimate the variable and fixed costs is to draw a straight line on the scattergraph plot. The intercept of the line with the vertical axis is the estimated total fixed cost. The slope of the line is the estimated variable cost per unit of activity.

G. The *high-low method* of analyzing a mixed cost is based on using the data at the highest and lowest levels of activity.

   1. The high-low method uses the "rise over run" formula for the slope of a straight line. The change in cost observed between the two extremes (i.e., the rise)

is divided by the change in activity (i.e., the run) to estimate the amount of variable cost. The formula is:

$$\frac{\text{Variable cost}}{\text{per unit of activity}} = \frac{\text{Change in cost}}{\text{Change in activity}}$$

2. The estimated variable cost per unit of activity is then used to estimate the fixed cost as follows:

Total cost at the high activity level........	$XXX
Less variable portion:	
High activity level × variable cost	XXX
Fixed portion of the mixed cost	$ XXX

3. The high-low method is quick, but it is not reliable because t is based on costs and activity for only two periods—the periods with the highest and lowest levels of activity. Other data are ignored and these two particular periods tend to be unusual and may not be representative of typical cost behavior.

H. The *least-squares regression method* of analyzing a mixed cost fits a straight line, called a *regression line*, to cost and activity data using a formula explained in the appendix to the chapter.

1. The least-squares regression formula calculates the slope and intercept of the straight line that minimizes the sum of the squared errors from the regression line. Since the computations are fairly complex, it is a good idea to use statistical software or a spreadsheet to do the calculations.

2. *Multiple regression* analysis should be used when more than one factor causes a cost to vary. This technique is, however, beyond the scope of the book.

I. The *contribution approach* to preparation of an income statement emphasizes cost behavior.

1. The *traditional format* for an income statement groups expenses into the functional categories—cost of goods sold on the one hand and administrative and selling expenses on the other hand:

Sales.......................................	$XXX
Less cost of goods sold	XXX
Gross margin.............................	XXX
Less administrative and selling expense ..	XXX
Net operating income............................	$XXX

2. In contrast, the *contribution approach* to the income statement groups expenses according to their cost behavior—variable or fixed.

Sales.......................................	$XXX
Less variable expenses	XXX
Contribution margin................................	XXX
Less fixed expenses.................................	XXX
Net operating income..............................	$XXX

3. Note that the *contribution margin* is determined by deducting all variable expenses from sales.

4. The contribution approach is very useful in internal reports since it emphasizes the behavior of costs. As you will see in later chapters, this is very important in planning, budgeting, controlling operations, and in performance evaluation. However, the traditional format that emphasizes cost by function must be used in external reports.

Appendix 5A: Least-Squares Regression

A. The formulas for computing the variable cost per unit, b, and total fixed cost, a, using the least-squares regression method are:

$$b = \frac{n\left(\sum XY\right)-\left(\sum X\right)\left(\sum Y\right)}{n\left(\sum X^2\right)-\left(\sum X\right)^2}$$

$$a = \frac{\left(\sum Y\right)-b\left(\sum X\right)}{n}$$

where n is the number of observations; X is the activity; and Y is the cost.

B. The appendix illustrates how to use built-in functions in Microsoft Excel to do a regression analysis.

REVIEW AND SELF-TEST
Questions and Exercises

True or False

Enter a T or an F in the blank to indicate whether the statement is true or false.

____ 1. A variable cost is a cost that changes, in total, in proportion to changes in the activity level.

____ 2. In cost analysis work, activity is known as the dependent variable.

____ 3. Within the relevant range, the higher the activity level, the lower the fixed cost per unit.

____ 4. Contribution margin and gross margin mean the same thing.

____ 5. Contribution margin is the difference between sales and variable expenses.

____ 6. Discretionary fixed costs arise from annual decisions by management to spend in certain areas.

____ 7. Advertising is a committed fixed cost.

____ 8. A mixed cost is a cost that contains both manufacturing and non-manufacturing costs.

____ 9. Within the relevant range, the relation between cost and activity is approximately a straight line.

____ 10. In order for a cost to be variable, it must vary with either units produced or services provided.

____ 11. The contribution approach to the income statement organizes costs according to behavior, rather than according to function.

Multiple Choice

Choose the best answer or response by placing the identifying letter in the space provided.

____ 1. A company's cost formula for maintenance is $Y = \$4,000 + \$3X$, where X is machine-hours. During a period in which 2,000 machine-hours are worked, the expected maintenance cost would be: a) $12,000; b) $6,000; c) $10,000; d) $4,000.

____ 2. The costs associated with a company's basic facilities, equipment, and organization are known as: a) committed fixed costs; b) discretionary fixed costs; c) mixed costs; d) variable costs.

____ 3. Last year, Barker Company's sales were $240,000, its fixed costs were $50,000, and its variable costs were $2 per unit. During the year, 80,000 units were sold. The contribution margin was: a) $200,000; b) $240,000; c) $30,000; d) $80,000.

____ 4. An example of a discretionary fixed cost would be: a) depreciation on equipment; b) rent on a factory building; c) salaries of top management; d) items a, b, and c are all discretionary fixed costs; e) none of the above.

____ 5. In March, Espresso Express had electrical costs of $225 when the total volume was 4,500 cups of coffee served. In April, electrical costs were $227.50 for 4,750 cups of coffee. Using the high-low method, what is the estimated fixed cost of electricity per month? a) $200; b) $180; c) $225; d) $150.

Exercises

5-1.   Data concerning the electrical costs at Doughboy Corporation follow:

	Machine hours	Electrical cost
Week 1..............	6,800 hours	$1,770
Week 2..............	6,000 hours	$1,650
Week 3..............	5,400 hours	$1,560
Week 4..............	7,900 hours	$1,935

a.   Plot the data on the following scattergraph:

b.   Is the relation between machine-hours and electrical costs approximately linear? Explain.

_____

_____

_____

_____

5-2.   Refer to the data for Doughboy in the previous exercise.

a.   Using the high-low method of cost analysis, what is the variable cost per machine-hour at Doughboy?

	Cost	*Machine Hours*
High activity level..	_____	_____
Low activity level...	_____	_____
Change	_____	_____

$$\frac{\text{Change in cost}}{\text{Change in activity}} = \frac{\rule{3cm}{0.4pt}}{\rule{3cm}{0.4pt}} = \$\rule{2cm}{0.4pt} \text{ per machine hour}$$

b.   Using the high-low method of cost analysis, what is the total fixed cost?

Total cost at the high activity level..   _____
Less variable cost element:

_____...................   _____

Fixed cost element ....   _____

c.   Express the cost formula for electrical costs in the form Y = a + bX: _____

5-3. (Appendix 5A) Data on a week's activity in the shipping department of Osan, Inc. are given below:

	Units Shipped X	Shipping Cost Y
Monday	12	$595
Tuesday	17	$640
Wednesday	10	$555
Thursday............................	7	$500
Friday	9	$545
Saturday...	5	$480

a. Estimate the fixed cost per day. (Use statistical software or see Appendix 5A for instructions of how to use Excel to compute this value.)

a = _____

b. Using the least-squares method, estimate the variable cost per unit shipped. (Use statistical software or see Appendix 5A for instructions of how to use Excel to compute this value.)

b = _____

c. Express the cost formula for shipping costs in the form $Y = a + bX$: _____

5-4.   During July, Cramer's, Inc., a wholesale distributor of a unique business software application, sold 500 units. The company's income statement for the month follows:

CRAMER'S, INC.
Income Statement
For the Month Ended July 31

Sales ($100 per unit)		$50,000
Less cost of goods sold ($60 per unit)		30,000
Gross margin		20,000
Less operating expenses:		
Commissions ($6 per unit)	$3,000	
Salaries	8,000	
Advertising	6,000	
Shipping ($2 per unit)	1,000	18,000
Net operating income		$ 2,000

Redo the company's income statement for the month in the contribution format. Assume that cost of goods sold, commissions, and shipping expenses are variable costs and salaries and advertising expenses are fixed costs.

CRAMER'S, INC.
Income Statement
For the Month Ended July 31

Sales .... $_____

Less _____ :

    _____.................. $_____

    _____..................   _____

    _____..................   _____   _____

Contribution margin..   _____

Less _____ :

    _____..................   _____

    _____..................   _____   _____

Net operating income.. $_____

Answers to Questions and Exercises

True or False

1. T   This is the definition of a variable cost.

2. F   Activity is the independent variable.

3. T   Fixed costs per unit vary inversely with changes in activity.

4. F   Contribution margin is sales less variable expenses; gross margin is sales less cost of goods sold.

5. T   This is true by definition.

6. T   Discretionary fixed costs are reevaluated each year by management.

7. F   Advertising is a discretionary fixed cost since the company's advertising budget is typically reevaluated on an annual basis.

8. F   Mixed costs contain both variable and fixed cost elements.

9. T   By definition, a straight line is a reasonable approximation to the real cost behavior within a relevant range.

10. F Activity can be measured in many ways besides units produced and units sold. Other measures include miles driven, number of beds occupied in a hospital, and number of flight hours.

11. T The contribution approach groups variable costs together and fixed costs together; thus, the income statement is organized according to cost behavior.

Multiple Choice

1. c
Fixed cost	$ 4,000
Variable cost:	
2,000 hours × $3 per hour	6,000
Total cost	$10,000

2. a   Committed fixed costs relate to basic facilities, equipment, and organization.

3. d
Sales	$240,000
Less variable costs:	
80,000 units × $2 per unit	160,000
Contribution margin	$ 80,000

4. e   All of the listed costs are generally considered to be committed fixed costs.

5. b

	Cost	Cups
High activity level	$227.50	4,750
Low activity level	225.00	4,500
Change	$ 2.50	250

$$\frac{\text{Change in cost}}{\text{Change in activity}} = \frac{\$2.50}{250} = \$0.01 \text{ per cup}$$

Total cost at the high activity	$227.50
Less variable cost element:	
4,750 cups × $0.01 per cup	47.50
Fixed cost element	$180.00

Chapter 5

Exercises

5-1. a. The scattergraph plot looks like this:

b. The relation between machine-hours and electrical costs is almost perfectly linear—a straight line can be drawn through all of the points on the scattergraph.

5-2. a. Variable cost per machine-hour:

	Cost	Machine Hours
High activity level	$1,935	7,900
Low activity level	1,560	5,400
Change	$ 375	2,500

$$\frac{\text{Change in cost}}{\text{Change in activity}} = \frac{\$375}{2,500 \text{ hours}} = \$0.15 \text{ per machine hour}$$

b. Total fixed cost:

Total cost at the high activity level............................	$1,935
Less variable cost element:	
7,900 hours × $0.15 per hour	1,185
Fixed cost element	$ 750

c. Cost formula for electrical costs: $750 per period, plus $0.15 per machine-hour, or
$$Y = \$750 + \$0.15X$$

5-3.   a.   Using statistical software or Excel will yield an estimate of the fixed cost of about $413 per day.

     b.   The least-squares regression estimate of the variable cost is about $13.92 per unit shipped.

     c.   The cost formula is $Y = \$413 + \$13.92X$.

5-4.

CRAMER'S, INC.
Income Statement
For the Month Ended July 31

Sales ($100 per unit)		$50,000
Less variable expenses:		
Cost of goods sold ($60 per unit)	$30,000	
Commissions ($6 per unit)	3,000	
Shipping ($2 per unit)	1,000	34,000
Contribution margin		16,000
Less fixed expenses:		
Salaries	8,000	
Advertising	6,000	14,000
Net operating income		$ 2,000

Chapter 6

Cost-Volume-Profit Relationships

Chapter Study Suggestions

✳

Chapter 6 is one of the key chapters in the book. Many of the chapters ahead depend on concepts developed here. You should study several sections in the chapter with particular attention. The first of these is the section titled, "Contribution Margin." Note how changes in the contribution margin affect net operating income. The next section you should study with particular care is titled "Contribution Margin Ratio." The contribution margin ratio is used in much of the analytical work in the chapter.

Another section warranting particular attention is titled "Some Applications of CVP Concepts." Much of the homework material is drawn from this section. The section titled "Break-Even Analysis" also forms the basis for much of the homework material. Finally, the section titled "The Concept of Sales Mix" shows how to use CVP analysis when the company has more than one product.

When studying this chapter, try especially hard to understand the logic behind the solutions rather than just memorizing formulas.

CHAPTER HIGHLIGHTS

A. The contribution margin is a key concept that will be used throughout the chapter and in subsequent chapters.

    1. The *contribution margin* is the difference between total sales and total variable expenses:

Sales	XXX
Less variable expenses	XXX
Contribution margin	XXX

    2. The *unit contribution margin* is the difference between the unit selling price and the unit variable expense:

Selling price per unit	XXX
Less variable expense per unit	XXX
Unit contribution margin	XXX

    3. The relation between the contribution margin and the unit contribution margin is simple. The contribution margin is equal to the unit contribution margin multiplied by the number of units sold:

Unit contribution margin	XXX
× Unit sales	XXX
Contribution margin	XXX

The term "total contribution margin" is also commonly used to refer to the contribution margin.

    4. Net operating income is equal to the contribution margin less fixed expenses.

Sales	XXX
Less variable expenses	XXX
Contribution margin	XXX
Less fixed expenses	XXX
Net operating income	XXX

    5. The *break-even point* is the level of sales at which profits are zero. This is also the point at which the total contribution margin just equals fixed expenses.

    6. The relation between contribution margin and net operating income provides a very powerful planning tool. It gives the manager the ability to predict what profits will be at various activity levels without the necessity of preparing detailed income statements.

    a. The contribution margin must first cover fixed expenses. If it doesn't, the company has a loss. Below the break-even point, every unit sold reduces the loss by the amount of the unit contribution margin.

    b. Once the break-even point is reached, net operating income will increase by the amount of the unit contribution margin for each additional unit sold.

B. The contribution margin ratio (CM ratio), which expresses the contribution margin as a percentage of sales, is another very powerful concept.

    1. The contribution margin ratio is defined as follows:

$$\text{CM ratio} = \frac{\text{Contribution margin}}{\text{Sales}}$$

    2. In a company with only a single product, the CM ratio can also be computed as follows:

$$\text{CM ratio} = \frac{\text{Unit contribution margin}}{\text{Unit selling price}}$$

    3. The contribution margin ratio is used to predict the change in total contribution margin that would result from a given change in dollar sales:

Change in dollar sales	XXX
× CM ratio	XXX
Change in contribution margin	XXX

    4. Assuming that fixed expenses are not affected, an increase (or decrease) in contribution margin will be reflected dollar-for-dollar in increased (or decreased) net operating income.

    5. The CM ratio is particularly useful when a company has multiple products. In such situations, volume is most conveniently expressed in terms of total dollar sales rather than in units sold.

C. Cost-volume-profit (CVP) concepts can be used in many day-to-day decisions. Carefully study the examples given under the heading "Some Applications of CVP Concepts" in the early part of the chapter.

    1. Notice that each solution makes use of either the unit contribution margin or the CM ratio. This underscores the importance of these two concepts.

    2. Also notice that several of the examples use *incremental analysis*. An incremental analysis is based on only those costs and revenues that *differ* between alternatives.

D. Two particular examples of CVP analysis, called *break-even analysis* and *target profit analysis*, are often used. Break-even analysis is a special case of target profit analysis, so target profit analysis is considered first below.

1. Target profit analysis is used to find out how much would have to be sold to attain a specific target profit. The analysis is based on the following equation:

Profits = Sales − Variable expenses − Fixed expenses

In CVP analysis, this equation is often rewritten in the following format:

Sales = Variable expenses + Fixed expenses + Profits

All of the problems can be worked using this basic equation and simple algebra. However, handy formulas are available for answering some of the more common questions. These formulas are discussed below.

2. Target profit analysis is used in two basic variations. In the first variation, the question is how many *units* would have to be sold to attain the target profit. In the second variation, the question is how much total dollar sales would have to be to attain the target profit. The formulas are:

$$\frac{\text{Unit sales to}}{\text{attain target profit}} = \frac{\text{Fixed expenses+Target profit}}{\text{Unit contribution margin}}$$

$$\frac{\text{Dollar sales to}}{\text{attain target profit}} = \frac{\text{Fixed expenses+Target profit}}{\text{CM ratio}}$$

E. Break-even occurs when profit is zero. Thus, break-even analysis is really just a special case of target profit analysis in which the target profit is zero. Therefore, the break-even formulas can be stated as follows:

$$\frac{\text{Break-even point}}{\text{in units sold}} = \frac{\text{Fixed expenses}}{\text{Unit contribution margin}}$$

$$\frac{\text{Break-even point}}{\text{in total sales dollars}} = \frac{\text{Fixed expenses}}{\text{CM ratio}}$$

F. CVP and break-even analysis can also be done graphically. Exhibits 6-1 and 6-2 show how a CVP graph is prepared and interpreted. A cost-volume-profit graph depicts the relations among sales, costs, and volume.

G. The *margin of safety* is the excess of budgeted (or actual) sales over the break-even volume of sales. It is the amount by which sales can drop before losses begin to be incurred. The margin of safety can be stated in terms of either dollars or as a percentage of sales:

Total budgeted (or actual) sales	XXX
Less break-even sales	XXX
Margin of safety	XXX

$$\frac{\text{Margin of safety}}{\text{percentage}} = \frac{\text{Margin of safety}}{\text{Total budgeted (or actual) sales}}$$

H. Cost structure—the relative proportion of fixed and variable costs—has an impact on how sensitive a company's profits are to changes in sales. A company with low fixed costs and high variable costs will tend to have a lower CM ratio than a company with a greater proportion of fixed costs. Such a company will tend to have less volatile profits, but at the risk of losing substantial profits if sales trend sharply upward.

I. *Operating leverage* refers to the effect a given percentage increase in sales will have on net operating income.

1. The degree of operating leverage is defined as:

$$\frac{\text{Degree of operating}}{\text{leverage}} = \frac{\text{Contribution margin}}{\text{Net operating income}}$$

2. To estimate the *percentage* change in net operating income that would occur as the result of a given percentage change in dollar sales, multiply the change in sales by the degree of operating leverage.

Percentage change in dollar sales	XXX
× Degree of operating leverage	XXX
Percentage change in net operating income	XXX

3. *The degree of operating leverage is not constant.* It changes as sales increase or decrease. In general, *the degree of operating leverage decreases the further a company moves away from its break-even point.*

J. When a company has more than one product, the *sales mix* can be crucial. The sales mix refers to the relative proportions in which the company's products are sold.

1. When CVP analysis involves more than one product, the analysis is normally based on the *overall contribution margin ratio*. This is computed exactly like the CM ratio is computed in a single product company except that overall figures are used for both the contribution margin and sales:

$$\text{Overall CM ratio} = \frac{\text{Overall contribution margin}}{\text{Overall sales}}$$

2. When the company has more than one product, the *overall* CM ratio is used in the target profit and break-even formulas instead of the CM ratio.

3. As the sales mix changes, *the overall CM ratio will also change.* If the shift is toward less profitable products, then the overall CM ratio will fall; if the shift

is toward more profitable products, then the overall CM ratio will rise.

K. CVP analysis ordinarily relies on the following assumptions:

1. The selling price is constant; it does not change as unit sales change.

2. Costs are linear. Costs can be accurately divided into variable and fixed elements. The variable cost per unit is constant and the total fixed cost is constant.

3. In multi-product situations, the sales mix is constant.

4. In manufacturing companies, inventories do not change.

REVIEW AND SELF-TEST
Questions and Exercises

True or False

Enter a T or an F in the blank to indicate whether the statement is true or false.

_____ 1. If product A has a higher unit contribution margin than product B, then product A will also have a higher CM ratio than product B.

_____ 2. The break-even point occurs where the contribution margin is equal to total variable expenses.

_____ 3. The break-even point can be expressed either in terms of units sold or in terms of total sales dollars.

_____ 4. If the sales mix changes, the break-even point may change.

_____ 5. For a given increase in sales dollars, a high CM ratio will result in a greater increase in profits than will a low CM ratio.

_____ 6. If sales increase by 8%, and the degree of operating leverage is 4, then profits can be expected to increase by 12%.

_____ 7. The degree of operating leverage remains the same at all levels of sales.

_____ 8. Once the break-even point has been reached, net operating income will increase by the unit contribution margin for each additional unit sold.

_____ 9. A shift in sales mix toward less profitable products will cause the overall break-even point to fall.

_____ 10. Incremental analysis focuses on the differences in costs and revenues between alternatives.

_____ 11. If a company's cost structure shifts toward higher fixed costs and lower variable costs, one would expect the company's CM ratio to fall.

_____ 12. One way to compute the break-even point is to divide total sales by the CM ratio.

_____ 13. When a company has more than one product, a key assumption in break-even analysis is that the sales mix will not change.

Multiple Choice

Choose the best answer or response by placing the identifying letter in the space provided.

_____ 1. Lester Company has a single product. The selling price is $50 and the variable cost is $30 per unit. The company's fixed expenses are $200,000 per month. What is the company's unit contribution margin? a) $50; b) $30; c) $20; d) $80.

_____ 2. Refer to the data for Lester Company in question 1 above. What is the company's contribution margin ratio? a) 60%; b) 40%; c) 167%; d) 20%.

_____ 3. Refer to the data for Lester Company in question 1 above. What is the company's break-even in sales dollars? a) $500,000; b) $33,333; c) $200,000; d) $400,000.

_____ 4. Refer to the data for Lester Company in question 1 above. How many units would the company have to sell to attain target profits of $50,000? a) 10,000; b) 12,500; c) 15,000; d) 13,333.

_____ 5. Parker Company has provided the following data for the most recent year: net operating income, $30,000; fixed expenses, $90,000; sales, $200,000; and CM ratio, 60%. The company's margin of safety in dollars is: a) $150,000; b) $30,000; c) $50,000; d) $80,000.

_____ 6. Refer to the data in question for Parker Company in 5 above. The margin of safety in percentage form is: a) 60%; b) 75%; c) 40%; d) 25%.

_____ 7. Refer to the data for Parker Company in question 5 above. What is the company's total contribution margin? a) $110,000; b) $120,000; c) $170,000; d) $200,000.

_____ 8. Refer to the data for Parker Company in question 5 above. What is the company's degree of operating leverage? a) 0.25; b) 0.60; c) 1.25; d) 4.00.

_____ 9. If sales increase from $400,000 to $450,000, and if the degree of operating leverage is 6, net operating income should increase by: a) 12.5%; b) 75%; c) 67%; d) 50%.

_____ 10. In multiple product companies, a shift in the sales mix from less profitable products to more profitable products will cause the company's break-even point to: a) increase; b) decrease; c) there will be no change in the break-even point; d) none of these.

_____ 11. Herman Corp. has two products, A and B, with the following total sales and total variable costs:

	Product A	Product B
Sales	$10,000	$30,000
Variable expenses	$4,000	$24,000

What is the overall contribution margin ratio? a) 70%; b) 50%; c) 30%; d) 40%.

Exercises

6-1.   Hardee Company sells a single product. The selling price is $30 per unit and the variable expenses are $18 per unit. The company's most recent annual contribution format income statement is given below:

Sales	$135,000
Less variable expenses	81,000
Contribution margin	54,000
Less fixed expenses	48,000
Net operating income	$ 6,000

a.   Compute the contribution margin per unit. $_____

b.   Compute the CM ratio. _____%

c.   Compute the break-even point in sales dollars. $_____

d.   Compute the break-even point in units sold. _____ units

e. How many units must be sold next year to double the company's profits? _____ units

f. Compute the company's degree of operating leverage. _____

g. Sales for next year (in units) are expected to increase by 5%. Using the degree
of operating leverage, compute the expected percentage increase in net operating income. _____%

h. Verify your answer to part g above by preparing a contribution format income statement showing a 5%
increase in sales.

    Sales .... $_____

    Less variable expenses .... _____

    Contribution margin .... _____

    Less fixed expenses .... _____

    Net operating income .... $_____

6-2. Using the data below, construct a cost-volume-profit graph like the one in Exhibit 6-1 in the text:

Sales: 15,000 units at $10 each.
Variable expenses: $6 per unit.
Fixed expenses: $40,000 total.

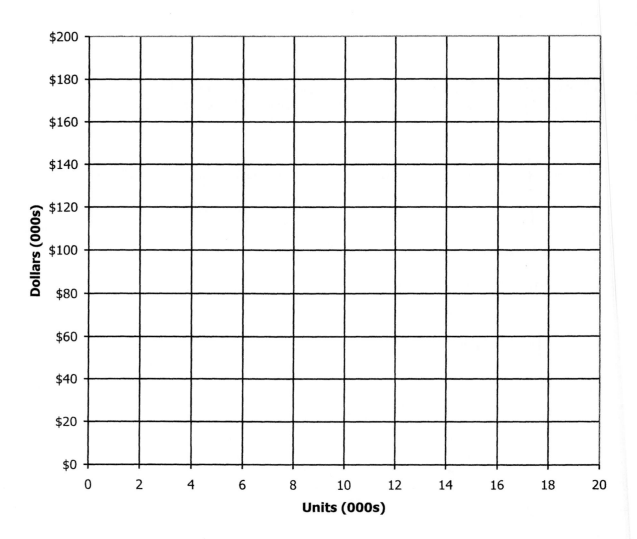

What is the break-even point in units? _____.

What is the break-even point in total sales dollars? _____

6-3. Seaver Company produces and sells two products, X and Y. Data concerning the products follow:

	Product X	*Product Y*
Selling price per unit	$10	$12
Variable expenses per unit	6	3
Contribution margin per unit	$ 4	$ 9

In the most recent month, the company sold 400 units of Product X and 600 units of Product Y. Fixed expenses are $5,000 per month.

a. Complete the following contribution format income statement for the most recent month (carry percentages to one decimal point):

	Product X		*Product Y*		*Total*	
	Amount	*%*	*Amount*	*%*	*Amount*	*%*
Sales..	$		$		$	
Less variable expenses						
Contribution margin	$		$			
Less fixed expenses						
Net operating income (loss)					$	

b. Compute the company's overall monthly break-even point in sales dollars. $ _____

c. If the company continues to sell 1,000 units, in total, each month, but the sales mix shifts so that an equal number of units of each product is being sold, would you expect monthly net operating income to rise or fall? Explain.

_____

_____

_____

_____

_____

d. Refer to the data in part c above. If the sales mix shifts as explained, would you expect the company's monthly break-even point to rise or fall? Explain.

_____

_____

_____

_____

_____

_____

6-4. **Critical thought writing exercise:** Able Company and Baker Company are competing companies that sell a product at the same price. Both companies are operating above the break-even point and have similar total profits. Able Company's costs are mostly variable, whereas Baker Company's costs are mostly fixed. In a time of increasing sales which company will tend to realize the most rapid increase in net operating income? Explain your answer.

_____

_____

_____

_____

_____

_____

_____

_____

_____

_____

_____

_____

Answers to Questions and Exercises

True or False

1. **F** The CM ratio is the unit contribution margin divided by the unit selling price. One product might have a higher unit contribution than another, but its selling price may be lower.

2. **F** The break-even point occurs where profit is zero.

3. **T** The break-even point can be computed in terms of units sold or sales dollars.

4. **T** A change in sales mix often results in a change in the overall CM ratio. If the overall CM ratio changes, the break-even point will also change.

5. **T** The CM ratio measures how much of a sales dollar is translated into increased contribution margin and profit.

6. **F** Profits should increase by 32% = 4 × 8%.

7. **F** The degree of operating leverage decreases as a company moves further and further from its break-even point.

8. **T** At the break-even point all fixed costs have been covered. All contribution margin generated from that point forward increases net operating income.

9. **F** The reverse is true—the overall break-even point will rise since the average CM ratio will be lower as a result of selling less profitable products.

10. **T** By definition, incremental analysis deals only with differences between alternatives.

11. **F** The reverse is true—one would expect the company's CM ratio to rise. Variable costs would be lower and hence the CM ratio would be higher.

12. **F** The break-even point is computed by dividing total *fixed expenses* by the CM ratio.

13. **T** This is a key assumption since a change in the sales mix will change the break-even point.

Multiple Choice

1. **c**

Unit selling price	$50
Less unit variable expenses	30
Unit contribution margin	$20

2. **b**

Unit contribution margin	$ 20
Unit selling price	÷ $ 50
Contribution margin ratio	40%

3. **a**

$$\frac{\text{Breakeven point}}{\text{in total sales dollars}} = \frac{\text{Fixed expenses}}{\text{CM ratio}}$$

$$= \frac{\$200,000}{0.40} = \$500,000$$

4. **b**

$$\frac{\text{Unit sales to}}{\text{attain target profit}} = \frac{\text{Fixed expenses+Target profit}}{\text{Unit contribution margin}}$$

$$= \frac{\$200,000+\$50,000}{\$20 \text{ per unit}} = 12,500 \text{ units}$$

5. **c**

$$\frac{\text{Break-even point}}{\text{in dollar sales}} = \frac{\text{Fixed expenses}}{\text{CM ratio}}$$

$$= \frac{\$90,000}{0.60} = \$150,000$$

Margin of safety = $200,000 − $150,000

= $50,000

6. **d** $50,000 ÷ $200,000 = 25%

7. **b**

Sales	$200,000
CM ratio	× 0.60
Contribution margin	$120,000

8. **d**

Contribution margin	$120,000
Net operating income	÷ $30,000
Operating leverage	4.0

9. **b** The computations are:

$$\frac{\text{Percentage}}{\text{change in sales}} = \frac{\$450,000-\$400,000}{\$400,000} = 12.5\%$$

Percentage change in dollar sales	12.5%
Degree of operating leverage	× 6.0
Percentage change in net operating income	75.0%

71

10. b A shift to more profitable products would result in an increase in the overall CM ratio. Thus, less sales would be needed to cover the fixed costs and the break-even point would therefore decrease.

11. c

	Product A	Product B	Total
Sales	$10,000	$30,000	$40,000
Variable expenses	4,000	24,000	28,000
Contribution margin	$ 6,000	$ 6,000	$12,000

Overall CM ratio = $12,000 ÷ $40,000 = 30%

Exercises

6-1. a.

	Per Unit	
Selling price.................................	$30	100%
Less variable expenses	18	60
Unit contribution margin	$12	40%

   b. $\text{CM ratio} = \dfrac{\text{Contribution margin}}{\text{Sales}} = \dfrac{\$54,000}{\$135,000} = 40\%$

   c. Sales = Variable expenses + Fixed expenses + Profits
   X = 0.60X + $48,000 + $0
   0.40X = $48,000
   X = $48,000 ÷ 0.40
   X = $120,000

   Alternative solution:

   $\dfrac{\text{Breakeven point}}{\text{in total sales dollars}} = \dfrac{\text{Fixed expenses}}{\text{CM ratio}} = \dfrac{\$48,000}{0.40} = \$120,000$

   d. Sales = Variable expenses + Fixed expenses + Profits
   $30Q = $18Q + $48,000 + $0
   $12Q = $48,000
   Q = $48,000 ÷ $12 per unit
   Q = 4,000 units

   Alternative solution:

   $\dfrac{\text{Breakeven point}}{\text{in units sold}} = \dfrac{\text{Fixed expenses}}{\text{Unit contribution margin}} = \dfrac{\$48,000}{\$12} = 4,000 \text{ units}$

   e. Sales = Variable expenses + Fixed expenses + Profits
   $30Q = $18Q + $48,000 + $12,000
   $12Q = $60,000
   Q = $60,000 ÷ $12 per unit
   Q = 5,000 units

   Alternative solution:

   $\dfrac{\text{Units sold to}}{\text{attain target profit}} = \dfrac{\text{Fixed expenses+Target profit}}{\text{Unit contribution margin}} = \dfrac{\$48,000 + \$12,000}{\$12 \text{ per unit}} = 5,000 \text{ units}$

   f. $\dfrac{\text{Degree of operating}}{\text{leverage}} = \dfrac{\text{Contribution margin}}{\text{Net income}} = \dfrac{\$54,000}{\$6,000} = 9.0$

g.
Percentage change in dollar sales	5%
Degree of operating leverage	× 9.0
Percentage change in net operating income ..	45%

h. New sales volume: 4,500 units × 105% = 4,725 units

Sales (4,725 units @ $30 per unit)	$141,750
Less variable expenses (4,725units @ $18 per unit) ..	85,050
Contribution margin	56,700
Less fixed expenses	48,000
Net operating income	$ 8,700

Present net income	$ 6,000
Expected increase: $6,000 × 45%	2,700
Expected net operating income (as above)	$ 8,700

6-2.   The completed CVP graph:

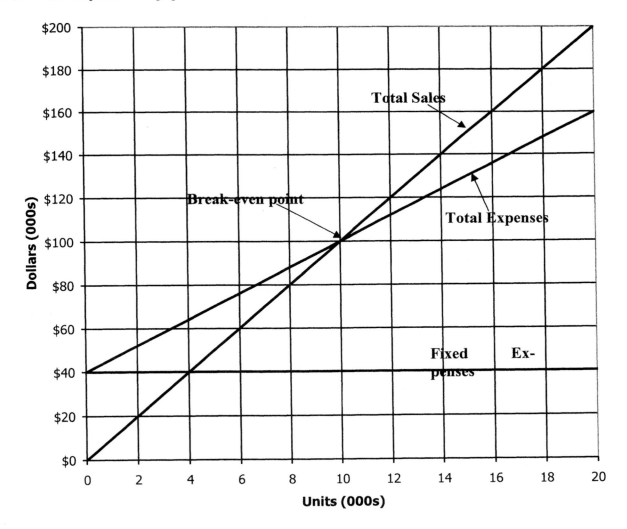

The break-even point is 10,000 units or $100,000 in sales.

6-3.   a.   The completed income statement:

	Product X		Product Y		Total	
	Amount	*%*	*Amount*	*%*	*Amount*	*%*
Sales	$4,000	100	$7,200	100	$11,200	100.0
Less variable expenses	2,400	60	1,800	25	4,200	37.5
Contribution margin	$1,600	40	$5,400	75	7,000	62.5
Less fixed expenses					5,000	
Net operating income					$ 2,000	

b. $$\frac{\text{Breakeven point}}{\text{in total sales dollars}} = \frac{\text{Fixed expenses}}{\text{CM ratio}} = \frac{\$5,000}{0.625} = \$8,000$$

c.   Monthly net operating income will fall. The shift in sales mix will mean that less of Product Y is being sold and more of Product X is being sold. Since Product Y has a higher contribution margin per unit than Product X, this means that less contribution margin in *total* will be available, and profits will therefore fall.

d.   The monthly break-even point will rise. As explained above, the shift in sales mix will be toward the less profitable Product X, which has a CM ratio of only 40% as compared to 75% for Product Y. Thus, the company's *overall* CM ratio will fall, and the break-even point will rise since less contribution margin will be available per unit to cover the fixed costs.

6-4.   Baker Company will have a higher contribution margin ratio (and contribution margin per unit) due to its lower variable costs. Thus, the company's contribution margin (and net operating income) will increase more rapidly than Able Company's as sales increase. Therefore, Baker Company will realize the most rapid increase in net operating income. The impact on net operating income can also be viewed in terms of operating leverage. Baker Company will have a higher degree of operating leverage than Able Company because of its higher contribution margin. Therefore, as sales increase, its net operating income will rise more rapidly than will Able Company's.

Chapter 7

Variable Costing — A Tool for Management

Chapter Study Suggestions

✳

This chapter introduces a method of determining unit product costs called variable costing. Throughout the chapter we compare variable costing with absorption costing, which was covered in Chapter 3.

In your study of Chapter 7, note that the difference between the two costing methods centers on how they handle the fixed portion of manufacturing overhead cost. This point is emphasized in Exhibit 7-1. Exhibits 7-2 through 7-6 are the heart of the chapter. These exhibits show how to compute unit product costs under both variable and absorption costing, and they show the impact of the two methods on net operating income. Be sure you understand the computations in these exhibits. You must thoroughly understand them to complete homework assignments.

CHAPTER HIGHLIGHTS

A. Two different methods can be used to determine unit product costs—*absorption costing* and *variable costing*.

1. Under *absorption costing*, all manufacturing costs, both variable and fixed, are included in unit product costs.

Direct materials	$XXX
Direct labor	XXX
Variable manufacturing overhead	XXX
Fixed manufacturing overhead	XXX
Unit product cost	$XXX

2. Under *variable costing*, only variable manufacturing costs—which usually consist of direct materials, direct labor, and variable manufacturing overhead—are included in unit product costs.

Direct materials	$XXX
Direct labor	XXX
Variable manufacturing overhead	XXX
Unit product cost	$XXX

    a. Variable costing focuses on cost behavior. The contribution approach and cost-volume-profit analysis discussed in prior chapters implicitly assumed that variable costing is used. Absorption costing data should not be used in cost-volume-profit calculations—the results can be very misleading.

    b. Under the variable costing method, fixed manufacturing costs are treated as period costs and are expensed in the period in which they are incurred, just like selling and administrative expenses.

B. Under absorption costing, fixed manufacturing costs may be shifted from one period to another due to changes in inventories.

1. A small portion of the period's fixed manufacturing overhead costs is assigned to each unit that is produced. If the unit is not sold during the period, the fixed manufacturing overhead assigned to the unit is part of the inventories on the balance sheet rather than cost of goods sold on the income statement. This is referred to as *deferral of fixed manufacturing overhead in inventory*.

2. Exhibit 7-3 is a key exhibit illustrating the differences between variable and absorption costing. *Study this exhibit carefully before going on.*

C. Exhibit 7-4 is also a key exhibit that summarizes the relations between variable and absorption costing. Any difference in net operating income between the two methods can be traced to changes in the level of inventories.

1. When production and sales (in units) are equal and hence inventories don't change, both variable and absorption costing will yield the same net operating income.

2. When production exceeds sales (in units) and hence inventories increase, greater net operating income will be reported under absorption costing than under variable costing.

    a. When inventories increase, some of the current period's *fixed manufacturing overhead costs are deferred in inventory*.

    b. The amount of fixed manufacturing overhead cost deferred is equal to the increase in units in inventory multiplied by the fixed manufacturing overhead cost per unit.

3. When production is less than sales (in units) and hence inventories decrease, less net operating income will be reported under absorption costing than under variable costing.

    a. *Fixed manufacturing overhead costs are released from inventory* when the units in inventory are sold.

    b. The amount of fixed manufacturing overhead cost released is equal to the decrease in units in inventory multiplied by the fixed manufacturing overhead cost per unit.

4. Over an extended period of time, the net operating income reported by the two costing methods will tend to be the same. Over the long run sales can't exceed production, nor can production much exceed sales. The shorter the period, the more the net operating income figures will tend to differ.

D. The following form, which is illustrated in Exhibit 7-5, can be used to reconcile the variable costing and absorption costing net operating income figures.

Variable costing net operating income	$XXX
Add: Fixed manufacturing overhead costs deferred in inventory under absorption costing	XXX
Deduct: Fixed manufacturing overhead costs released from inventory under absorption costing	(XXX)
Absorption costing net operating income	$XXX

E. Exhibit 7-6 shows the effects of changes in production on net operating income—holding sales constant— under both variable and absorption costing.

1. Net operating income under variable costing *is not* affected by changes in production.

2. Net operating income under absorption costing *is* affected by changes in production.

    a. Under absorption costing, net operating income increases as production increases, and decreases as production decreases. This occurs because of changes in ending inventories. As inventories grow, fixed manufacturing overhead is deferred in inventories. As inventories shrink, fixed manufacturing overhead is released to the income statement.

    b. The effects of changes in production on net operating income are a major drawback of absorption costing, since managers can manipulate reported profits by simply changing the number of units produced.

F. A number of factors should be considered by a manager when choosing between the variable and absorption costing methods.

1. Advantages of variable costing and the contribution approach are as follows:

    a. The contribution approach works well with cost-volume-profit analysis. The data for the analysis can be taken directly from the contribution format income statement since it categorizes costs by how they behave.

    b. Unlike absorption costing, variable costing profits are unaffected by changes in production (and inventories).

    c. Under variable costing, unit product costs are variable costs. Under absorption costing, unit product costs are a mixture of variable and fixed costs. This can be confusing to managers who tend to think of unit product costs as variable costs.

    d. Under variable costing, fixed costs are highlighted rather than buried in cost of goods sold and in inventories.

    e. As discussed in later chapters, variable costing data make it easier to estimate the profitability of products.

    f. Also as discussed in later chapters, variable costing works well with cost control methods such as standard cost variance analysis and flexible budgets.

    g. Variable costing net operating income is closer to net cash flows than absorption costing net operating income. This can be important for organizations that need to closely monitor their cash resources.

2. Nevertheless, absorption costing is the generally accepted method for preparing external financial reports and for preparing income tax returns. Variable costing is usually limited to internal use in a company. And because of the cost and possible confusion of maintaining two separate costing systems, most companies use absorption costing for internal as well as for external reports.

G. When companies employ Just-in-Time (JIT) inventory methods, differences in net operating income between variable costing and absorption costing are reduced or eliminated.

1. The sometimes erratic movement of net operating income under absorption costing, and the differences in net operating income between absorption and variable costing, arise because of changing levels of inventory. Under JIT, goods are produced strictly to customers' orders, so inventories are largely eliminated.

2. Since inventories are largely eliminated under JIT, there is little opportunity for fixed manufacturing overhead costs to be shifted between periods under absorption costing. Thus, net operating income is essentially the same whether variable and absorption costing is used, and the sometimes erratic movement of net operating income under absorption costing is largely eliminated.

REVIEW AND SELF-TEST
Questions and Exercises

True or False

Enter a T or an F in the blank to indicate whether the statement is true or false.

____ 1. Product costs under the absorption costing method consist of direct materials, direct labor, and both variable and fixed manufacturing overhead.

____ 2. Selling and administrative expenses are treated as period costs under both variable costing and absorption costing.

____ 3. Fixed manufacturing overhead costs are treated the same way under both the variable costing and absorption costing methods.

____ 4. Under absorption costing it is possible to defer some of the fixed manufacturing overhead costs of the current period to future periods.

____ 5. Variable costing will always produce higher net operating income than absorption costing.

____ 6. When production and sales are equal, the same net operating income will be reported regardless of whether variable costing or absorption costing is used.

____ 7. When production exceeds sales, the net operating income reported under absorption costing will generally be greater than the net operating income reported under variable costing.

____ 8. When production exceeds sales, fixed manufacturing overhead costs are released from inventory under absorption costing.

____ 9. Changes in the level of production do not affect net operating income under the variable costing method.

____ 10. When sales are constant but the level of production fluctuates, absorption costing will produce a more stable net operating income pattern than variable costing.

____ 11. The variable costing method is not generally accepted for external reporting or for income tax purposes.

____ 12. Absorption costing data are generally better suited for cost-volume-profit analysis than variable costing data.

Multiple Choice

Choose the best answer or response by placing the identifying letter in the space provided.

____ 1. White Company manufactures a single product and has the following cost structure:

Variable costs per unit:
Direct materials $3
Direct labor $4
Variable manufacturing overhead $1
Variable selling and admin. expense $2
Fixed costs per month:
Fixed manufacturing overhead $100,000
Fixed selling & admin. Expense $60,000

The company produces 20,000 units each month. The unit product cost under absorption costing is: a) $10; b) $13; c) $15; d) $12.

____ 2. Refer to the data in question 1 above. The unit product cost under variable costing would be: a) $8; b) $10; c) $13; d) $11.

____ 3. Refer to the data in question 1 above. Assume beginning inventories are zero, 20,000 units are produced, and 19,000 units are sold in a month. If the unit selling price is $20, what is the net operating income under absorption costing for the month? a) $30,000; b) $38,000; c) $35,000; d) $42,000.

____ 4. Refer to the data in question 1 above. Assume beginning inventories are zero, and 20,000 units are produced, and 19,000 units are sold in a month. If the unit selling price is $20, what is the net operating income under variable costing for the month? a) $30,000; b) $38,000; c) $35,000; d) $42,000.

____ 5. Refer to your answers to parts 3 and 4 above. The net operating income differs between variable and absorption costing in this situation because: a) variable costs are $5,000 higher under variable costing; b) $5,000 in fixed manufacturing overhead has been deferred in inventories under absorption costing; c) $5,000 in fixed manufacturing overhead has been released from inventories under absorption costing; d) none of the above.

____ 6. Which of the following costs are treated as period costs under the variable costing method? a) fixed manufacturing overhead and both variable and fixed selling and administrative expenses; b) both variable and fixed manufacturing overhead; c) only fixed manufacturing overhead and fixed selling and administrative expenses.

_____ 7. When production exceeds sales, fixed manufacturing overhead costs: a) are released from inventory under absorption costing; b) are deferred in inventory under absorption costing; c) are released from inventory under variable costing; d) are deferred in inventory under variable costing.

_____ 8. When sales are constant but production fluctuates: a) net operating income will be erratic under variable costing; b) absorption costing will always show a net loss; c) variable costing will always show a positive net operating income; d) net operating income will be erratic under absorption costing.

_____ 9. Last year, Peck Company produced 10,000 units and sold 9,000 units. Fixed manufacturing overhead costs were $20,000, and variable manufacturing overhead costs were $3 per unit. For the year, one would expect net operating income under the absorption costing method to be: a) $2,000 more than net operating income under the variable costing method; b) $5,000 more than net operating income under the variable costing method; c) $2,000 less than net operating income under the variable costing method; d) $5,000 less than net operating income under the variable costing method.

Chapter 7

Exercises

7-1.   Selected data relating to the operations of Dover Company for last year are given below:

Units in beginning inventory	0
Units produced	40,000
Units sold	35,000
Units in ending inventory	5,000

Selling price per unit	$27
Variable costs per unit:	
Direct materials	$7
Direct labor	$6
Variable manufacturing overhead	$3
Variable selling and administrative	$2
Fixed costs:	
Fixed manufacturing overhead	$160,000
Fixed selling and administrative	$140,000

a.   Assume that the company uses absorption costing.

Compute the unit product cost. .... $_____

Determine the value of the ending inventory. .... $_____

Complete the following absorption costing income statement:

Sales		$_____
Cost of goods sold:		
Beginning inventory	_____	
Add cost of goods manufactured	_____	
Goods available for sale	_____	
Less ending inventory	_____	
Cost of goods sold		_____
Gross margin		_____
Less selling and administrative expenses:		
Variable selling and administrative	_____	
Fixed selling and administrative............................	_____	_____
Net operating income		$_____

b. Assume that the company uses variable costing.

Compute the unit product cost. .... $_____

Determine the value of the ending inventory. .... $_____

Complete the following contribution format income statement using variable costing:

Sales   .... $_____

Less variable expenses:

Variable cost of goods sold:

Beginning inventory .... $_____

Add variable manufacturing costs ....   _____

Goods available for sale ....   _____

Less ending inventory ....   _____

Variable cost of goods sold ....   _____

Variable selling and administrative ....   _____   _____

Contribution margin ....   _____

Less fixed expenses:

Fixed manufacturing overhead ....   _____

Fixed selling and administrative ....   _____   _____

Net operating income .... $_____

c. Reconcile the net operating incomes under the two methods by filling in the following form:

Variable costing net operating income .... $_____
Add fixed manufacturing overhead cost deferred
    in inventory under absorption costing ....   _____
Deduct fixed manufacturing overhead cost released
    from inventory under absorption costing ....   _____

Absorption costing net operating income .... $_____

Chapter 7

7-2.   Hodex Corporation manufactures and sells a unique product that has enjoyed brisk sales. The results of last month's operations are shown below (absorption costing basis):

Sales (10,000 units @ $20 per unit)	$200,000
Less cost of goods sold (10,000 units @ $14 per unit)	140,000
Gross margin	60,000
Less selling and administrative expenses	45,000
Net operating income	$ 15,000

Variable selling and administrative expenses are $2 per unit. Variable manufacturing costs are $10 per unit and fixed manufacturing overhead costs are $48,000 per month. There was no beginning inventory. The company produced 12,000 units during the month.

a.   Redo the company's income statement in the contribution format, using variable costing.

Sales   .... $_____

Less variable expenses:

  Variable cost of goods sold:

    Beginning inventory .... $_____

    Add variable manufacturing costs ....   _____

    Goods available for sale ....   _____

    Less ending inventory ....   _____

  Variable cost of goods sold ....   _____

  Variable selling and administrative ....   _____   _____

Contribution margin ....   _____

Less fixed expenses:

  Fixed manufacturing overhead ....   _____

  Fixed selling and administrative ....   _____   _____

  Net operating income .... $_____

b.   Reconcile the variable costing and absorption costing net operating incomes:

Variable costing net operating income .... $_____

_____

_____.......   _____

Absorption costing net operating income .... $_____

7-3.   **Critical thought writing exercise:** Lake Corporation uses absorption costing to prepare its financial statements for the annual report to stockholders. Last year, the company had $10,000,000 in sales and reported a $400,000 loss in its annual report. According to a CVP analysis prepared for management's use (using variable costing), $10,000,000 in sales is the break-even point for the company. Based on these data, was the company's ending inventory greater than, less than, or equal to its beginning inventory? Explain your answer.

_____

_____

_____

_____

_____

_____

_____

_____

_____

_____

_____

_____

_____

_____

_____

_____

_____

_____

_____

Answers to Questions and Exercises

True or False

1. T   All manufacturing costs are included as product costs under absorption costing.

2. T   Selling and administrative expenses are never treated as product costs under either costing method.

3. F   Under variable costing, fixed manufacturing overhead costs are treated as period costs; under absorption costing, fixed manufacturing overhead costs are treated as product costs.

4. T   Fixed manufacturing overhead costs are deferred to the future under absorption costing whenever production exceeds sales.

5. F   Variable costing will produce higher net operating income than absorption costing only when sales exceed production.

6. T   When sales and production are equal, fixed manufacturing overhead cost is neither deferred in nor released from inventory under absorption costing.

7. T   When production exceeds sales, fixed manufacturing overhead cost is deferred in inventory under absorption costing. Consequently, net operating income is higher under absorption costing than under variable costing.

8. F   When production exceeds sales, fixed manufacturing overhead costs are deferred in inventory under absorption costing.

9. T   Changes in the number of units sold—not produced—affect net operating income under the variable costing method.

10. F   If production fluctuates, absorption costing will produce erratic net operating income. The reason is that fixed manufacturing overhead cost will be shifted into and out of inventory as production goes up and down.

11. T   Variable costing is used internally by managers for planning and decision-making purposes.

12. F   The reverse is true—variable costing data are better suited for CVP analysis than absorption costing data.

Multiple Choice

1. b   Variable manufacturing costs
      ($3 + $4 + $1) .... $ 8
   Fixed manufacturing costs
      ($100,000 ÷ 20,000 units) .... $\underline{5}$
   Unit product cost .... $\underline{\$13}$

2. a   Only the variable manufacturing costs are treated as product costs under variable costing. Thus, the unit product cost is $3 + $4 + $1 = $8.

3. c   The absorption costing net operating income is computed as follows:

Sales	$380,000
Cost of goods sold:	
Beginning inventory	0
Add COGM	260,000
Goods available for sale	260,000
Less ending inventory............	13,000
Cost of goods sold....................	247,000
Gross margin	133,000
Less selling & admin.	
Variable selling & admin........	38,000
Fixed selling & admin.	60,000
Total selling & admin..............	98,000
Net operating income	$ 35,000

4. a   The variable costing net operating income is computed as follows:

Sales	$380,000
Less variable expenses:	
Variable cost of goods sold:	
Beginning inventory	0
Add variable manuf. costs	160,000
Goods available for sale	160,000
Less ending inventory..........	8,000
Variable cost of goods sold	152,000
Variable selling & admin........	38,000
Total variable expenses	190,000
Contribution margin	190,000
Less fixed expenses:	
Fixed manuf. overhead...........	100,000
Fixed selling & admin.	60,000
Total fixed expenses.................	160,000
Net operating income	$ 30,000

5. b   Inventories increased by 1,000 units. Under absorption costing, $5 (=$100,000 ÷ 20,000 units) of fixed manufacturing overhead cost is applied to each unit that is produced. Thus, $5,000 in fixed manufacturing overhead costs are deferred in inventories and do not appear on the income statement as part of cost of goods sold.

6. a   Fixed manufacturing overhead cost is expensed as incurred under variable costing. Also, both variable and fixed selling and administrative expenses are always treated as period costs under both variable and absorption costing.

7. b   When production exceeds sales, units are added to inventory. Thus, fixed manufacturing overhead costs are deferred in inventory under absorption costing.

8. d   When production fluctuates, net operating income will be erratic under absorption costing since fixed manufacturing overhead costs will be shifted into and out of inventory as production goes up and down.

9. a   Under absorption costing, fixed manufacturing overhead cost per unit will be $2 (= $20,000 ÷ 10,000 units). If only 9,000 units are sold, then 1,000 units will go into inventory. Thus, under absorption costing, $2,000 in fixed manufacturing overhead cost will be deferred in inventory ($2 per unit × 1,000 units = $2,000). Net operating income will therefore be $2,000 more under absorption costing than under variable costing.

Exercises

7-1.   a.   Direct materials .... $ 7
            Direct labor   6
            Variable manufacturing overhead   3
            Fixed manufacturing overhead ($160,000 ÷ 40,000 units)   4
            Unit product cost $20

            Ending inventory (5,000 units × $20 per unit) $100,000

Absorption costing income statement

Sales (35,000 units × $27 per unit)		$945,000
Cost of goods sold:		
Beginning inventory	$ 0	
Add cost of goods manufactured		
(40,000 units × $20 per unit)	800,000	
Goods available for sale	800,000	
Less ending inventory (5,000 units × $20 per unit).......	100,000	
Cost of goods sold		700,000
Gross margin		245,000
Less selling & admin. expenses:		
Variable selling & admin. (35,000 units × $2 per unit) 70,000		
Fixed selling & admin.	140,000	210,000
Net operating income		$ 35,000

       b.   Direct materials .... $ 7
            Direct labor   6
            Variable manufacturing overhead   3
            Unit product cost $16

            Ending inventory (5,000 units × $16 per unit) $80,000

Variable costing income statement

Sales (35,000 units × $27 per unit)		$945,000
Less variable expenses:		
Variable cost of goods sold:		
Beginning inventory	$ 0	
Add variable manufacturing costs		
(40,000 per unit × $16 per unit)	640,000	
Goods available for sale	640,000	
Less ending inventory (5,000 per unit × $16 per unit) ..	80,000	
Variable cost of goods sold	560,000	
Variable selling & admin. (35,000 units × $2 per unit)	70,000	630,000
Contribution margin		315,000
Less fixed expenses:		
Fixed manufacturing overhead	160,000	
Fixed selling and administrative	140,000	300,000
Net operating income		$ 15,000

c. Reconciliation of variable costing and absorption costing net operating incomes:

Variable costing net operating income	$15,000
Add fixed manufacturing overhead cost deferred	
in inventory under absorption costing (5,000 units × $4 per unit)	20,000
Deduct fixed manufacturing overhead cost released	
from inventory under absorption costing	0
Absorption costing net operating income	$35,000

7-2.   a.

Sales (10,000 units × $20 per unit)		$200,000
Less variable expenses:		
Variable cost of goods sold:		
Beginning inventory	$ 0	
Add variable manufacturing costs		
(12,000 units × $10 per unit)	120,000	
Goods available for sale	120,000	
Less ending inventory	20,000	
Variable cost of goods sold		
(10,000 units × $10 per unit)	100,000	
Variable selling & admin.		
(10,000 units × $2 per unit)	20,000	120,000
Contribution margin		80,000
Less fixed expenses:		
Fixed manufacturing overhead	48,000	
Fixed selling and administrative	25,000*	73,000
Net operating income		$ 7,000

*$45,000 - (l0,000 units × $2 per unit) = $25,000

b.

Variable costing net operating income	$ 7,000
Add fixed manufacturing overhead cost deferred	
in inventory under absorption costing	
(2,000 units × $4 per unit*)	8,000
Absorption costing net operating income	$ 15,000

*$48,000 ÷ 12,000 units produced = $4 per unit.

7-3.   Since Lake Company reported a loss when its sales were at the break-even level, fixed manufacturing overhead costs must have been released from inventory under the absorption costing approach. (The break-even point is computed assuming either that variable costing is used or that there is no change in inventory.) Therefore, the company's inventory level for the year decreased. When inventory levels decrease, fixed manufacturing overhead costs are released from inventory under absorption costing. Thus, the fixed manufacturing overhead costs released from inventory would have resulted in a loss for the year, even though from a variable costing point of view the company would have broken even.

Chapter 8

Activity-Based Costing:
A Tool to Aid Decision Making

Chapter Study Suggestions

✳

Activity-based costing is very similar to the methods you learned in Chapter 3. The biggest change is the use of many overhead cost pools rather than a single overhead cost pool. However, within each overhead cost pool, the procedures are the same as they were in Chapter 3.

Your instructor may assign the appendix, which is concerned with the construction of action analyses. Exhibit 8A-6 provides a very useful roadmap to the appendix. The procedures are somewhat complex, so it is a good idea to frequently consult Exhibit 8A-6 as you work through the appendix.

CHAPTER HIGHLIGHTS

A.   As discussed in Chapters 2 and 3, traditional costing systems in manufacturing companies are primarily designed to provide product cost data for external financial reports rather than for internal decision-making.

  1. For external financial reports, all manufacturing costs must be assigned to products—even manufacturing costs that are not actually caused by any particular product. For example, the rent on the factory building is the same (within limits) regardless of which products are produced and how much is produced.

  2. For external financial reports, selling and administrative costs are not assigned to products even if the products directly cause the costs. For example, sales commissions are not included in product costs in traditional costing systems.

  3. Since all manufacturing costs must be assigned to products for external financial reports, this means that the costs of idle capacity must also be assigned to products. As a consequence, products are charged for the costs of resources they don't use as well as for the costs of resources they do use.

  4. In traditional costing systems, overhead costs are usually allocated to products using a single measure of activity such as direct labor-hours. This approach assumes that overhead costs are highly correlated with direct labor-hours; that is, it assumes that overhead costs and direct labor-hours tend to move together. If this assumption is not valid, product costs will be distorted.

B.   *Activity-based costing (ABC)* attempts to remedy these deficiencies of traditional costing systems. The key concept in activity-based costing is that products (and customers) cause activities. These activities result in the consumption of resources, which in turn result in costs. Consequently, if we want to accurately assign costs to products and customers, we must identify and measure the activities that link products and customers to costs.

C.   The distinction between manufacturing and non-manufacturing costs is critical in traditional costing systems. This distinction is much less important in activity-based costing. Like variable costing, activity-based costing is concerned with how costs behave. And like variable costing, activity-based costing is primarily used in internal reports and is intended to help managers in making decisions.

D.   Many companies have experimented with some form of activity-based costing. Activity-based costing originated in manufacturing companies, but is now be-ing widely applied in service companies and in government.

E.   Activity-based costing differs from traditional costing in five major ways:

  1. Non-manufacturing costs, as well as manufacturing costs, may be assigned to products.

  2. Some manufacturing costs—the costs of idle capacity and organization-sustaining costs—may be excluded from products.

  3. A number of activity cost pools are used in activity-based costing. Each cost pool has its own unique measure of activity that is used as the basis for allocating its costs to products, customers, and other cost objects.

    a. An *activity* is an event that causes consumption of overhead resources such as processing a purchase order.

    b. An *activity cost pool* is a "bucket" in which costs are accumulated that relate to a single activity such as processing purchase orders.

  4. The allocation bases in activity-based costing (i.e., measures of activity) often differ from those used in traditional costing systems.

  5. The overhead rates in activity-based costing (which are called *activity rates*), may be based on the level of activity at capacity rather than on the budgeted level of activity.

F.   Implementing activity-based costing involves six steps:

  1. Identify and define activities and activity cost pools.

  2. Wherever possible, trace costs directly to activities and cost objects. For example, direct materials and direct labor costs are often traced directly to products.

  3. Assign costs to activity cost pools.

  4. Calculate activity rates, which function like predetermined overhead rates in a traditional costing system.

  5. Assign costs to cost objects using the activity rates and measures of activity.

  6. Prepare management reports.

G. It is useful to think in terms of a hierarchy of costs:

1. *Unit-level activities* are performed each time a unit is produced. An example is testing a completed unit.

2. *Batch-level activities* are performed each time a batch is handled or processed. For example, tasks such as placing purchase orders and setting up equipment are batch-level activities. These activities occur no matter how many units are produced in a batch.

3. *Product-level activities* are required to have a product at all. An example is maintaining an up-to-date parts list and instruction manual for the product. These activities must be performed regardless of how many batches are run or units produced.

4. *Customer-level activities* relate to specific customers and include sales calls and catalog mailings that are not tied to a specific product.

5. *Organization-sustaining activities* are carried out regardless of which customers are served, which products are produced, how many batches are run, or how many units are produced. Examples include providing a computer network for employees, preparing financial reports, providing legal advice to the board of directors, and so on. Organization-sustaining costs should not be allocated to products or customers for purposes of making decisions.

H. To understand the mechanics of activity-based costing, there is no good substitute for working through the example in the book step-by-step. Nevertheless, the process can be briefly summarized as follows:

1. Prepare the *first-stage allocation* of costs to the activity cost pools.

    a. Begin with a listing of the costs that will be included in the activity-based costing system and the results of interviews with employees that indicate how these costs are to be distributed across the activity cost pools. The interview results indicate what percentage of a specific cost such as indirect factory wages should be allocated to the first activity cost pool, the second activity cost pool, and so on.

    b. For example, the results of the interviews might indicate that 20% of the resources associated with office staff wages are consumed in processing purchase orders. If the office staff wages are $200,000 per year, then 20% of $200,000, or $40,000, would be allocated to the activity cost pool called processing purchase orders.

2. Calculate the activity rates.

    a. An *activity rate* is a cost per unit of activity. For example, the activity rate for machine set-ups might be $14 per machine set-up.

    b. Suppose that 2,000 purchase orders are processed per year. If the total cost of processing purchase orders is $60,000, then the average cost would be $30 per purchase order. ($60,000 ÷ 2,000 = $30.) This is the activity rate for the "processing purchase orders" activity cost pool.

    c. Activity rates are important in *activity-based management*. Activity rates can be compared across organizations or across different locations in the same organization. For example, the cost of $30 for processing a purchase order may be higher at some locations in a company and lower at others. The higher cost locations may learn how to better process purchase orders by studying the techniques used at the lower cost locations.

3. Prepare the *second-stage allocation of costs to products*, customers, and other cost objects.

    a. To allocate costs to products or other cost objects, multiply the amount of activity caused by the cost object's by the activity rate.

    b. For example, if a product requires two purchase orders and the activity rate is $30 per purchase order, the product would be allocated $60 (2 purchase orders × $30 per purchase order). Sum all of the costs of all of the activities associated with the product to determine the total cost of the product.

I. Product costs computed under activity-based costing and traditional costing systems differ for a number of reasons. They differ in *what* costs are allocated to products as well as in *how* they are allocated. Focusing just on *how* the costs are allocated, some general patterns emerge.

1. An activity-based costing system will typically shift costs away from high-volume products that are produced in large batches to low-volume products that are produced in small batches. Traditional costing systems apply batch-level and product-level costs uniformly to all products and the high-volume products absorb the bulk of such costs. In an activity-based costing system, such costs are assigned to the products that cause the costs rather than spreading them uniformly over all products on the basis of volume.

2. The unit costs of the low-volume products usually increase more than the unit costs of the high-volume products decrease. The reason is that if X dollars are shifted from high-volume products to low-volume products, the cost savings for the high-volume products is spread over many units whereas the in-

crease in costs for the low-volume products is spread over few units.

J. *(Appendix 8A) Action analysis report.* Before taking an action such as dropping a product or a customer, managers should prepare an action analysis report. The action analysis report does two things. First, it identifies where in the organization any cost savings would have to come from. Second, it provides a simple coding scheme—red, yellow, and green—that can be used to highlight how easy or difficult it would be to adjust a cost if there is a change in activity.

1. *Green costs* adjust automatically to changes in activity without any action by managers. For example, the power to run production equipment would automatically decrease if fewer units were made.

2. *Yellow costs* could be adjusted in response to changes in activity, but such adjustments require management action. The adjustment is not automatic. Many wages would be classified as yellow costs since managers would have to explicitly lay off workers or redeploy them to more profitable uses to actually save any money.

3. *Red costs* could be adjusted to changes in activity only with a great deal of difficulty and the adjustment would require management action. For example, staff salaries are often a red cost.

REVIEW AND SELF-TEST
Questions and Exercises

True or False

Enter a T or an F in the blank to indicate whether the statement is true or false.

____ 1. If direct labor is used as the base for overhead cost assignment and direct labor is not highly correlated with the overhead cost, the result will be distorted product costs.

____ 2. In activity-based costing, some manufacturing costs may not be assigned to products.

____ 3. In activity-based costing, nonmanufacturing costs are not assigned to products.

____ 4. In designing an activity-based costing system, managers should keep in mind that the system must conform to Generally Accepted Accounting Principles (GAAP).

____ 5. In activity-based costing, activity rates should be based on budgeted or estimated activity rather than activity at capacity.

____ 6. In activity-based costing, the first-stage allocation of costs to activity cost pools is often based on the results of interviews with employees.

____ 7. In activity-based costing, the overhead costs of the entire company are distributed to product and other cost objects on the basis of a single well-chosen measure of activity.

____ 8. Direct labor-hours should never be used as an allocation base in activity-based costing.

____ 9. An action analysis report helps managers identify which costs may be relevant in a decision.

Multiple Choice

Choose the best answer or response by placing the identifying letter in the space provided.

____ 1. Advertising a product would be considered a: a) unit-level activity; b) batch-level activity; c) product-level activity; d) customer-level activity; e) organization-sustaining activity.

____ 2. Providing legal advice to the president concerning a possible merger with another company would be considered a: a) unit-level activity; b) batch-level activity; c) product-level activity; d) customer-level activity; e) organization-sustaining activity.

____ 3. Writing software for a new computer game at a software company would be considered a: a) unit-level activity; b) batch-level activity; c) product-level activity; d) customer-level activity; e) organization-sustaining activity.

____ 4. A software company orders 100,000 copies of a CD-ROM from a supplier. This CD-ROM will be enclosed in a computer game designed and published by the software company. Ordering the CD-ROMs would be considered a: a) unit-level activity; b) batch-level activity; c) product-level activity; d) customer-level activity; e) organization-sustaining activity.

____ 5. A company that provides photocopying services has an activity-based costing system with three activity cost pools—making photocopies, serving customers, and setting up machines. The activity rates are $0.02 per photocopy, $2.15 per customer, and $0.75 per machine-setup. If a customer requires setups on two different machines and makes 200 copies in total, how much cost would be assigned to the job for the customer by the activity-based costing system? a) $4.00; b) $2.15; c) $1.50; d) $7.65.

Exercises

8-1.   Lambert Fabrication, Inc., uses activity-based costing data for internal decisions. The company has four activity cost pools, which are listed below:

Activity Cost Pool	Annual Activity
Producing units	5,000 machine-hours
Processing orders	1,000 orders
Customer support	200 customers
Other	Not applicable

The "Other" activity cost pool consists of the costs of idle capacity and organization-sustaining costs.

The company traces the costs of direct materials and direct labor to jobs (i.e., orders). Overhead costs—both manufacturing and non-manufacturing—are allocated to jobs using the activity-based costing system. The company's overhead costs for the year are listed below:

Annual Overhead Costs

Indirect factory wages	$100,000
Other factory overhead	200,000
Selling and administrative overhead	400,000
Total overhead cost	$700,000

To develop the company's activity-based costing system, employees were asked how they distributed their time and resources across the four activity cost pools. The results of those interviews appear below:

Results of Interviews of Employees

	Distribution of Resource Consumption Across Activities				
	Producing Units	Processing Orders	Customer Support	Other	Totals
Indirect factory wages	40%	30%	10%	20%	100%
Other factory overhead	30%	10%	0%	60%	100%
Selling and administrative overhead	0%	25%	40%	35%	100%

a.   Using the results of the interviews, carry out the first-stage allocation of costs to the activity cost pools.

First-Stage Allocations

	Producing Units	Processing Orders	Customer Support	Other	Total
Indirect factory wages					
Other factory overhead					
Selling and administrative overhead	_____	_____	_____	_____	_____
Total overhead cost	_____	_____	_____	_____	_____

b. Using the results of the first-stage allocation, compute the activity rates for each of the activity cost pools. (Activity rates are not computed for the "Other" activity cost pool since these costs will not be allocated to products or customers.)

Computation of Activity Rates

Activity Cost Pools	Total Cost	Total Activity	Activity Rate
Producing units..........		5,000 machine-hours	per machine-hour
Processing orders.......		1,000 orders	per order
Customer support		200 customers	per customer

c. Using the activity rates you derived in part (b) above, compute the total amount of overhead cost that would be allocated to an order that requires 20 machine-hours.

The Overhead Cost of An Order Requiring 20 Machine-Hours

Activity Cost Pools	Activity Rate	Activity	ABC Cost
Producing units	per machine-hour	machine-hours	
Processing orders	per order	orders	
Customer support	per customer	customers	_____
Total			$_____

d. The order in part (c) above required $685 in direct materials and $975 in direct labor costs. The revenue from the job was $2,500. Prepare a report from an activity view that shows the margin from the order.

Margin on the Order from an Activity View

Revenue		$2,500
Costs:		
Direct materials	$685	
Direct labor	975	
Producing units		
Processing orders		
Customer support	_____	_____
Margin		_____

e. Using the activity rates, compute the total amount of overhead cost that would be allocated to a customer who had two orders during the year requiring a total of 100 machine-hours.

The Overhead Cost of Serving the Customer

Activity Cost Pools	Activity Rate	Activity	ABC Cost
Producing units..........	per machine-hour	100 machine-hours	
Processing orders.......	per order	2 orders	
Customer support	per customer	1 customer	_____
Total			$_____

f. The orders in part (e) above required $3,500 in direct materials and $1,750 in direct labor costs. The revenue from the orders was $8,000. Prepare a report from an activity view that shows the margin on the business with this customer.

Margin on the Customer from an Activity View

Revenue		$8,000
Costs:		
Direct materials	$3,500	
Direct labor	1,750	
Producing units......................		
Processing orders		
Customer support	_____	_____
Margin		_____

8-2.   (Appendix 8A) This exercise is a continuation of the previous exercise. Lambert Fabrication's managers would like action analysis reports in addition to the reports you have already completed. For the purpose of this report, management classifies the company's costs as follows:

> **Green:** *Costs that adjust automatically to changes in activity without management action.*
> Direct materials
> **Yellow:** *Costs that could, in principle, be adjusted to changes in activity, but management action would be required.*
> Direct labor
> Indirect factory wages
> **Red:** *Costs that would be very difficult to adjust to changes in activity and management action would be required.*
> Other factory overhead
> Selling and administrative overhead

a.   Using the results of the first-stage allocation, compute the activity rates for each of the activity cost pools. (Activity rates are not computed for the "Other" activity cost pool. These costs will not be allocated to products or customers.)

Computation of Activity Rates

	Producing Units	Processing Orders	Customer Support
Total activity	5,000 machine-hours	1,000 orders	200 customers
Indirect factory wages			
Other factory overhead			
Selling and administrative overhead	_____	_____	_____
Total overhead cost	========	========	========

b.   Using the activity rates you derived in part (a) above, compute the total amount of overhead cost that would be allocated to an order that requires 20 machine-hours.

The Overhead Cost of An Order Requiring 20 Machine-Hours

	Producing Units	Processing Orders	Customer Support	Total
Total activity	20 machine-hours	1 order	Not applicable	
Indirect factory wages				
Other factory overhead				
Selling and administrative overhead	_____	_____	_____	_____
Total overhead cost	========	========	========	========

c. Prepare an action analysis report for the order in part (b) above.

Action Analysis of the Order Requiring 20 Machine-Hours

Revenue		$2,500
Green costs:		
Direct materials	$685	685
Green margin		1,815
Yellow costs:		
Direct labor	975	
Indirect factory wages	_____	_____
Yellow margin		
Red costs:		
Other factory overhead		
Selling and administrative overhead	_____	_____
Red margin		_____

d. Compute the total amount of overhead cost that would be allocated to a customer who had two orders during the year requiring a total of 100 machine-hours.

The Overhead Cost of Serving the Customer

	Producing Units	Processing Orders	Customer Support	Total
Total activity	100 machine-hours	2 orders	1 customer	
Indirect factory wages				
Other factory overhead				
Selling and administrative overhead	_____	_____	_____	_____
Total overhead cost	_____	_____	_____	_____

e. Prepare an action analysis report concerning the customer in part (d) above.

Action Analysis of the Customer

Revenue		$8,000
Green costs:		
Direct materials	$3,500	3,500
Green margin		5,500
Yellow costs:		
Direct labor	1,750	
Indirect factory wages	_____	_____
Yellow margin		
Red costs:		
Other factory overhead		
Selling and administrative overhead	_____	_____
Red margin		_____

f. Based on your analysis of the margin on this customer's business in Exercises 8-1 and 8-2, what recommendation, if any, would you make to management? Which report would you prefer to rely on for making decisions—the activity view report from Exercise 8-1 or the action analysis report in Exercise 8-2?

_____

_____

_____

_____

_____

_____

_____

_____

_____

_____

_____

Answers to Questions and Exercises

True or False

1. T It is implicitly assumed that overhead cost is proportional to whatever allocation base is used. If this assumption is not valid, overhead costs will be incorrectly assigned to products and other cost objects.

2. T Organization-sustaining costs and the costs of idle capacity should not be assigned to products in activity-based costing.

3. F In activity-based costing, some non-manufacturing costs may be assigned to products. What matters is whether a cost is caused by the product, not whether it is a manufacturing or non-manufacturing cost.

4. F An activity-based costing system should be designed to aid decision making, not to conform to GAAP. Under GAAP, manufacturing costs that are not caused by any specific products must be assigned to products anyway and non-manufacturing costs that are caused by products cannot be assigned to them.

5. F The practice of basing overhead rates on estimated or budgeted activity results in assigning the costs of idle capacity to products that are made during the period.

6. T Since employee time is a resource, the activity-based costing system requires information about how people spend their time. There may be no better way to get this information than to ask people how they spend their time at work.

7. F One of the characteristics of activity-based costing is the use of multiple measures of activity.

8. F Direct labor-hours can be used as an allocation base if it provides a valid measure of activity for an activity cost pool. Direct labor-hours might, for example, be an appropriate measure of activity for an activity cost pool in which the costs of miscellaneous production supplies are accumulated.

9. T Costs that would not be affected by a decision are irrelevant. Some costs that are assigned to products in an activity-based costing system—particularly red costs that are difficult or impossible to adjust—are likely to be irrelevant.

Multiple Choice

1. c The advertising is incurred on behalf of the product and is not caused by running any particular batch or making any particular unit of that product.

2. e Providing legal advice, unless it is about a specific product or customer, would be considered an organization-sustaining activity.

3. c Writing software for a new computer game is a product-level activity. It only has to be done once for the product and does not have to be repeated to make more units of the software.

4. b This is a batch-level activity since the process of writing an order is the same whether 1 or 1 million copies of the CD-ROM are ordered.

5. d The costs would be assigned as follows:

Making photocopies (200 copies @ $0.02)	$4.00
Setting up machines (2 set-ups @ $0.75)	1.50
Serving customers (1 customer @ $2.15)	2.15
Total cost	$7.65

Chapter 8

Exercises

8-1. a.

	Producing Units	Processing Orders	Customer Support	Other	Totals
Indirect factory wages	$ 40,000	$ 30,000	$ 10,000	$ 20,000	$100,000
Other factory overhead	60,000	20,000	0	120,000	200,000
Selling and administrative overhead	0	100,000	160,000	140,000	400,000
Total overhead cost	$100,000	$150,000	$170,000	$280,000	$700,000

Example: 30% of $100,000 = $30,000

↑

Percentage of indirect factory wages attributable to
processing orders according to the interview results.

b.

Computation of Activity Rates

Activity Cost Pools	Total Cost	Total Activity	Activity Rate
Producing units..........	$100,000	5,000 machine-hours	$20 per machine-hour
Processing orders.......	$150,000	1,000 orders	$150 per order
Customer support	$170,000	200 customers	$850 per customer

c.

The Overhead Cost of An Order Requiring 20 Machine-Hours

Activity Cost Pools	Activity Rate	Activity	ABC Cost
Producing units..........	$20 per machine-hour	20 machine-hours	$400
Processing orders.......	$150 per order	1 order	150
Customer support	$850 per customer	Not applicable	
Total			$550

d.

Margin on the Order from an Activity View

Revenue		$2,500
Costs:		
Direct materials	$685	
Direct labor	975	
Producing units..................	400	
Processing orders	150	
Customer support	0	2,210
Margin		$ 290

e. The overhead cost allocated to a customer can be determined in exactly the same way as for an order. The only difference is that customer support costs are also allocated along with the costs of producing units and processing orders.

The Overhead Cost of Serving the Customer

Activity Cost Pools	Activity Rate	Activity	ABC Cost
Producing units..........	$20 per machine-hour	100 machine-hours	$2,000
Processing orders.......	$150 per order	2 orders	300
Customer support	$850 per customer	1 customer	850
Total			$3,150

f.

Margin on the Customer from an Activity View

Revenue		$8,000
Costs:		
Direct materials	$3,500	
Direct labor	1,750	
Producing units................	2,000	
Processing orders	300	
Customer support	850	8,400
Margin		($ 400)

8-2. a.

Computation of Activity Rates

	Producing Units	*Processing Orders*	*Customer Support*
Total activity	5,000 machine-hours	1,000 orders	200 customers
Indirect factory wages	$ 8	$ 30	$ 50
Other factory overhead	12	20	0
Selling and administrative overhead	0	100	800
Total overhead cost	$20	$150	$850

Example: $30,000 ÷ 1,000 orders = $30 per order

Indirect factory wages allocated to the processing orders
activity cost pool in the first-stage allocation above.

b.

The Overhead Cost of An Order Requiring 20 Machine-Hours

	Producing Units	*Processing Orders*	*Customer Support*	*Total*
Total activity	20 machine-hours	1 order	Not applicable	
Indirect factory wages	$160	$ 30		$190
Other factory overhead	240	20		260
Selling and administrative overhead	0	100		100
Total overhead cost	$400	$150		$550

Example: $30 per order × 1 order = $30

Cost per order from part (b) above.

c. The overhead costs for the action analysis can be taken directly from the row totals in the overhead cost analysis in part (b) above.

Action Analysis of the Order Requiring 20 Machine-Hours

Revenue		$2,500
Green costs:		
Direct materials	$685	685
Green margin		1,815
Yellow costs:		
Direct labor	975	
Indirect factory wages	190	1,165
Yellow margin		650
Red costs:		
Other factory overhead	260	
Selling and administrative overhead	100	360
Red margin		$ 290

d. The overhead cost allocated to a customer can be determined in exactly the same way as for an order. The only difference is that customer support costs are also allocated along with the costs of producing units and processing orders.

The Overhead Cost of Serving the Customer

	Producing Units	Processing Orders	Customer Support	Total
Total activity	100 machine-hours	2 orders	1 customer	
Indirect factory wages	$ 800	$ 60	$ 50	$ 910
Other factory overhead	1,200	40	0	1,240
Selling and administrative overhead	0	200	800	1,000
Total overhead cost	$2,000	$300	$850	$3,150

e. The overhead costs for the action analysis can be taken directly from the row totals in the overhead cost analysis in part (d) above.

Action Analysis of the Customer

Revenue		$8,000
Green costs:		
Direct materials	$3,500	3,500
Green margin		4,500
Yellow costs:		
Direct labor	1,750	
Indirect factory wages	910	2,660
Yellow margin		1,840
Red costs:		
Other factory overhead	1,240	
Selling and administrative overhead	1,000	2,240
Red margin		($ 400)

f.   The analysis in Exercise 8-1 (the activity view) indicates that the company is losing $400 on this customer. This suggests that the company might be better off financially if the customer were dropped. However, if this were done, many of the costs that have been allocated to the customer might not go away. The activity view does not indicate where the costs need to be cut in the organization. For example, the customer support cost of $850 cuts across several departments, but that is not at all clear in the activity view. Since these costs cut across several departments, it would be difficult to pin the responsibility for making cuts on individual managers.

The action analysis provides a much clearer view of the nature of the costs that would have to be cut if the customer were dropped. The manager in charge of the selling and administrative overhead, for example, should be held responsible for cutting $1,000 if this customer were dropped. If the manager would not commit to cutting these costs, there would be no point in dropping the customer. The Green and Yellow margins are positive, so it makes sense to drop this customer only if *at least* $1,840 of the Red costs would be eliminated if the customer were dropped and *all* of the Green and Yellow costs would be eliminated.

Chapter 9

Profit Planning

Chapter Study Suggestions

✳

Carefully study the flow of budget data in Exhibit 9-2. This exhibit provides a good overview of the chapter and the budgeting process. Notice particularly how all the budgets depend in some way on the sales budget and that nearly all budgets eventually impact on the cash budget. As suggested by this exhibit, the cash budget is a key budget that serves to tie together much of the budget process. Schedule 8 in the text contains an example of a cash budget.

Schedules 1 and 2, containing the sales and production budgets, are also very important and your homework assignments are very likely to concentrate on these two budgets.

CHAPTER HIGHLIGHTS

A. Profit planning is accomplished in most organizations with budgets. A *budget* is a detailed plan for the acquisition and use of financial and other resources over a specified time period.

1. The master budget is a summary of the company's plans and goals for the future. It sets specific targets for sales, production, and financing activities and indicates the resources that will be supplied to meet those targets. The master budget culminates with a cash budget and a budgeted income statement and budgeted balance sheet.

2. The budgeting process is concerned with both planning and control.

a. *Planning* involves developing objectives and formulating steps to achieve these objectives.

b. *Control* involves the steps taken by management to increase the likelihood that the objectives set down at the planning stage are attained.

3. Budgeting provides a number of benefits:

a The budget *communicates* management's plans throughout the entire organization.

b. The budgeting process forces managers to *think ahead* and to *formalize* their planning efforts.

c. The budgeting process provides a means of *allocating resources* to those parts of the organization where they can be used most effectively.

d. Budgeting uncovers potential *bottlenecks* before they occur.

e. The budget *coordinates* the activities of the entire organization by *integrating* the plans and objectives of the various parts.

f. The budget provides goals and objectives that serve as *benchmarks* for evaluating subsequent performance.

B. This chapter and the next three chapters are concerned with *responsibility accounting*. The basic idea behind responsibility accounting is that each manager's performance should be judged by how well he or she manages those items—and only those items—under his or her control. Each manager is assigned responsibility for those items of revenues and costs in the budget that the manager is able to control to a significant extent. The manager is then held responsible for deviations between the budget and actual results.

C. Budget preparation is a complex task requiring the cooperative effort of many managers.

1. Operating budgets (the budgets discussed in this chapter) ordinarily cover a one-year period divided into quarters and months.

2. Rather than impose a budget on a manager, managers should be involved in setting their own budgets. There are two reasons for this. First, managers are likely to have the best information concerning their own operations. Second, a manager is more likely to be committed to attaining a budget if the manager is given a major role in developing the budget.

D. The *master budget* consists of a number of separate but interdependent budgets. Exhibit 9-2 provides an overview of the master budget and shows how the parts of the master budget are linked together. Study this exhibit carefully.

1. The *sales budget* (Schedule 1 in the text) is the beginning point in the budgeting process. It details the expected sales, in both units and dollars, for the budget period.   The sales budget is accompanied by a *Schedule of Expected Cash Collections*, which shows the anticipated cash inflow from sales and collections of accounts receivable for the budget period.

2. In a manufacturing company, the sales budget is followed by the *production budget* (Schedule 2 in the text) that shows what must be produced to meet sales forecasts and to provide for desired levels of inventory.

a. The production budget has the following format:

Budgeted unit sales	XXX
Add desired ending inventory	XXX
Total needs	XXX
Less beginning inventory	XXX
Required production	XXX

b. Study Schedule 2 in the text carefully. Note that the "Year" column is not simply the sum of the figures for the Quarters in Schedule 2. The desired ending inventory for the year is the desired ending inventory for the 4th Quarter. And the beginning inventory for the year is the beginning inventory for the 1st Quarter. Warning: Students often overlook this important detail.

3. In a merchandising company such as a clothing store, the sales budget is followed by a *merchandise purchases budget* instead of a production budget. This budget details the amount of goods that must be purchased from suppliers to meet customer demand and to maintain adequate stocks of ending inventory.

    a. The format for the merchandise purchases budget is (in units or dollars):

Budgeted unit sales	XXX
Add desired ending inventory	XXX
Total needs	XXX
Less beginning inventory	XXX
Required purchases	XXX

    b. Note the similarity between the production budget in a manufacturing company and the merchandise purchases budget in a merchandising company.

4. In a manufacturing company, the *direct materials budget* follows the production budget. It details the amount of raw materials that must be acquired to support production and to provide for adequate inventories.

    a. The format for the direct materials budget is:

Raw materials required for production	XXX
Add desired ending inventory	XXX
Total raw materials needs	XXX
Less beginning inventory	XXX
Raw materials to be purchased	XXX

    b. The direct materials budget should be accompanied by a *Schedule of Expected Cash Disbursements* for raw materials.

    c. An example of the direct materials budget appears in Schedule 3 in the text. Note that the "Year" column is not simply the sum of the amounts for the Quarters.

5. In a manufacturing company, a *direct labor budget* (Schedule 4 in the text) also follows the production budget.

6. In a manufacturing company, a *manufacturing overhead budget* (Schedule 5 in the text) also follows the production budget and details all of the production costs that will be required other than direct materials and direct labor.

7. In a manufacturing company, the *ending finished goods inventory budget* (Schedule 6 in the text) provides computations of unit product costs and of the carrying value of the ending inventory.

8. In all types of companies, a *selling and administrative expense* budget (Schedule 7 in the text) is prepared.

9. The *cash budget* (Schedule 8 in the text) summarizes all of the cash inflows and cash outflows appearing on the various budgets. In many companies the cash budget is the single most important result of the budgeting process because it can provide critical advance warnings of potential cash problems. The cash budget allows managers to arrange for financing *before* a crisis develops. Potential lenders are more likely to provide financing if managers appear to be in control and looking ahead rather than simply reacting to crises.

    a. The cash budget has the following format:

Cash balance, beginning	XXX
Add receipts	XXX
Total cash available	XXX
Less disbursements	XXX
Excess (deficiency) of cash available over disbursements	XXX
Financing	XXX
Cash balance, ending	XXX

    b. Study Schedule 8 with care, noting particularly how the financing section is handled.

    c. As with the production budget and the direct materials budget, the "Year" column in Schedule 8 is not simply the sum of the amounts for the Quarters. The beginning cash balance for the year is the beginning cash balance for the first month or quarter. And the ending cash balance for the year is the ending cash balance for the final month or quarter.

10. The budgeting process culminates with the preparation of a *budgeted income statement* (Schedule 9 in the text) and a *budgeted balance sheet* (Schedule 10 in the text.)

REVIEW AND SELF-TEST
Questions and Exercises

True or False

Enter a T or an F in the blank to indicate whether the statement is true or false.

____ 1. The usual starting point in budgeting is to make a forecast of sales.

____ 2. A self-imposed budget is one prepared by top management and imposed on other management levels as it is passed downward through an organization.

____ 3. Budgets are planning devices rather than control devices.

____ 4. The basic idea behind responsibility accounting is that each manager's performance should be judged by how well he or she manages those items under his or her control.

____ 5. Ending inventories occur because an organization is unable to sell all that it had planned to sell during a period.

____ 6. The required production in units for a budget period is equal to the expected unit sales for the period.

____ 7. Because of the technical nature of budgeting, it is best to leave budgeting entirely in the capable hands of the accounting staff.

____ 8. The required raw materials purchases for a period equals the raw materials required for production.

Multiple Choice

Choose the best answer or response by placing the identifying letter in the space provided.

____ 1. Ward Corp.'s actual sales were $30,000 in June, $50,000 in July, and $70,000 in August. Sales in September are expected to be $60,000. Thirty percent of a month's sales are collected in the month of sale, 50% in the first month after sale, 15% in the second month after sale, and the remaining 5% is uncollectible. Budgeted cash receipts for September should be: a) $60,500; b) $62,000; c) $57,000; d) $70,000.

____ 2. Beecher Inc. is planning to purchase inventory for resale costing $90,000 in October, $70,000 in November, and $40,000 in December. The company pays for 40% of its purchases in the month of purchase and 60% in the month following purchase. What would be the budgeted cash disbursements for purchases of inventory in December? a) $40,000; b) $70,000; c) $58,000; d) $200,000.

____ 3. Archer Company has budgeted sales of 30,000 units in April, 40,000 units in May, and 60,000 units in June. The company has 6,000 units on hand on April 1. If the company requires an ending inventory equal to 20% of the following month's sales, production during May should be: a) 32,000 units; b) 44,000 units; c) 36,000 units; d) 40,000 units.

____ 4. Refer to the data for Archer Company in question 3. Each unit requires 3 pounds of a material. A total of 24,000 pounds of the material were on hand on April 1, and the company requires materials on hand at the end of each month equal to 25% of the following month's production needs. The company plans to produce 32,000 units of finished goods in April. How many pounds of the material should the company plan to purchase in April? a) 105,000; b) 19,000; c) 87,000; d) 6,000.

____ 5. If the beginning cash balance is $15,000, the required ending cash balance is $12,000, cash disbursements are $125,000, and cash collections from customers are $90,000, the company must borrow: a) $32,000; b) $20,000; c) $8,000; d) $38,000.

Exercises

9-1.   Billings Company produces and sells a single product. Expected sales for the next four months are given below:

	April	May	June	July
Sales in units	10,000	12,000	15,000	9,000

The company needs a production budget for the second quarter. Experience indicates that end-of-month inventories should equal 10% of the following month's sales in units. At the end of March, 1,000 units were on hand. Complete the following production budget for the quarter:

	April	May	June	Quarter
Budgeted sales				
Add desired ending inventory				
Total needs				
Less beginning inventory				
Required production				

9-2.   Dodero Company's production budget for the next four months is given below:

	July	August	September	October
Required production	15,000	18,000	20,000	16,000

Each unit of product uses five ounces of raw materials. At the end of June, 11,250 ounces of material were on hand. The company wants to maintain an inventory of materials equal to 15% of the following month's production needs.

Complete the following materials purchases budget for the third quarter:

	July	August	September	Quarter
Required production (units)				
Raw material needed per unit (ounces)				
Production needs (ounces)				
Add desired ending inventory (ounces)				
Total needs (ounces)				
Less beginning inventory (ounces)				
Raw materials to be purchased (ounces)				

9-3.   Whitefish Company budgets its cash two months at a time. Budgeted cash disbursements for March and April, respectively, are: for inventory purchases, $90,000 and $82,000; for selling and administrative expenses (includes $5,000 depreciation each month), $75,000 and $70,000; for equipment purchases, $15,000 and $6,000; and for dividend payments, $5,000 and $0. Budgeted cash collections from customers are $150,000 and $185,000 for March and April, respectively. The company will begin March with a $10,000 cash balance on hand. The minimum cash balance at the end of each month should be $5,000. If needed, the company can borrow money at 12% per year. All borrowings are at the beginning of a month, and all repayments are at the end of a month. Interest is paid only when principal is being repaid.

Complete the following cash budget for March and April:

	March	April	Two Months
Cash balance, beginning			
Add collections from customers			
Total cash available			
Less disbursements:			
_____			
_____			
_____			
_____			
Total disbursements			
Excess (deficiency) of cash available over			
disbursements			
Financing:			
Borrowings (at beginning)			
Repayments (at ending)			
Interest (12% per year)			
Total financing			
Cash balance, ending			

Answers to Questions and Exercises

True or False

1. T   A sales forecast is the basis for the company's sales budget. The sales budget, in turn, is the basis for most of the other parts of the master budget.

2. F   A self-imposed budget is one in which a manager prepares his or her own budget with review by higher-level managers.

3. F   Budgeting involves both planning and control. Once a budget is set, it then becomes a control device. It is the benchmark for assessing actual results.

4. T   This is a clear, straightforward statement of the purpose of responsibility accounting.

5. F   Ending inventories are carefully planned if a company is following good budget procedures.

6. F   Production requirements are determined by the level of beginning inventory and the desired level of ending inventory as well as by the expected unit sales.

7. F   The accounting staff may provide help in preparing budgets, but the underlying estimates and data should come from operating managers. There are two reasons for this. First, the operating managers generally have better information about their own operations than the accounting staff. Second, the operating managers must be involved in preparing their own budgets or they will not be committed to them.

8. F   Raw materials purchases do not simply equal the raw materials required for production because of inventories. Beginning inventories decrease the amount of raw materials that must be purchased; desired ending inventories increase the purchases.

Multiple Choice

1. a   The computations are:

September sales, ($60,000 × 30%)	$18,000
August sales, ($70,000 × 50%)	35,000
July sales, ($50,000 × 15%)	7,500
Total cash receipts	$60,500

2. c   The computations are:

November purchases ($70,000 × 60%)	$42,000
December purchases ($40,000 × 40%)	16,000
Total cash disbursements	$58,000

3. b   The computations are:

Budgeted sales	40,000
Desired ending inventory (20% × 60,000).....	12,000
Total needs	52,000
Less beginning inventory (20% × 40,000).....	8,000
Required production	44,000

4. a   The computations are:

Required production (units)........................	32,000
Material per unit (pounds)	× 3
Production needs (pounds)	96,000
Desired ending inventory	
(25% × 44,000 × 3 pounds)	33,000
Total needs	129,000
Less beginning inventory	
(25% × 96,000 pounds)	24,000
Required purchases (pounds)......................	105,000

5. a   The computations are:

Beginning cash balance	$ 15,000
Cash receipts	90,000
Cash available	105,000
Cash disbursements	125,000
Deficiency of cash	$(20,000)

Since the company desires an ending cash balance of $12,000, the company must borrow $32,000 to make up for the cash deficiency of $20,000.

Exercises

9-1.

	April	*May*	*June*	*Quarter*
Budgeted sales	10,000	12,000	15,000	37,000
Add desired ending inventory	1,200	1,500	900	900
Total needs	11,200	13,500	15,900	37,900
Less beginning inventory	1,000	1,200	1,500	1,000
Required production	10,200	12,300	14,400	36,900

9-2.

	July	*August*	*September*	*Quarter*
Required production (units)	15,000	18,000	20,000	53,000
Raw material needs per unit (ounces)	× 5	× 5	× 5	× 5
Production needs (ounces)	75,000	90,000	100,000	265,000
Add desired ending inventory (ounces)	13,500	15,000	12,000*	12,000
Total needs (ounces)	88,500	105,000	112,000	277,000
Less beginning inventory (ounces)	11,250	13,500	15,000	11,250
Raw materials to be purchased (ounces)	77,250	91,500	97,000	265,750

*16,000 units for October × 5 ounces per unit = 80,000 ounces;
80,000 ounces × 15% = 12,000 ounces

9-3.

	March	*April*	*Two Months*
Cash balance, beginning	$ 10,000	$ 5,000	$ 10,000
Add collections from customers	150,000	185,000	335,000
Total cash available	160,000	190,000	345,000
Less disbursements:			
Inventory purchases	90,000	82,000	172,000
Selling and administrative expenses (net of depreciation)	70,000	65,000	135,000
Equipment purchases	15,000	6,000	21,000
Dividends	5,000	—	5,000
Total disbursements	180,000	153,000	333,000
Excess (deficiency) of cash available over cash disbursements	(20,000)	37,000	12,000
Financing:			
Borrowings (at beginning)	25,000	—	25,000
Repayments (at ending)	—	(25,000)	(25,000)
Interest (12% per year)	—	(500)*	(500)
Total financing	25,000	(25,500)	(500)
Cash balance, ending	$ 5,000	$ 11,500	$11,500

* $25,000 × 12% × 2/12 = $500

Chapter 10

Standard Costs and the Balanced Scorecard

Chapter Study Suggestions

✳

The first part of the chapter covers setting standard costs. Exhibit 10-2 shows a standard cost card, which is the final product of the standard setting process. You will be using a standard cost card in the homework assignments in both this chapter and in Chapter 11, so be sure you understand what a standard cost card contains and how it is constructed.

The second part of the chapter covers standard cost variance analysis. Exhibit 10-3 provides a general model for variance analysis, and Exhibits 10-4 through 10-7 give detailed examples of the analysis of materials, labor, and variable overhead. Note that the data from the standard cost card in Exhibit 10-2 are used in Exhibits 10-4, 10-5, and 10-6. As you study, follow the data from Exhibit 10-2 into the following exhibits. This will help you tie the various parts of the chapter together into one integrated whole.

The third part of the chapter discusses the balanced scorecard and operational performance measures. Most of this material is conceptual, but make sure you understand the computations of delivery cycle time, throughput, and manufacturing cycle efficiency.

Chapter 10

CHAPTER HIGHLIGHTS

A. A *standard* is a benchmark or norm for evaluating performance. Manufacturing companies commonly set exacting standards for materials, labor, and overhead for each product. Service companies, such as auto repair shops and fast food outlets, also set standards.

1. Standards are set for both the quantity and the price (cost) of inputs.

2. Actual quantities and prices of inputs are compared to the standards. Differences are called variances. Under *management by exception,* only the significant variances are brought to the attention of management.

B. Setting accurate quantity and price standards is an important step in the control process.

1. Many persons should be involved in setting standards: accountants, purchasing agents, industrial engineers, production supervisors, and line managers.

2. Standards are either *ideal* or *practical.*

a. Ideal standards can only be attained by the best employees working at top efficiency 100% of the time. Ideal standards allow for no machine breakdowns, rest breaks or other lost time.

b. Practical standards, by contrast, allow for breakdowns and normal lost time (such as for rest breaks). Practical standards are tight, but attainable.

c. The use of ideal standards can easily lead to frustration, so most managers feel that practical standards provide better motivation than ideal standards.

3. Direct material standards are set for both the price and quantity of inputs.

a. Price standards should reflect the final, delivered cost of materials, net of any cash discounts allowed.. This price should include freight, handling, and other costs necessary to get the material into a condition ready to use.

b. Quantity standards should reflect the amount of material that is required to make one unit of product, including allowances for unavoidable waste and spoilage.

4. Direct labor price and quantity standards are expressed in terms of a labor rate and the labor-hours required to make a unit of product.

a. The standard direct labor rate per hour should include wages, fringe benefits, employment taxes, and other labor-related costs.

b. The standard labor-hours per unit should include allowances for rest breaks, personal needs of employees, clean-up, and machine down time.

5. As with direct labor, the price and quantity standards for variable overhead are generally expressed in terms of a rate and hours. The rate is the variable portion of the predetermined overhead rate. The quantity standard is expressed in terms of whatever basis is used for applying variable overhead to products. Most frequently, this is direct labor-hours.

6. The price and quantity standards for materials, labor, and overhead for a product are summarized on the product's *standard cost card*.

a. Study the standard cost card in Exhibit 10-2. Trace the numbers on the standard cost card back to the preceding pages in the text.

b. Essentially, the standard cost per unit represents the budgeted variable production cost for a single unit of product.

C. The General Variance Model. A *variance* is a difference between standard and actual prices or standard and actual quantities. The general model in Exhibit 10-3 is very helpful in variance analysis. Study this model with care.

1. A price variance and a quantity variance can be computed for each of the three variable cost categories—materials, labor, and overhead.

2. The *standard quantity allowed for the output* represents the amount of an input that *should have been used* to complete the output of the period. This is a key concept in the chapter!

D. Direct Materials Variances. Exhibit 10-4 illustrates the variance analysis of direct materials. As you study the exhibit, notice that the center column (Actual Quantity of Inputs, at Standard Price) plays a part in the computation of both the price and quantity variances.

1. The *materials price variance* can be expressed in formula form as:

$$\text{Price variance} = (AQ \times AP) - (AQ \times SP)$$
or
$$\text{Price variance} = AQ(AP - SP)$$

where:
  AQ = Actual quantity of the input purchased
  AP = Actual price of the input purchased
  SP = Standard price of the input

An unfavorable materials price variance has many possible causes, including excessive freight costs, loss of quantity discounts, the wrong grade or type of materials, rush orders, and inaccurate standards.

  2. The *materials quantity variance* can be expressed in formula form as:

$$\text{Quantity variance} = (AQ \times SP) - (SQ \times SP)$$
$$\text{or}$$
$$\text{Quantity variance} = SP (AQ - SQ)$$

where:
  AQ = Actual quantity of the input used
  SQ = Standard quantity of the input allowed for the actual output
  SP = Standard price of the input

Possible causes of an unfavorable materials quantity variance include untrained workers, faulty machines, low quality materials, and inaccurate standards.

  3. The materials price variance is usually computed when materials are purchased, whereas the materials quantity variance is computed when materials are used in production. Consequently, the price variance is computed based on the amount of material purchased whereas the quantity variance is computed based on the amount of material used in production.

E. Direct Labor Variances. Exhibit 10-6 shows the variance analysis of direct labor. Notice that the format is the same as for direct materials, but the terms "rate" and "hours" are used in place of the terms "price" and "quantity".

  1. The price variance for labor is called the *labor rate variance*. The formula is:

$$\text{Rate variance} = (AH \times AR) - (AH \times SR)$$
$$\text{or}$$
$$\text{Rate variance} = AH (AR - SR)$$

where:
  AH = Actual labor-hours
  AR = Actual labor rate
  SR = Standard labor rate

Possible causes of an unfavorable labor rate variance include poor assignment of workers to jobs, unplanned overtime, pay increases, and inaccurate standards.

  2. The quantity variance for labor is called the *labor efficiency variance*. The formula is:

$$\text{Efficiency variance} = (AH \times SR) - (SH \times SR)$$
$$\text{or}$$
$$\text{Efficiency variance} = SR (AH - SH)$$

where:
  AH = Actual labor-hours
  SH = Standard labor-hours allowed for the actual output
  SR = Standard labor rate

Possible causes of an unfavorable labor efficiency variance include poorly trained workers, low quality materials, faulty equipment, poor supervision, insufficient work to keep everyone busy, and inaccurate standards.

F. Variable Manufacturing Overhead Variances. Exhibit 10-7 illustrates the variance analysis of variable manufacturing overhead. Note that the format is the same as for direct labor.

  1. The price or rate variance for variable manufacturing overhead is called the *variable overhead spending variance*. The formula for this variance is:

$$\text{Spending variance} = (AH \times AR) - (AH \times SR)$$
$$\text{or}$$
$$\text{Spending variance} = AH (AR - SR)$$

where:
  AH = Actual hours (usually labor-hours)
  AR = Actual variable manufacturing overhead rate
  SR = Standard variable manufacturing overhead rate

  2. The quantity, or efficiency, variance for variable manufacturing overhead is called the *variable overhead efficiency variance*. The formula for this variance is:

$$\text{Efficiency variance} = (AH \times SR) - (SH \times SR)$$
$$\text{or}$$
$$\text{Efficiency variance} = SR (AH - SH)$$

where:
  AH = Actual hours (usually labor-hours)
  SH = Standard hours allowed for the actual output
  SR = Standard variable manufacturing overhead rate

G. Exhibit 10-8 shows how reports should be structured in a standard costing system.

1. Performance reports build upward, with each manager receiving information on his or her own performance, as well as on the performance of subordinates.

2. Each manager is responsible *only* for those costs over which he or she has control.

H. Not all variances warrant investigation. Managers should be interested only in the variances that are significant. Statistical control charts, such as the one in Exhibit 10-9, can be used to identify the variances that are worth investigating.

I. There are some potential problems with the use of standard costs. Most of these problems result from improper use of standard costs or from using standard costs in situations in which they are not appropriate.

1. Standard cost variance reports are usually prepared on a monthly basis and may be released too late to be really useful. Some companies are now reporting variances and other key operating data daily or even more frequently.

2. Managers must avoid using variance reports as a way to find someone to blame. Management by exception, by its nature, tends to focus on the negative. Managers should remember to reward workers for a job well done.

3. If labor is fixed, the only way to avoid an unfavorable labor efficiency variance may be to keep workers busy all the time producing output—even if there is no demand. This can lead to excess work in process and finished goods inventories.

4. A favorable variance may not be good. For example, Pizza Haven has a standard for the amount of mozzarella cheese in a 9-inch pizza. A favorable variance means that less cheese was used than the standard specifies. The result is a substandard pizza.

5. A standard cost reporting system may lead to an emphasis on meeting standards to the exclusion of other important objectives such as maintaining and improving quality, on-time delivery, and customer satisfaction.

6. Just meeting standards may not be sufficient; continual improvement may be necessary.

J. The Balanced Scorecard. A *balanced scorecard* is an integrated set of performance measures that are derived from and support the company's strategy.

1. Each company's balanced scorecard should be different because each company's strategy is different.

2. The balanced scorecard emphasizes continual improvement and trends rather than meeting preset targets or standards.

3. The performance measures on a balanced scorecard should be linked on a cause-and-effect basis. The cause-and-effect links are essentially hypotheses of the form "If there is an improvement in this performance measure, then there will be improvement in that performance measure."

   a. For example, managers of a fast-food restaurant might reason that if the amount of time hamburgers sit on the warming rack before being served is reduced, then customers will like the hamburgers better. And if customers like the hamburgers better, then more hamburgers will be sold. The performance measures on the balanced scorecard would be "time on the warming rack", "customer satisfaction with hamburgers," and "sales of hamburgers."

   b. Most performance measures fall into four categories: financial, customer, internal business processes, and learning and growth. "Time on the warming rack" is a measure of internal business process performance. "Customer satisfaction" is a customer-oriented performance measure. And "sales of hamburgers" is a financial measure of performance.

   c. The performance measures and the hypotheses underlying them should tell a story about how improvements in internal business processes will ultimately lead to improvements in meeting the company's objectives.

   d. If real, sustained improvement in one performance measure does not lead to the predicted improvement in another performance measure, then the company's strategy should be reconsidered. The assumptions underlying the strategy may be false.

4. The entire company should have a comprehensive balanced scorecard. In addition, individuals should have scorecards that contain only those performance measures they can actually influence.

K. Measures of Internal Business Process Performance. Many measures of internal business process performance, such as the percentage of orders that are delivered on time, are self-explanatory. Some are not.

1. Study Exhibit 10-11 carefully to understand the definitions of *Wait Time, Process Time, Inspection Time, Move Time*, and *Queue Time*.

2. *Throughput time* measures the amount of time required to make a completed product. It is also known as the manufacturing cycle time. Throughput time is the sum of process time, inspection time, move time, and queue time as shown below:

Throughput Time = Process Time + Inspection Time + Move Time + Queue Time

3. *Delivery cycle time* represents the amount of time that elapses between the time when a customer submits an order and when the order is shipped.

Delivery Cycle Time = Wait Time + Throughput Time

4. *Manufacturing cycle efficiency (MCE)* is a measure of the efficiency of the production process. It is computed as follows:

$$MCE = \frac{\text{Value-added (Process) Time}}{\text{Throughput (Manufacturing Cycle) Time}}$$

If the MCE is less than 1, non-value-added time is present in the production process. An MCE of 0.25 for example, would mean that 75% of the total production time consisted of Inspection Time, Move Time, and Queue Time—all non-value-added activities.

Appendix 10A: General Ledger Entries to Record Variances

A. Many companies carry inventories at standard cost and record standard cost variances in the general ledger. This simplifies bookkeeping.

B. Favorable variances are recorded as credits, and unfavorable variances are recorded as debits.

1. The entry to record an unfavorable material price variance upon purchase of materials on account would be:

Raw Materials	XXX	
Materials Price Variance (U)	XXX	
Accounts Payable		XXX

2. The entry to record a favorable material quantity variance would be:

Work in Process	XXX	
Materials Quantity Variance (F)		XXX
Raw Materials		XXX

3. The entry to record an unfavorable labor efficiency variance and a favorable labor rate variance would be:

Work in Process	XXX	
Labor Efficiency Variance (U)	XXX	
Labor Rate Variance (F)		XXX
Wages Payable		XXX

REVIEW AND SELF-TEST
Questions and Exercises

True or False

Enter a T or an F in the blank to indicate whether the statement is true or false.

____ 1. Practical standards are generally viewed as better than ideal standards for motivating employees.

____ 2. Ideal standards allow for machine breakdown time and other normal inefficiencies.

____ 3. In determining a material price standard, any freight or handling costs should be excluded.

____ 4. The standard rate for variable overhead consists of the variable portion of the predetermined overhead rate.

____ 5. Raw materials price variances should be computed and reported only when materials are placed into production.

____ 6. Waste on the production line will result in a materials price variance.

____ 7. If the actual price or quantity exceeds the standard price or quantity, the variance is unfavorable.

____ 8. Labor rate variances are generally out of the control of management.

____ 9. Managers should thoroughly investigate all differences (variances) between standard cost and actual cost.

____ 10. In a company with fixed labor, an undue focus on labor efficiency variances may result in the production of excess inventories.

____ 11. The balanced scorecard approach focuses more on improvement over time than on meeting specific standards.

____ 12. Any two companies should have basically the same balanced scorecard.

____ 13. If the MCE is less than 1, the production process includes non-value-added time.

____ 14. (Appendix 10A) The use of standard costs simplifies bookkeeping.

____ 15. (Appendix 10A) An unfavorable variance would be recorded as a debit in the general ledger.

Multiple Choice

Choose the best answer or response by placing the identifying letter in the space provided.

____ 1. The labor rate variance is determined by multiplying the difference between the actual labor rate and the standard labor rate by: a) the standard hours allowed; b) the actual hours worked; c) the budgeted hours allowed; d) none of these.

____ 2. If inferior-grade materials are purchased, the result may be: a) an unfavorable materials price variance; b) a favorable materials price variance; c) an unfavorable labor efficiency variance; d) a favorable labor efficiency variance; e) responses b and c are both correct; f) responses a and d are both correct.

____ 3. During June, Bradley Company produced 4,000 units of product. The standard cost card indicates the following labor standards per unit of output: 3.5 hours @ $6 per hour = $21. During the month, the company worked 15,000 hours. The standard hours allowed for the month were: a) 14,000 hours; b) 15,000 hours; c) 24,000 hours; d) 18,000 hours.

____ 4. Refer to the data in question 3 above. What was the labor efficiency variance for June? (F indicates a Favorable variance and U indicates an Unfavorable variance.) a) $1,000 F; b) $1,000 U; c) $6,000 F; d) $6,000 U.

____ 5. Refer to the data in question 3 above. The total labor cost during June was $88,000 for the 15,000 hours that were worked. What was the labor rate variance for June? a) $6,000 F; b) $6,000 U; c) $2,000 F; d) $2,000 U.

____ 6. During July, Bradley Company produced 3,000 units. The standard cost card indicates the following materials standards per unit of output: 2 pounds @ $0.50 per pound = $1. During July, 8,000 pounds of material were purchased at a cost of $3,900. The materials price variance for July was: a) $100 F; b) $100 U; c) $4,100 F; d) $4,100 U.

____ 7. Refer to the data in question 6 above. 6,100 pounds of material were used in July to produce the output of 3,000 units. The materials quantity variance for July was: a) $1,550 F; b) $1,550 U; c) $50 F; d) $50 U.

____ 8. During August, Bradley Company produced 3,500 units of product using 12,750 labor-hours. The standard cost card indicates the following variable manufacturing overhead standards per unit of output: 3.5 labor-hours @ $2 per labor-hour = $7. During the month, the actual variable manufacturing overhead cost incurred was $25,000. The variable overhead spending variance was: a) $500 U; b) $500 F; c) $24,500 U; d) $24,500 F.

____ 9. Refer to the data in question 8 above. The variable overhead efficiency variance was: a) $7,000 F; b) $7,000 U; c) $1,000 F; d) $1,000 U.

____ 10. The "price" variance for variable overhead is called a: a) rate variance; b) spending variance; c) budget variance; d) none of these.

____ 11. The delivery cycle time consists of: a) the time required to get a product to a customer after production is complete; b) the time required to get delivery of raw materials; c) the velocity of production plus the throughput time; d) the time required from receipt of an order from a customer to shipment of the completed goods.

____ 12. The following data are average times per order over the last month.

Wait time to start production	15.0 days
Inspection time	0.6 days
Process time	3.0 days
Move time	1.4 days
Queue time	7.0 days

The throughput time would be: a) 12.0 days; b) 7.0 days; c) 5.0 days; d) 20.0 days.

____ 13. Refer to the data in question 12 above. The MCE would be: a) 75%; b) 30%; c) 25%; d) 42%.

____ 14. Refer again to the data in question 12 above. What percentage of the throughput time is spent in non-value-added activities: a) 25%; b) 70%; c) 75%; d) 58%.

Chapter 10

Exercises

10-1.   Selected data relating to Miller Company's operations for April are given below:

Number of units produced .... 500 units
Number of actual direct labor-hours worked .... 1,400 hours
Total actual direct labor cost $10,850

The standard cost card indicates that 2.5 hours of direct labor time is allowed per unit, at a rate of $8 per hour.

a.   Complete the following analysis of direct labor cost for the month:

Actual Hours of Input, at the Actual Rate $(AH \times AR)$	*Actual Hours of Input, at the Standard Rate* $(AH \times SR)$	*Standard Hours Allowed for Output, at the Standard Rate* $(SH \times SR)$
_____	_____	_____
_____	_____	_____
_____	_____	_____

b.   Redo the above analysis of direct labor cost for the month, using the following formulas:

Labor Rate Variance = $AH\,(AR - SR)$

Labor Efficiency Variance = $SR\,(AH - SH)$

10-2. The following activity took place in Solo Company during May:

Number of units produced .... 450 units
Material purchased .... 1,500 feet
Material used in production .... 720 feet
Cost per foot for material purchased $3

The standard cost card indicates that 1.5 feet of materials are allowed for each unit of product. The standard cost of the materials is $4 per foot.

a. Complete the following analysis of direct materials cost for the month:

Actual Quantity of Inputs, at Actual Price (AQ × AP)	*Actual Quantity of Inputs, at Standard Price (AQ × SP)*	*Standard Quantity Allowed for Output, at Standard Price (SQ × SP)*

b. Redo the above analysis of direct materials cost for the month, using the following formulas:

Materials Price Variance = AQ (AP – SP)

Materials Quantity Variance = SP (AQ – SQ)

10-3.   (Appendix 10A) Refer to the data for Solo Company in exercise 10-2 on the previous page. Prepare journal entries to record all activity relating to direct materials for the month:

	Debit	Credit

10-4.   During the last quarter, Scott Company recorded the following average times per order received and processed:

Wait time to start production	9.0 days
Inspection time	0.8 days
Process time	3.0 days
Move time	0.2 days
Queue time	6.0 days

a.   Compute the throughput time.

Throughput time =

b.   Compute the manufacturing cycle efficiency (MCE).

MCE =

c.   What percentage of the production time is spent in non-value-added activities?

d.   Compute the delivery cycle time.

Delivery Cycle Time =

Answers to Questions and Exercises

True or False

1. T Practical standards are considered to provide better motivation than ideal standards because they are attainable by workers.

2. F Ideal standards do not allow for either machine breakdowns or other normal inefficiencies.

3. F Freight and handling costs should be included in the material price standard.

4. T This statement is true by definition.

5. F The purchasing manager is responsible for the materials price variance. This variance should be computed when the purchasing manager does his or her work—not when the materials are put into production.

6. F Waste will result in a materials quantity variance.

7. T This statement is true by definition.

8. F Labor rate variances can arise from overtime and other causes that are within the control of management.

9. F Managers should not waste time investigating insignificant variances.

10. T When labor is fixed, the only way to generate a more favorable labor efficiency variance may be to keep everyone busy producing output—even if there is no demand.

11. T The balanced scorecard approach emphasizes continual improvement.

12. F Since companies have different strategies, their balanced scorecards should be different.

13. T Since the MCE is measured by value-added time divided by throughput time, an MCE of less than 1 means that the throughput time contains some amount of non-value-added time.

14. T The use of standard costs simplifies the bookkeeping process since standards permit all units to be carried at the same cost.

15. T Unfavorable variances have the effect of decreasing income. Therefore, they are debit entries just as an expense is a debit entry.

Multiple Choice

1. b This point is illustrated in Exhibit 10-6.

2. e The materials price variance will probably be favorable, since the inferior grade materials probably will cost less. The labor efficiency variance will probably be unfavorable, since the inferior grade materials will probably require more work.

3. a 4,000 units × 3.5 hours per unit = 14,000 hours.

4. d Efficiency variance = SR (AH − SH)
$$= \$6\ (15,000 - 14,000)$$
$$= \$6,000\ U$$

5. c Rate variance = (AH × AR) −(AH × SR)
$$= (\$88,000) - (15,000 \times \$6)$$
$$= \$2,000\ F$$

6. a Price variance = (AQ × AP) − (AQ × SP)
$$= (\$3,900) - (8,000 \times \$0.50)$$
$$= \$100\ F$$

7. d Quantity variance = SP (AQ − SQ)
$$= \$0.50\ (6,100 - 2 \times 3,000)$$
$$= \$50\ U$$

8. b Spending variance
$$= (AH \times AR) - (AH \times SR)$$
$$= (\$25,000) - (12,750 \times \$2)$$
$$= \$500\ F$$

9. d Efficiency variance = SR (AH − SH)
$$= \$2\ (12,750 - 3.5 \times 3,500)$$
$$= \$1,000\ U$$

10. b This point is illustrated in Exhibit 10-3.

11. d This point is illustrated in Exhibit 10-11.

12. a Throughput time = Process time + Inspection time + Move time + Queue time
$$= 3.0\ days + 0.6\ days + 1.4\ days + 7.0\ days$$
$$= 12.0\ days$$

13. c
$$MCE = \frac{\text{Value-added time}}{\text{Throughput time}} = \frac{3.0\ days}{12.0\ days} = 25\%$$

14. c If the MCE is less than one, non-value-added time is present in the production process. In this case, since the MCE is 25%, 75% of the time is spent in non-value-added activities (1.00− 0.25 = 0.75 or 75%).

Exercises

10-1.   a.

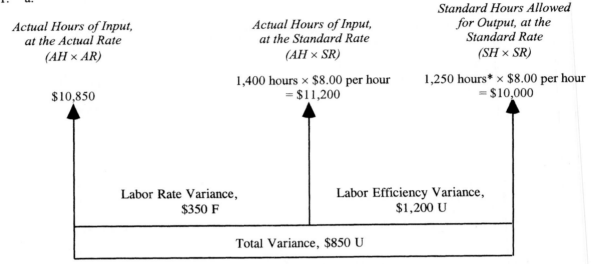

| | *Actual Hours of Input, at the Standard Rate (AH × SR)* | *Standard Hours Allowed for Output, at the Standard Rate (SH × SR)* |

Actual Hours of Input, at the Actual Rate (AH × AR)

$10,850

1,400 hours × $8.00 per hour = $11,200

1,250 hours* × $8.00 per hour = $10,000

Labor Rate Variance, $350 F

Labor Efficiency Variance, $1,200 U

Total Variance, $850 U

*500 units × 2.5 hours per unit = 1,250 hours

b.   AR = $10,850 ÷ 1,400 hours = $7.75 per hour
Labor Rate Variance = AH (AR – SR)
= 1,400 hours ($7.75 per hour – $8.00 per hour) = $350 F

Labor Efficiency Variance = SR (AH – SH)
= $8.00 per hour (1,400 hours – 1,250 hours) = $1,200 U

10-2. a.

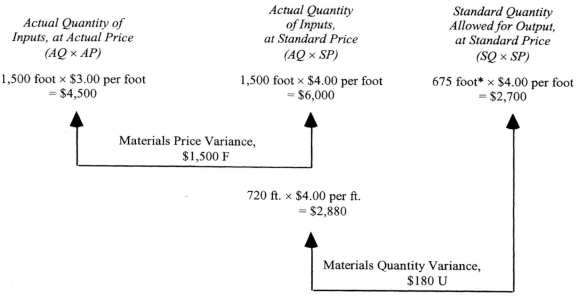

Actual Quantity of Inputs, at Actual Price (AQ × AP)	Actual Quantity of Inputs, at Standard Price (AQ × SP)	Standard Quantity Allowed for Output, at Standard Price (SQ × SP)
1,500 foot × $3.00 per foot = $4,500	1,500 foot × $4.00 per foot = $6,000	675 foot* × $4.00 per foot = $2,700

Materials Price Variance, $1,500 F

720 ft. × $4.00 per ft. = $2,880

Materials Quantity Variance, $180 U

*450 units × 1.5 feet per unit = 675 feet

b.   Materials Price Variance = AQ (AP − SP)
              = 1,500 feet ($3.00 per foot − $4.00 per foot) = $1,500 F
       Materials Quantity Variance = SP (AQ − SQ)
              = $4.00 per foot (720 feet − 675 feet) = $180 U

Note that more materials were purchased (1,500 feet) than were used in production (720 feet). When computing the price variance, use the quantity of materials purchased. When computing the quantity variance, use the quantity of materials used in production.

10-3.   Raw Materials   6,000
                   Materials Price Variance   1,500
                   Accounts Payable   4,500
             Work in Process   2,700
             Materials Quantity Variance   180
                   Raw Materials   2,880

10-4. a.   Throughput time = Process time + Inspection time + Move time + Queue time
                      = 3.0 days + 0.8 days + 0.2 days + 6.0 days
                      = 10.0 days

       b.   MCE= $\dfrac{\text{Value-added time}}{\text{Throughput time}} = \dfrac{3.0\ \text{days}}{10.0\ \text{days}} = 30\%$

       c.   Since 30% of throughput time is value-added time, 70% represents non-value-added time.

       d.   Delivery cycle time = Wait time + Throughput time
                      = 9.0 days + 10.0 days
                      = 19.0 days

Chapter 11

Flexible Budgets and Overhead Analysis

Chapter Study Suggestions

*

The chapter is divided into three parts. The first part covers flexible budgets, with Exhibit 11-3 providing a comprehensive example of how a flexible budget is prepared. Pay close attention to the differences between a flexible budget and a static budget.

The middle part of the chapter expands on the variance analysis of variable overhead that was introduced in Chapter 10. Exhibits 11-6 and 11-7 are the key exhibits here.

The last part of the chapter covers fixed overhead analysis. Pay particular attention to three items in this part of the chapter. First, understand what the "denominator activity" is, and how it is used. Second, understand the difference between a "normal cost system" and a "standard cost system," as illustrated in Exhibit 11-9. Third, be sure you understand the fixed overhead variances illustrated in Exhibit 11-10.

The chapter concludes with a detailed example of flexible budgets and fixed overhead analysis. Follow the example step by step before attempting your homework.

CHAPTER HIGHLIGHTS

A. The sales budgets, production budgets, and cash budgets in Chapter 9 are *static budgets*. They are static in the sense that they represent costs at a single level of activity—the originally budgeted level of activity. The static budget can't be used to assess how well individuals were able to control costs after the period is over. For example, if activity is higher than was assumed in the original budget, variable costs should be higher than originally budgeted.

B. A *flexible budget* is geared to a range of activity, rather than to a single level. This can be seen from the flexible budget presented in Exhibit 11-3. Notice especially how a "cost formula" is used in the flexible budget for the variable costs.

   1. A flexible budget is a dynamic tool. It can be used to quickly develop a budget for any level of activity within the relevant range. The variable costs are adjusted by multiplying the cost per unit by the activity level. Fixed costs remain unchanged within the relevant range.

   2. The activity base underlying the flexible budget must be carefully chosen. Three general criteria are used in selecting an activity base:

      a. The flexible budget assumes that the variable costs change in proportion to changes in the activity base, so the activity base should actually drive the variable costs.

      b. The activity base should not be expressed in dollars. For example, direct labor cost should not be used as an activity base. A change in the labor wage rate would change the measure of activity, but may have little real effect on the costs in the flexible budget.

      c. The activity base should be simple and easy to understand.

C. A *flexible budget performance report* can be easily constructed to evaluate how well costs were controlled.

   1. Compute the amount for each variable cost in the flexible budget by multiplying its cost per unit by the actual level of activity for the period.

   2. If the actual activity is within the relevant range, the fixed cost amounts can be copied from the static budget since they should not change.

   3. Variances are computed for each of the costs. If the actual cost exceeds the flexible budget cost for the actual level of activity, the variance is unfavorable. If the actual cost is less than the flexible budget cost for the actual level of activity, the variance is favorable.

   4. Fixed costs can have variances because actual fixed costs can differ from budgeted fixed costs.

      a. A cost is fixed if it does not depend on the level of activity. However, that does not mean a fixed cost cannot change for other reasons or that it cannot be controlled.

      b. For example, the cost of heating and lighting an administrative office is fixed—it does not depend on how many goods or services the company sells. Nevertheless, this cost can change from period to period due to seasonal factors, how conscientious people are in turning off lights, the thermostat setting they use, and so on.

      c. It is often easier to control fixed costs than variable costs. Many fixed costs involve discretionary activities such as travel costs, entertainment, and executive seminars.

D. The middle portion of the chapter focuses on variable manufacturing overhead. Two types of *variable overhead performance reports* are illustrated. One type of report shows just a spending variance. The other type of report shows both a spending and an efficiency variance. Both of these variances were discussed in Chapter 10.

   1. If the flexible budget allowances in the performance report are based on the actual number of hours worked during the period, then there will be just a spending variance. Exhibit 11-6 illustrates this procedure. The overhead spending variance combines both price and quantity variances. An unfavorable variance could occur because the standard is in error, prices paid for overhead items were too high, or too many overhead resources were used.

   2. If the flexible budget allowances in the performance report are based on both the actual number of hours worked and the standard hours allowed for the output of the period, both a spending and an efficiency variance can be computed.

      a. Exhibit 11-7 contains a performance report using this approach. Study the column headings in this exhibit carefully.

      b. The term "variable overhead efficiency variance" is a misnomer. This variance has nothing to do with how efficiently or inefficiently variable overhead resources were used. The inefficiency is really in the base underlying the application of overhead. For example, if direct labor-hours are used as the activity base, an unfavorable variable overhead efficiency variance will occur whenever the actual direct labor-hours exceeds the standard number of direct labor-hours allowed for the actual output.

E. The flexible budget can serve as the basis for computing predetermined overhead rates for product costing purposes. The formula is:

$$\text{Predetermined overhead rate} = \frac{\text{Overhead from the flexible budget at the denominator level of activity}}{\text{Denominator level of activity}}$$

1. The denominator level of activity is the level of activity (usually in direct labor-hours or machine-hours) that is assumed when the predetermined overhead rate is computed. The numerator in the rate is the amount of manufacturing overhead from the flexible budget at that level of activity.

2. The predetermined overhead rate can be divided into two parts, one for the variable overhead costs and the other for the fixed overhead costs.

　　a. The fixed portion of the predetermined overhead rate depends on the level of the denominator activity that is chosen. The larger the denominator activity, the lower the rate will be.

　　b. The variable portion of the predetermined overhead rate does not depend on the level of the denominator activity; it is constant. [This can be confusing.]

F. Exhibit 11-9 is an extremely important exhibit. It shows that overhead is applied to work in process differently under a *standard cost system* than it is under a *normal cost system.*

1. We studied normal cost systems in Chapter 3. In a normal cost system, overhead is applied by multiplying the predetermined overhead rate by the actual hours of activity for a period.

2. In contrast, under a standard cost system overhead is applied to work in process by multiplying the predetermined overhead rate by the *standard hours allowed for the output of the period.* As in Chapter 10, the standard hours allowed for the output are computed by multiplying the standard hours per unit of output by the actual output of the period.

G. The last part of the chapter is concerned with the two fixed manufacturing overhead variances—the budget variance and the volume variance.

1. The *fixed overhead budget variance*, or simply "budget variance," is the difference between actual fixed overhead costs and budgeted fixed overhead costs. The formula for the variance is:

$$\text{Budget variance} = \frac{\text{Actual fixed}}{\text{overhead cost}} - \frac{\text{Budgeted fixed}}{\text{overhead cost}}$$

2. The formula for the *fixed overhead volume variance*, is:

$$\text{Volume variance} = \frac{\text{Fixed overhead rate}}{} \times \left(\frac{\text{Denominator hours}}{} - \frac{\text{Standard hours allowed}}{} \right)$$

The "fixed overhead rate" is the fixed portion of the predetermined overhead rate. The volume variance does not measure how well spending was controlled. It is completely determined by the relation between the denominator hours and the standard hours allowed for the actual output.

　　a. If the denominator hours exceed the standard hours allowed for the output of the period, the volume variance is an unfavorable.

　　b. If the denominator hours are less than the standard hours allowed for the output of the period, the volume variance is favorable.

I. In a standard cost system, the amount of overhead applied to products is determined by the standard hours allowed for the actual output.

1. As in Chapter 3, if the actual overhead cost exceeds the amount of overhead cost applied to units of product, then the overhead is underapplied. If the actual overhead cost incurred is less than the amount of overhead cost applied to units, then the overhead is overapplied.

2. In a standard cost system, the sum of the overhead variances equals the amount of under- or overapplied overhead.

Overhead under- or overapplied =
　　　Variable overhead spending variance
　+　Variable overhead efficiency variance
　+　Fixed overhead budget variance
　+　Fixed overhead volume variance

If the sum of the variances is unfavorable, the overhead is underapplied. If the sum of the variances is favorable, the overhead is overapplied.

REVIEW AND SELF-TEST
Questions and Exercises

True or False

Enter a T or an F in the blank to indicate whether the statement is true or false.

____ 1. A budget prepared for a single level of activity is called a static budget.

____ 2. Fixed costs are not controllable and therefore should be omitted from performance reports.

____ 3. A manger should be judged on the basis of how well he or she is able to keep costs to their originally budgeted levels.

____ 4. Direct labor cost would generally be a better base to use in preparing a flexible budget than direct labor-hours.

____ 5. A variable overhead spending variance is affected by waste and excessive usage as well as price.

____ 6. The term "overhead efficiency variance" is really a misnomer since this variance has nothing to do with efficiency in the use of overhead.

____ 7. If overhead is applied to production on the basis of direct labor-hours, the labor efficiency variance and the overhead efficiency variance will always be favorable or unfavorable together.

____ 8. The fixed overhead volume variance measures how well fixed overhead spending was controlled.

____ 9. If the denominator activity level exceeds the standard hours allowed for the output, the volume variance will be favorable.

____ 10. In a standard cost system, if overhead is overapplied, then the sum of the four manufacturing overhead variances will be favorable.

Multiple Choice

Choose the best answer or response by placing the identifying letter in the space provided.

____ 1. In a standard cost system, overhead is applied to production on the basis of: a) the actual hours required to complete the output of the period; b) the standard hours allowed to complete the output of the period; c) the denominator hours chosen for the period; d) none of these.

____ 2. If the standard hours allowed for the output of a period exceed the denominator hours used in setting overhead rates, there will be: a) a favorable budget variance; b) an unfavorable budget variance; c) a favorable volume variance; d) an unfavorable volume variance.

____ 3. Baxter Company uses a standard cost system in which manufacturing overhead is applied to units of product on the basis of direct labor-hours. The variable portion of the company's predetermined overhead rate is $3 per direct labor-hour. The standards call for 2 direct labor-hours per unit of output. In March, the company produced 2,000 units using 4,100 direct labor-hours and the actual variable overhead cost incurred was $12,050. What was the variable overhead spending variance? a) $250 U; b) $250 F; c) $6,050 U; d) $6,050 F.

____ 4. Refer to the data in part (3) above concerning Baxter Company. What was the variable overhead efficiency variance for March? a) $6,300 F; b) $6,300 U; c) $300 F; d) $300 U.

____ 5. Baxter Company's flexible budget for manufacturing overhead indicates that the fixed overhead should be $30,000 at the denominator level of 3,000 standard direct labor-hours. In March, the actual fixed overhead cost incurred was $33,000. Recall from the above data concerning Baxter Company that the standards call for 2 direct labor-hours per unit of output and that in March, the company produced 2,000 units using 4,100 direct labor-hours (DLHs). What is the fixed portion of the predetermined overhead rate? a) $10 per DLH; b) $11 per DLH; c) $30 per DLH; d) $2 per DLH.

____ 6. Refer to the data in parts (3) and (5) above concerning Baxter Company. How much overhead (both variable and fixed) was applied to units of product during March? a) $12,000; b) $30,000; c) $52,000; d) $42,000.

____ 7. Refer to the data in part (5) above concerning Baxter Company. What was the fixed overhead budget variance for March? a) $10,000 F; b) $10,000 U; c) $3,000 U; d) $3,000 F.

____ 8. Refer to the data in part (5) above concerning Baxter Company. What was the fixed overhead volume variance for March? a) $10,000 F; b) $10,000 U; c) $3,000 U; d) $3,000 F.

Exercises

11-1. Herbold Corporation uses the following cost formulas in its flexible budget for manufacturing overhead:

Item	*Cost Formula*
Utilities	$ 6,000 per year, plus $0.30 per machine-hour (MH)
Supplies	$10,000 per year, plus $0.80 per machine-hour
Depreciation	$25,000 per year
Indirect labor	$21,000 per year, plus $0.40 per machine-hour

Using these cost formulas, complete the following flexible budget:

Overhead Costs	*Cost Formula (per MH)*	*Machine-hours*		
		8,000	*10,000*	*12,000*
Variable overhead costs:				
_____	____	____	____	____
_____	____	____	____	____
_____	____	____	____	____
Total variable costs	____	____	____	____
Fixed overhead costs:				
_____		____	____	____
_____		____	____	____
_____		____	____	____
_____		____	____	____
Total fixed costs		____	____	____
Total overhead costs		____	____	____

11-2. Refer to the flexible budget data in Exercise 11-1. The standard time to complete one unit of product is 1.6 machine-hours. Last year the company budgeted to operate at the 10,000 machine-hour level of activity. During the year the following actual activity took place:

Number of units produced	5,000 units
Actual machine-hours worked	8,500 hours

Actual overhead costs:

	Variable	*Fixed*
Utilities	$2,600	$5,900
Supplies	$6,700	$10,300
Indirect labor	$3,300	$21,700
Depreciation		$25,000

Prepare a performance report for the year using the format that appears below. Do not compute efficiency variances for variable overhead items.

Performance Report
Herbold Corporation

Budgeted machine-hours .... _____

Actual machine-hours .... _____

Standard machine-hours .... _____

	Cost Formula (per MH)	*Actual Costs 8,500 MHs*	*Budget Based on ____ MHs*	*Spending or Budget Variance*
Variable overhead costs:				
_____	_____	_____	_____	_____
_____	_____	_____	_____	_____
_____	_____	_____	_____	_____
Total variable costs	=======	_____	_____	_____
Fixed overhead costs:				
_____		_____	_____	_____
_____		_____	_____	_____
_____		_____	_____	_____
Total fixed costs		_____	_____	_____
Total overhead costs		=======	=======	=======

11-3.   The flexible budget for manufacturing overhead for Marina Company is given below:

MARINA COMPANY
Flexible Budget

Overhead Costs	Cost Formula (per DLH)	Direct Labor-hours 10,000	12,000	14,000
Variable costs:				
Electricity	$0.15	$ 1,500	$ 1,800	$ 2,100
Indirect materials	0.50	5,000	6,000	7,000
Indirect labor	0.25	2,500	3,000	3,500
Total variable costs	$0.90	9,000	10,800	12,600
Fixed costs:				
Depreciation		11,500	11,500	11,500
Property taxes		8,500	8,500	8,500
Insurance		4,000	4,000	4,000
Total fixed costs		24,000	24,000	24,000
Total overhead costs		$33,000	$34,800	$36,600

Marina Company uses a standard cost system in which manufacturing overhead is applied to units of product on the basis of standard direct labor-hours (DLHs). The denominator activity level used in setting predetermined overhead rates is 12,000 direct labor-hours. The standard time to complete one unit of product is 1.5 direct labor-hours.

For the company's most recent year, the following actual operating data are available:

Units produced	9,000 units
Actual direct labor-hours worked	14,000 hours
Actual variable overhead cost	$12,880
Actual fixed overhead cost	$23,750

a.   Compute the predetermined overhead rate that would be used by the company, and break it down into variable and fixed cost elements:

Predetermined overhead rate ....   _____

Variable cost element ....   _____

Fixed cost element ....   _____

b.   How much overhead would have been applied to work in process during the year? _____

   c.   Complete the following variance analysis of variable overhead cost for the company's most recent year (see Chapter 10):

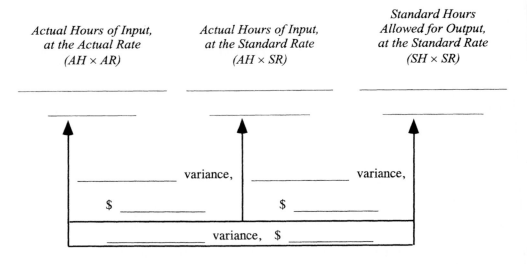

Actual Hours of Input, at the Actual Rate (AH × AR)   *Actual Hours of Input, at the Standard Rate (AH × SR)*   *Standard Hours Allowed for Output, at the Standard Rate (SH × SR)*

_____ variance, $ _____   _____ variance, $ _____

_____ variance, $ _____

   d.   Complete the following variance analysis of fixed overhead cost for the company's most recent year:

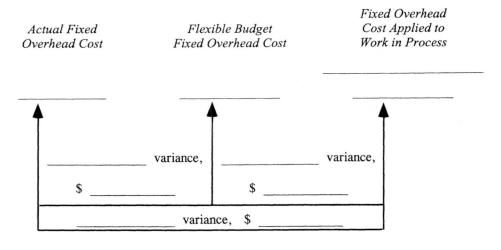

Actual Fixed Overhead Cost   *Flexible Budget Fixed Overhead Cost*   *Fixed Overhead Cost Applied to Work in Process*

_____ variance, $ _____   _____ variance, $ _____

_____ variance, $ _____

Answers to Questions and Exercises

True or False

1. T   A static budget is prepared for only one level of activity.

2. F   Many fixed costs are controllable and must be on someone's performance report or no one will control them.

3. F   This may be true in government, but is not true in commercial enterprises. Costs will be higher or lower than budgeted simply due to changes in activity. It is unreasonable to expect , for example, that a production manager will be able to make 10% more units than budgeted (if requested by marketing) without spending more than was originally budgeted.

4. F   It is generally best to avoid using dollars in the activity base.

5. T   The overhead spending variance contains elements of both price and quantity variances.

6. T   The overhead efficiency variance really reflects efficiency in the base underlying the application of overhead.

7. T   The reason for the close relationship is that both variances are based on the difference between the actual direct labor-hours and the standard direct labor-hours allowed for actual output.

8. F   The fixed overhead volume variance results from a difference between the denominator level of activity and the standard hours allowed for the actual output of the period. It has nothing to do with spending.

9. F   The reverse is true—the volume variance would be unfavorable.

10. T   Overapplied overhead is equivalent to favorable variances and underapplied overhead is equivalent to unfavorable variances.

Multiple Choice

1. b   This point is illustrated in Exhibit 11-9.

2. c   The volume variance is favorable any time the standard hours allowed for the actual output of the period exceeds the denominator level of activity.

3. b

Spending var. $= (AH \times AR) - (AH \times SR)$
$= (\$12,050) - (4,100 \times \$3)$
$= \$250$ F

4. d

Efficiency var. $= (AH \times SR) - (SH \times SR)$
$= (4,100 \times \$3) - (4,000^* \times \$3)$
$= \$300$ U

* 2,000 units $\times$ 2 DLHs per unit = 4,000 DLHs

5. a

$$\begin{matrix}\text{Fixed portion of} \\ \text{the predetermined} \\ \text{overhead rate}\end{matrix} = \frac{\$30,000}{3,000 \text{ DLHs}}$$

$= \$10$ per DLH

6. c

$$\begin{matrix}\text{Prdetermined} \\ \text{overhead rate}\end{matrix} = \$3 + \$10$$

$= \$13$ per DLH

$$\begin{matrix}\text{Standard hours} \\ \text{allowed for} \\ \text{the output}\end{matrix} = \frac{2,000}{\text{units}} \times \frac{2 \text{ DLHs}}{\text{per unit}}$$

$= 4,000$ DLHs

Overhead applied $= \$13 \times 4,000$
$= \$52,000$

7. c

$$\begin{matrix}\text{Budget} \\ \text{variance}\end{matrix} = \begin{matrix}\text{Actual fixed} \\ \text{overhead cost}\end{matrix} - \begin{matrix}\text{Budgeted fixed} \\ \text{overhead cost}\end{matrix}$$

$= \$33,000 - \$30,000$
$= \$3,000$ U

8. a

$$\begin{matrix}\text{Volume} \\ \text{variance}\end{matrix} = \begin{matrix}\text{Fixed} \\ \text{overhead} \\ \text{rate}\end{matrix} \times \left(\begin{matrix}\text{Denominator} \\ \text{hours}\end{matrix} - \begin{matrix}\text{Standard} \\ \text{hours} \\ \text{allowed}\end{matrix} \right)$$

$= \$10 \times (3,000 - 4,000) = \$10,000$ F

Exercises

11-1.

Overhead Costs	Cost Formula (per MH)	Machine-hours		
		8,000	10,000	12,000
Variable overhead costs:				
Utilities....................................	$0.30	$ 2,400	$ 3,000	$ 3,600
Supplies....................................	0.80	6,400	8,000	9,600
Indirect labor...........................	0.40	3,200	4,000	4,800
Total variable costs....................	$1.50	12,000	15,000	18,000
Fixed overhead costs:				
Utilities....................................		6,000	6,000	6,000
Supplies....................................		10,000	10,000	10,000
Depreciation.............................		25,000	25,000	25,000
Indirect labor...........................		21,000	21,000	21,000
Total fixed costs		62,000	62,000	62,000
Total overhead costs...................		$74,000	$77,000	$80,000

11-2.

Performance Report
Herbold Corporation

Budgeted machine-hours...........................	10,000
Actual machine-hours..............................	8,500
Standard machine-hours..........................	8,000

	Cost Formula (per MH)	Actual Costs 8,500 MHs	Budget Based on 8,500 MHs	Spending or Budget Variance
Variable overhead costs:				
Utilities	$0.30	$ 2,600	$ 2,550	$ 50 U
Supplies	0.80	6,700	6,800	100 F
Indirect labor	0.40	3,300	3,400	100 F
Total variable costs	$1.50	12,600	12,750	150 F
Fixed overhead costs:				
Utilities		5,900	6,000	100 F
Supplies		10,300	10,000	300 U
Depreciation		25,000	25,000	0
Indirect labor		21,700	21,000	700 U
Total fixed costs		62,900	62,000	900 U
Total overhead costs...........................		$75,500	$74,750	$750 U

11-3.   a.   Predetermined overhead rate ($34,800 ÷ 12,000 DLHs)........... $2.90 per DLH
            Variable element ($10,800 ÷ 12,000 DLHs) .... $0.90 per DLH
            Fixed element ($24,000 ÷ 12,000 DLHs)................................. $2.00 per DLH

       b.   Overhead applied:
            9,000 units × 1.5 DLHs per unit = 13,500 DLHs allowed
            13,500 DLHs × $2.90 per DLH = $39,150 overhead applied

       c.   Variable overhead variance analysis:

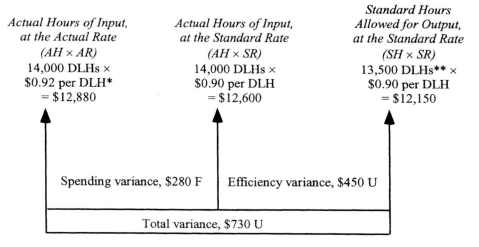

	Actual Hours of Input, at the Actual Rate (AH × AR)	Actual Hours of Input, at the Standard Rate (AH × SR)	Standard Hours Allowed for Output, at the Standard Rate (SH × SR)
	14,000 DLHs × $0.92 per DLH* = $12,880	14,000 DLHs × $0.90 per DLH = $12,600	13,500 DLHs** × $0.90 per DLH = $12,150
	Spending variance, $280 F	Efficiency variance, $450 U	
		Total variance, $730 U	

       * $12,880 ÷ 14,000 DLHs = $0.92 per DLH
       ** 9,000 units × 1.5 DLHs per unit = 13,500 DLHs

       d.   Fixed overhead variance analysis:

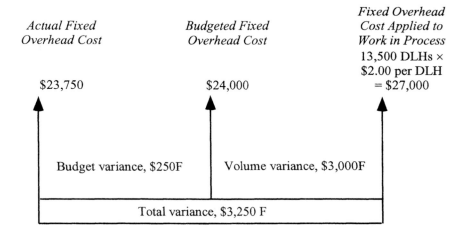

	Actual Fixed Overhead Cost	Budgeted Fixed Overhead Cost	Fixed Overhead Cost Applied to Work in Process
			13,500 DLHs × $2.00 per DLH = $27,000
	$23,750	$24,000	
	Budget variance, $250F	Volume variance, $3,000F	
		Total variance, $3,250 F	

Chapter 12

Segment Reporting and Decentralization

Chapter Study Suggestions

✳

In the first part of the chapter that covers segment reporting, make sure that you carefully study Exhibits 12-3 and 12-4. Notice particularly that on a segmented report the company is divided into progressively smaller parts. Make sure you fully understand the difference between traceable and common costs, and the difference between segment margin and contribution margin. You should memorize the format for a segment report.

The second part of the chapter covers return on investment (ROI) and residual income. Memorize the formulas for ROI and residual income since they are used extensively in the homework material.

The appendix to the chapter covers transfer pricing. The key ideas in the appendix are the lower limits and the upper limits for a negotiated transfer price. Make sure you understand how these limits are determined.

CHAPTER HIGHLIGHTS

A. A *responsibility accounting* system functions best in a decentralized organization. A *decentralized organization* is one in which decision making is spread throughout the organization, with managers at all levels making decisions. In a decentralized organization the responsibility accounting system is structured around cost centers, profit centers, and investment centers.

  1. A *cost center* is any responsibility center where a manager has control over cost but not over revenues or investments. A cost center manager is usually held responsible for minimizing cost while providing quality goods and services as requested.

  2. The manager of a *profit center* has control over both cost and revenue. A profit center manager is usually held responsible for maximizing profit.

  3. The manager of an *investment center* has control over cost, revenue, and investments in operating assets. An investment center manager is ordinarily evaluated on the basis of return on investment or residual income, as explained later.

B. To operate effectively, management needs much more information than is provided by a single income statement. Management needs information about the segments of the organization.

  1. A *segment* is any part or activity of an organization about which the manager seeks cost or revenue data. Examples of segments include sales territories, manufacturing divisions, departments, and groups or lines of products.

  2. Segmented reports for the use of managers should be prepared in the contribution format with which you are already largely familiar from chapters 6 and 7.

  3. Exhibit 12-3 contains an illustration of a series of segmented reports. Notice that as you go from one segmented report to another in the exhibit, the reports focus on smaller and smaller parts of the company.

  4. A segmented report such as the one illustrated in Exhibit 12-3 may uncover problems and opportunities that otherwise would have remained hidden from view. For example, some product lines may be unprofitable; some sales territories may have a poor sales mix; other sales territories may be using ineffective promotional strategies, etc. Such problems can be spotted with segmented reports.

C. Two general guidelines should be used in assigning costs to the various segments when the contribution approach is used.

  1. First, costs are assigned according to cost behavior patterns; that is, according to whether they are variable or fixed.

  2. Second, costs are assigned according to whether they are traceable or common to the various segments.

    a. Only *traceable costs* should be charged to segments. The traceable costs of a segment consist of those costs—including fixed costs—that arise because of the existence of the segment. The general rule is to treat as traceable costs only those costs that would disappear over time if the segment were eliminated.

    b. *Common costs* should not be charged to the segments. Common costs are costs that support more than one segment, but are not traceable, in whole or in part, to any one of those segments. Common costs would not disappear over time if a segment were eliminated and therefore should not be allocated to segments for decision-making purposes. For example, the cost of the company's executive jet is a common cost of the products the company sells. Even if a product were dropped entirely, it is unlikely that there would be any significant change in the costs of owning and operating the executive jet.

D. The format of a segmented income statement is:

	Total	Segment A	Segment B
Sales	$XXX	$XXX	$XXX
Less variable expenses	XXX	XXX	XXX
Contribution margin	XXX	XXX	XXX
Less traceable fixed expenses	XXX	XXX	XXX
Segment margin	XXX	$XXX	$ XXX
Less common fixed expenses not traceable to individual segments	XXX		
Net operating income.	$ XXX		

  1. A segmented income statement emphasizes the distinctions between variable and fixed costs and between traceable and common costs.

  2. As an organization is segmented into smaller and smaller pieces, some costs that were previously traceable will become common to the smaller segments. There are limits to how finely a cost can be divided.

3. The *segment margin* shows the profitability of a segment after it has covered all of the costs that can be traced directly to it.

4. Common costs should not be allocated to segments, since such an allocation would convey the misleading impression that the cost can be avoided by eliminating the segment.

E. Performance in an investment center is often measured by *return on investment (ROI),* which is defined as:

$$ROI = \frac{Net\ operating\ income}{Average\ operating\ assets}$$

ROI can also be expressed in terms of margin and turnover:

$$ROI = Margin \times Turnover$$

where:

$$Margin = \frac{Net\ operating\ income}{Sales}$$

$$Turnover = \frac{Sales}{Average\ operating\ assets}.$$

1. *Net operating income* is income before interest and taxes.

2. *Operating assets* include cash, accounts receivable, inventory, and all other assets held for productive use within the organization. Operating assets do *not* include, for example, investments in other companies and investments in undeveloped land.

3. A company's return on investment can be improved by doing at least one of the following: (1) increasing sales, (2) reducing expenses, or (3) reducing assets.

4. ROI is criticized for several reasons. One of the most important criticisms is that a division manager who is evaluated based on ROI will tend to reject a project whose ROI is less than the division's current ROI but greater than the company's minimum rate of return. However, from the standpoint of the entire company such a project should be accepted.

F. Residual income is another approach to measuring performance in an investment center.

1. *Residual income* is the net operating income that an investment center earns above the minimum required rate of return on operating assets and is defined as follows:

$$Residual\ income = Net\ operating\ income - \left(\begin{array}{c}Required\ rate\ of\ return \times Average\ operating\ assets\end{array}\right)$$

2. The residual income approach to performance evaluation encourages investment in worthwhile projects—overcoming the major difficulty with ROI. Any project whose rate return exceeds the company's required rate of return will be favored by managers—even a project whose rate of return is less than the division's current ROI.

3. A major disadvantage of the residual income approach is that it can't be easily used to compare divisions of different sizes. Larger divisions naturally tend to have larger residual incomes.

Appendix 12A: Transfer Pricing

A. One part of a company often provides goods or services to another part of the company. For example, the General Motors truck division sells delivery trucks to the Chevrolet Division. The price that is charged for such a sale inside a company is called a *transfer price.*

1. If the divisions are profit or investment centers, then the selling division would like the transfer price to be high and the buying division would like the transfer price to be low.

2. Three general approaches are used in setting transfer prices: (1) allow the involved managers to negotiate their own transfer price; (2) set the transfer price equal to cost; or (3) set the transfer price equal to the outside market price.

B. When an organization relies on negotiated transfer prices, managers are free to work out transfer prices on their own. The managers of the divisions involved in the proposed transfer can choose whether to agree to the transfer or not. If they do agree to a transfer, then they must agree on the transfer price. Presumably, neither manager would agree to a transfer price unless it increases his or her division's profit.

1. From the viewpoint of the selling division, the transfer price must cover at least variable costs plus any opportunity costs. This sets a limit on how low the transfer price can go in negotiations.

$$\frac{Transfer}{price} \geq \frac{Variable}{cost} + \frac{Opportunity}{cost}$$

a. There is an opportunity cost if there is a constraint. In that case, filling the buying division's order would result in lost sales to other customers.

b. The opportunity cost per unit transferred internally can be computed as follows:

$$\text{Opportunity cost} = \frac{\text{Total contribution margin on lost sales}}{\text{Number of units transferred}}$$

2. If the buying division can purchase what it needs from an outside supplier, then the manager of the buying division clearly would not want to pay a higher price within the company. From the viewpoint of the buying division, the upper limit on the transfer price is given by:

$$\text{Transfer price} \leq \text{Cost of buying from an outside supplier}$$

3. In principle, negotiated transfer prices should work. If it is in the best interests of the company for the transfer to be made, it will always be possible for the managers to find a transfer price between the lower and upper limits that would make them both better off.

4. However, in practice, managers may not understand what is in their own best interests or they may be uncooperative. In either case, negotiations my drag on and even fail. Perhaps for that reason, most companies use rules to set transfer prices that are based on either cost or market price.

C. Cost-based transfer prices are convenient to use, but may lead to bad decisions.

1. If variable cost is used as the transfer price, it will understate the real cost to the company of the transfer when there are opportunity costs. In essence, the manager of the buying division will be getting the transferred good or service at a discounted price below true cost to the company. This can lead to unwise decisions such as pricing products too low.

2. If full absorption cost is used as the transfer price, the cost will never reflect the true cost to the company of making the transfer. If the transfer has no effect on total fixed costs, then the true cost to the company of the transfer is variable cost plus, possibly, opportunity cost. This would very rarely equal full absorption cost.

3. When the transfer price is set equal to cost, the only division that will show any profit on the transaction is the one that makes a final sale to an outside party. Other divisions will show no profit for their efforts.

4. When transfers are priced at the selling division's actual cost, there is no incentive to control costs. The selling division simply passes its costs on to the next division. For this reason, if transfer prices are based on cost, standard costs rather than actual costs should be used.

D. Market prices are often used as transfer prices. This solution works very well when the selling division has no idle capacity. However, when the selling division has idle capacity, the market price overstates the real cost of the transfer.

REVIEW AND SELF-TEST
Questions and Exercises

True or False

Enter a T or an F in the blank to indicate whether the statement is true or false.

____ 1. Common costs should be allocated to segments on the basis of sales dollars.

____ 2. The terms "traceable cost" and "variable cost" mean the same thing.

____ 3. As an organization is broken down into smaller segments, costs that were traceable to the larger segments may become common to the smaller segments.

____ 4. A decentralized organization is one in which decision making is confined to top management.

____ 5. Residual income is equal to the difference between total revenues and operating expenses.

____ 6. Using ROI to evaluate managers may lead managers to reject investment opportunities that would be beneficial to the company as a whole.

____ 7. A profit center manager is responsible for generating revenue, but is not responsible for controlling costs.

____ 8. A reduction in operating assets will increase a division's ROI if sales and expenses remain unchanged.

____ 9. In computing residual income, expenses incurred in operating corporate headquarters should be allocated to the separate divisions on the basis of the contribution margins of the divisions.

____ 10. Under the residual income approach, the objective is to maximize the rate of return on operating assets.

____ 11. An increase in total sales would typically increase turnover but would have no effect on the margin.

____ 12. (Appendix 12A) When a division is operating at capacity, the cost of transferring a product or service to another division includes an element of opportunity cost.

____ 13. (Appendix 12A) Transfer prices based on actual cost are superior in that they provide incentive for the control of costs between transferring divisions.

Multiple Choice

Choose the best answer or response by placing the identifying letter in the space provided.

____ 1. Armco, Inc., produces and sells five products. Which of the following costs would typically be a traceable fixed cost of a product? a) advertising costs of the product; b) the salary of the company's president; c) depreciation of facilities jointly used to produce several products; d) responses a, b, and c, are all correct.

____ 2. If a segment has a negative segment margin: a) the segment should be dropped; b) the segment should be retained only if it has a positive contribution margin; c) the segment is not covering its own traceable costs, but it still may be of benefit to the company; d) none of these.

____ 3. Rumberger, Inc. sells two products: X and Y. Data concerning the company for July follow:

	Product X	Product Y
Sales	$200,000	$300,000
Variable expenses	$50,000	$100,000
Traceable fixed expenses	$80,000	$150,000

In addition, common fixed expenses of $70,000 were incurred in July. What is the segment margin for Product X? a) $70,000; b) $120,000; c) $150,000; d) $38,000.

____ 4. Refer to the data for Rumberger, Inc. in exercise (3) above. What is the net operating income for the entire company? a) $120,000; b) $(4,000); c) $70,000; d) $50,000.

____ 5. Refer to the data for Rumberger, Inc. in exercise (3) above. Suppose advertising for Product Y is increased by $20,000 per month, which results in increased sales of $90,000 per month. This should have the following effect on Product Y's monthly segment margin: a) increase by $70,000; b) increase by $40,000; c) increase by $60,000; d) decrease by $20,000.

____ 6. Refer to the data for Rumberger, Inc. in exercise (5) above. What would be the effect of the increase in advertising and sales of Product Y on the company's overall net operating income? a) increase by $70,000; b) increase by $40,000; c) increase by $60,000; d) decrease by $20,000.

_____ 7. If the level of inventory in a company is reduced, and if sales and expenses remain unchanged, one would expect the company's ROI to: a) increase; b) decrease; c) remain unchanged; d) it is impossible to tell what would happen to ROI.

_____ 8. A company reported the following results:

Average operating assets.............	$45,000
Sales..	$180,000
Contribution margin....................	$21,600
Net operating income..................	$9,000

The company's ROI is: a) 48%; b) 12%; c) 20%; d) 30%.

_____ 9. The purpose of the residual income approach is to: a) maximize a segment's overall rate of return; b) maximize the ROI that a segment is able to get on its operating assets; c) maximize the total amount of the residual income; d) none of these.

_____ 10. A company reported the following results:

Average operating assets	$300,000
Stockholders' equity	$50,000
Sales..	$900,000
Net operating income..............................	$75,000
Minimum required rate of return	18%

The company's residual income is: a) $25,000; b) $15,000; c) $21,000; d) 475,000.

_____ 11. (Appendix 12A) Division A produces a part that it sells to outside customers. Data concerning this part appear below:

Selling price to outside customers..........	$60
Variable cost per unit..............................	$40
Total fixed cost	$100,000
Capacity in units......................................	20,000

Division B of the same company now purchases 5,000 units of a similar part from an outside supplier at a price of $58 per unit. Division B wants to purchase these 5,000 units from Division A instead, but Division A has no idle capacity. Division A should insist on a transfer price of at least: a) $60; b) $58; c) $40; d) $45.

_____ 12. (Appendix 12A) Refer to the data in question (11) above. If Division A has idle capacity, the manager of Division A should insist that the transfer price be at least: a) $60; b) $40; c) between $45 and $58; d) between $40 and $58.

Exercises

12-1.   The following data, pertain to Bylund Company's operations for July.

	Total	Product X	Product Y
Number of units sold		10,000	12,000
Selling price per unit		$20.00	$25.00
Variable cost per unit:			
Production		$9.00	$10.00
Selling and administrative		$3.00	$3.75
Fixed costs:			
Production	$155,000		
Selling and administrative	$20,000		

Of the fixed costs, only $50,000 of the fixed production costs is traceable to the production of Product X and $75,000 is traceable to Product Y.

a.   Prepare a segmented income statement for Bylund Company using the following form:

BYLUND COMPANY
Income Statement
For the Month Ended July 31

	Total		Product X		Product Y	
	Amount	%	Amount	%	Amount	%
Sales	$_____	____	$_____	____	$_____	____
Less variable expenses:						
Production	_____	____	_____	____	_____	____
Selling and administrative	_____	____	_____	____	_____	____
Total variable expenses	_____	____	_____	____	_____	____
Contribution margin	_____	____	_____	____	_____	____
Less traceable fixed expenses	_____	____	_____	____	_____	____
Product line segment margin	_____	____	$_____	____	$_____	____
Less common fixed expenses not						
traceable to individual products:						
Production	_____	____				
Selling and administrative	_____	____				
Total common fixed expenses	_____	____				
Net operating income	$_____	____				

b. Should either Product X or Product Y be dropped? Why?

_____

_____

_____

_____

c. Product X can be enhanced by incurring an additional $25,000 in fixed production costs. Instead of raising the price of Product X to reflect the enhancement, Bylund Company would seek to increase sales. If sales increased by $80,000, should the product be enhanced?

_____

_____

_____

_____

_____

_____

_____

_____

12-2. Fill in the missing data for Biggerstaff, Inc.

	Total Amount	%	Southwest Division Amount	%	Central Division Amount	%
Sales	$1,000,000	___	$ _____	___	$ _____	___
Variable expenses	_____	___	_____	___	_____	___
Contribution margin	_____	___	360,000	60	_____	___
Traceable fixed expenses	_____	___	150,000	___	200,000	___
Division segment margin	_____	___	$ _____	___	$ 120,000	30
Common fixed expenses not traceable to individual divisions	_____	___				
Net operating income	$ 40,000	___				

Hint: The contribution margin ratio for the Southwest Division can be used to determine its sales.

12-3.   Frankel Company has the following data for its Connectors Division for last year:

Sales	$2,000,000
Net operating income	$160,000
Average operating assets	$800,000
Minimum rate of return	16%

a.   Compute the return on investment (ROI) for the Connectors Division, using margin and turnover.

b.   Compute the residual income for the Connectors Division.

12-4.   Fill in the missing information for the three different companies below:

	Company 1	*Company 2*	*Company 3*
Sales	$600,000	$600,000	$_____
Net operating income	$60,000	_____	$27,000
Average operating assets	$300,000	$200,000	_____
Margin	_____	7.5%	_____
Turnover	_____	_____	1.8
Return on investment (ROI)	_____	_____	27%

12-5. (Appendix 12A) Perchon Company's Regulator Division produces a small valve used by other companies as a key part in their products. Cost and sales data relating to the valve are given below:

Selling price per unit $50
Variable costs per unit $30
Fixed costs per unit $12*

*Based on the Regulator Division's capacity of 40,000 valves per year.

Perchon Company's Boiler Division is introducing a new product that will use a valve such as the one produced in the Regulator Division. An outside supplier has quoted the Boiler Division a price of $48 per valve for the 10,000 valves the Boiler Division needs every year. The Boiler Division would like to purchase the valves from the Regulator Division instead if an acceptable transfer price can be worked out.

a.   Assume that the Regulator Division is presently selling all the valves it can produce to outside customers. What is the lowest acceptable transfer price from the viewpoint of the selling division?

b.   From the standpoint of the entire company, should the Boiler Division purchase the valves from the Regulator Division or from the outside supplier? Explain.

_____

_____

_____

_____

c.   Assume the Regulator Division is presently selling 35,000 valves per year to outside customers. What would be the impact on Perchon Company's overall profits if all 10,000 valves were acquired from the Regulator Division rather than from the outside supplier?

d.   Assume that the Regulator Division has ample idle capacity to handle all the Boiler Division's needs. What is the lowest acceptable transfer price from the viewpoint of the selling division?

Answers to Questions and Exercises

True or False

1. F   Common costs should never be allocated to segments since such allocated costs could lead managers to believe that they could be avoided by dropping the segment.

2. F   A traceable cost can be either variable or fixed.

3. T   As an organization is divided into smaller and smaller segments, there are limits to how finely a cost can be divided.

4. F   In a decentralized organization, decision making is spread through all levels of management.

5. F   Residual income is the difference between net operating income and the minimum return that must be generated on operating assets.

6. T   This is a major criticism of the ROI method.

7. F   A profit center is responsible for controlling costs as well as generating revenues.

8. T   A reduction in assets will result in an increase in the turnover figure, and an increase in the ROI.

9. F   Common expenses, such as those associated with operating corporate headquarters, should not be allocated to segments when making either residual income or ROI computations.

10. F   Under the residual income approach, the objective is to maximize residual income, not return on investment.

11. F   The margin would also typically increase, since the net operating income would generally increase more rapidly than sales due to the effects of operating leverage discussed in an earlier chapter.

12. T   The opportunity cost is the contribution margin lost from giving up outside sales.

13. F   The opposite is true. When actual cost is used as a transfer price there is little or no incentive to control costs since whatever cost is incurred can simply be transferred on to the next division.

0Multiple Choice

1. a   The cost of advertising a specific product could be eliminated if the product were dropped.

2. c   A negative segment margin means that a segment is not covering its own traceable costs. However, the segment may still be of value to the company if it is necessary to the sale of other products.

3. a   The segment margin for Product X can be read directly from the segmented income statement that appears below:

	Total	Product X	Product Y
Sales	$500,000	$200,000	$300,000
Variable expenses	150,000	50,000	100,000
Contribution margin	350,000	150,000	200,000
Traceable fixed expenses	230,000	80,000	150,000
Segment margin	120,000	$ 70,000	$ 50,000
Common fixed expenses	70,000		
Net operating income	$ 50,000		

4. d   See the segmented income statement above in the answer to exercise (3).

5. b   The following statement will help in solving this exercise:

	Product Y	Percentage of Sales
Sales	$300,000	100 %
Variable expenses	100,000	$33\frac{1}{3}$ %
Contribution margin	200,000	$66\frac{2}{3}$ %
Traceable fixed expenses	150,000	50 %
Segment margin	$ 50,000	$16\frac{2}{3}$ %

Using the contribution margin ratio method, the $90,000 increase in sales should lead to a $60,000 (= 66 2/3% × $90,000) increase in contribution margin. This would be offset by the $20,000 increase in advertising expenses, a traceable fixed expense, to yield a net $40,000 increase in segment margin.

6. b   Since there is no mention of any change in common fixed expenses, the change in the company's overall net operating income should be the same as the change in Product Y's segment margin.

7. a   If the level of inventory is reduced, then operating assets are reduced. The result will be a higher turnover figure and an increase in the ROI.

8. c   The computations are:

$$\text{ROI} = \frac{\$9,000}{\$180,000} \times \frac{\$180,000}{\$45,000} = 5\% \times 4 = 20\%$$

9. c   Residual income has nothing to do with ROI; moreover, as residual income increases ROI frequently decreases (as shown in examples in the chapter).

10. c   The computations are:

Average operating assets	$300,000
Net operating income	$ 75,000
Minimum required return	
(18% × $300,000)	54,000
Residual income	$ 21,000

11. a   The computations are:

Transfer price = Variable costs + Opportunity cost
Transfer price = $40 + ($60 − $40)
Transfer price = $60

12. b   The computations are:

Transfer price = Variable costs + Opportunity cost
Transfer price = $40 + $0
Transfer price = $40

Exercises

12-1.

a.

BYLUND COMPANY
Income Statement
For the Month Ended July 31

	Total Amount	%	Product X Amount	%	Product Y Amount	%
Sales	$500,000	100	$200,000	100	$300,000	100
Less variable expenses:						
Production	210,000	42	90,000	45	120,000	40
Selling and administrative	75,000	15	30,000	15	45,000	15
Total variable expenses	285,000	57	120,000	60	165,000	55
Contribution margin	215,000	43	80,000	40	135,000	45
Less traceable fixed expenses	125,000	25	50,000	25	75,000	25
Product line segment margin	90,000	18	$ 30,000	15	$ 60,000	20
Less common fixed expenses not traceable to individual products:						
Production	30,000	6				
Selling and administrative	20,000	4				
Total common fixed expenses	50,000	10				
Net operating income	$ 40,000	8				

b. Neither product should be dropped. They are both covering all of their own traceable costs and are contributing to covering the fixed common costs and to overall profits of the company.

c.
Increase in sales	$80,0000
Contribution margin ratio	× 40%
Increase in contribution margin	$ 32,000
Increase in fixed production costs	25,000
Increase in net operating income	$ 7,000

Yes, the product should be enhanced

Chapter 12

12-2.

	Total		Southwest Division		Central Division	
	Amount	%	Amount	%	Amount	%
Sales	$1,000,000	100	$600,000[5]	100	$400,000[6]	100
Variable expenses	320,000[10]	32	240,000[7]	40	80,000[9]	20
Contribution margin	680,000[11]	68	360,000	60	320,000[8]	80
Traceable fixed expenses	350,000[2]	35	150,000	25	200,000	50
Division segment margin	330,000[3]	33	$210,000[1]	35	$120,000	30
Common fixed expenses not						
traceable to divisions	290,000[4]	29				
Net operating income	$ 40,000	4				

Note: This problem can be solved in many different ways. The following is one sequence that can be followed:

1. $360,000 − $150,000 = $210,000
2. $150,000 + $200,000 = $350,000
3. $210,000 + $120,000 = $330,000
4. $330,000 + $40,000 = $290,000
5. $360,000 ÷ 60% = $600,000
6. $1,000,000 − $600,000 = $400,000
7. $600,000 − $360,000 = $240,000
8. $200,000 + $120,000 = $320,000
9. $400,000 − $320,000 = $80,000
10. $240,000 + $80,000 = $320,000
11. $360,000 + $320,000 = $680,000

12-3.   a. $\text{Margin} = \dfrac{\text{Net operating income}}{\text{Sales}} = \dfrac{\$160,000}{\$2,000,000} = 8\%$

$\text{Turnover} = \dfrac{\text{Sales}}{\text{Average operating assets}} = \dfrac{\$2,000,000}{\$800,000} = 2.5$

ROI = Margin × Turnover
     = 8% × 2.5 = 20%

b.

Average operating assets	$800,000
Net operating income	$160,000
Minimum required return	
(16% × $800,000)	$128,000
Residual income	$ 32,000

12-4.

	Company 1	Company 2	Company 3
Sales	$600,000*	$600,000*	$180,000
Net operating income	$60,000*	$45,000	$27,000*
Average operating assets	$300,000*	$200,000*	$100,000
Margin	10%	7.5%*	15%
Turnover	2	3.0	1.8*
Return on investment (ROI)	20%	22.5%	27%*

*Given

12-5.

a. If the Regulator Division transfers a valve to the Boiler Division, it cannot be sold on the outside market. Therefore, the Regulator Division loses $50 in revenue. Thus, the lowest transfer price the Regulator Division could accept is $50. This is verified by using the formula approach as follows:

$$\frac{\text{Transfer}}{\text{price}} \geq \frac{\text{Variable}}{\text{cost}} + \frac{\text{Total contribution margin on lost sales}}{\text{Number of units transferred}}$$

$$\frac{\text{Transfer}}{\text{price}} \geq \$30 + \frac{(\$50\text{-}\$30) \times 10,000}{10,000} = \$30 + (\$50 - \$30) = \$50$$

b. The valves should be purchased from the outside supplier, since the price will be only $48 per valve. In contrast, the company will give up $50 in revenue for each valve transferred internally rather than sold on the outside market.

c.

Regulator Division capacity	40,000 valves
Less Boiler Division's requirements............................	10,000 valves
Valves available for sale to outsiders	30,000 valves
Potential sales to outsiders..	35,000 valves
Valves available for sale to outsiders	30,000 valves
Lost sales...	5,000 valves

Cost of transferring internally:	
Variable cost $30 × 10,000	$300,000
Lost contribution margin ($50 – $30) × 5,000	$100,000
Total cost of transferring internally............................	$400,000
Cost of purchasing from an outside supplier	$480,000

Profits will be $80,000 higher if the valves are acquired internally rather than purchased outside.

d. Transfer Price = $30 + $0 = $30
There is no lost contribution margin, since the Regulator Division has idle capacity.

Chapter 13

Relevant Costs for Decision Making

Chapter Study Suggestions

The concept of relevant costs is covered in the first few pages of the chapter. Study these pages carefully, since this idea underpins almost everything in the chapter. A number of specific decision-making situations are covered in the chapter, but the relevant cost concept is the key to the solution in every case.

CHAPTER HIGHLIGHTS

A. Every decision involves a choice from among at least two alternatives. A *relevant cost* or benefit is a cost or benefit that differs between alternatives. If a cost or benefit does not differ between alternatives, it is not relevant in the decision and can be ignored. *Avoidable cost, differential cost,* and *incremental cost* are synonyms for relevant cost.

  1. Two broad classifications of costs are irrelevant in decisions: (a) sunk costs; and (b) future costs that do not differ between alternatives. *Sunk costs* are costs that have already been incurred and are irrevocable. Thus, they cannot differ between alternatives and are always irrelevant.

  2. To make a decision, you should:

    a. Eliminate the costs and benefits that do not differ between alternatives. These irrelevant costs consist of sunk costs and future costs that do not differ between alternatives.

    b. Make a decision based on the remaining costs and benefits–those that differ between alternatives.

  3. Costs that are relevant in one situation may not be relevant in another. There are no rules for identifying what costs are relevant and what costs are irrelevant except that costs that do not differ between alternatives are irrelevant.

B. You should disregard irrelevant costs and benefits in decisions for three reasons:

    a. In any given situation, the irrelevant costs greatly outnumber the relevant costs. Focusing just on the relevant costs takes less time and effort.

    b. Intermingling irrelevant with relevant costs may draw attention away from the really critical data.

    c. Including irrelevant costs often leads to mistakes. This happens when an irrelevant cost is incorrectly computed for one or both of the alternatives—making it appear that the cost differs between the alternatives when it does not.

C. *Adding or dropping a segment* such as a product line is one of the decision-making situations covered in the chapter. In making this decision, compare the contribution margin of the segment to the fixed costs that could be avoided by dropping the segment. If the contribution margin lost by dropping a segment is greater than the fixed costs that can be avoided, then the segment should be retained. If the contribution margin lost

by dropping a segment is less than the fixed costs that can be avoided, then the segment should be dropped.

  1. Exhibit 13-3 illustrates an alternative approach to deciding whether to retain or drop a product line or other segment of a company. In this approach two income statements are prepared—one for each alternative.

  2. The decision to keep or drop a product line or other segment of a company is often clouded by the allocation of common fixed costs as discussed in Chapter 12.

    a. Allocations of common costs can make a profitable product line or other segment *appear* to be unprofitable.

    b. Common fixed costs should never be allocated to segments of a company; segments should be charged only with those costs that would be eliminated if the segment were eliminated.

D. A decision to produce a part (or a service) internally rather than to buy it from a supplier is called a *make or buy decision*. The relevant costs in such a decision, as always, are the costs that differ between the alternatives.

  1. Exhibit 13-5 contains an example of a make or buy decision. Notice from the exhibit that the costs that are relevant in a make or buy decision are the costs that *differ* between the make or buy alternatives.

  2. Opportunity cost may be a key factor in a make or buy decision as well as in other decisions.

    a. If the resources that are currently being used to make a part or a product all have excess capacity, then the opportunity cost is zero.

    b. On the other hand, if there is no excess capacity, then there is an opportunity cost. This opportunity cost is the incremental profit that could be obtained from the best alternative use of the capacity. The opportunity cost should be included in the analysis.

E. Another decision concerns *special orders*—one-time orders that don't affect regular sales. Such an order should be accepted if the incremental revenue from the special order exceeds the incremental (i.e., avoidable) costs of the order. Any opportunity costs should be taken into account.

F. A *constraint* is anything that limits the organization's ability to further its goals. For example, when a profit-making company is unable to satisfy the demand for its products with its existing capacity, it has a production constraint. When the constraint is a machine or a workstation, it is called a *bottleneck*. For example, a company may be able to sell 1,000 units of a product per week, but the product may require a machine that is capable of only producing 800 units a week. The machine would be a bottleneck.

1. When demand exceeds capacity, the company has a production constraint. In that case, managers must decide what the company *will* and *will not* do since the company cannot do everything. The problem is how to best utilize a constrained resource.

2. Fixed costs are likely to be unaffected by the decision of how best to utilize the constrained resource. If the fixed costs are unaffected by the decision and hence irrelevant, maximizing the company's total contribution margin is equivalent to maximizing the company's profit. Given capacity and the company's fixed costs, the problem is how to best use that capacity to maximize total contribution margin and profit.

3. The key to the efficient utilization of a scarce resource is *the contribution margin per unit of the constrained resource*. The products with the greatest contribution margin per unit of the constrained resource are the most profitable; they generate the greatest profit from a given amount of the constrained resource. These products should be emphasized over products with a lower contribution margin per unit of the constrained resource.

4. Since the constraint limits the output of the entire organization, increasing the amount of the constrained resource can yield a huge payoff. This is called "elevating the constraint" and can be accomplished in a variety of ways including working overtime on the bottleneck, buying another machine, subcontracting work, and so on.

5. The contribution margin per unit of the constrained resource is also a measure of opportunity cost. For example, when considering whether to accept an order for a product that uses the constrained resource, the opportunity cost of using the constrained resource should be considered. That opportunity cost is the lost contribution margin for the job that would be displaced if the order were accepted.

G. In some industries, such as petroleum refining, a number of end products are produced from a single raw material input. Such products are known as *joint products*. The *split-off point* is that point in the manufacturing process at which the joint products can be recognized as separate products.

1. Decisions as to whether a joint product should be sold at the split-off point or processed further and then sold are known as *sell or process further* decisions.

2. Costs incurred up to the split-off point are called *joint costs*. These costs are irrelevant in decisions concerning whether a product should be processed further after the split-off point, since they will be incurred regardless of what is done after the split-off point.

3. It is profitable to continue processing joint products after the split-off point so long as the incremental revenue from such processing exceeds the incremental processing costs.

REVIEW AND SELF-TEST
Questions and Exercises

True or False

Enter a T or an F in the blank to indicate whether the statement is true or false.

____ 1. All costs are relevant in a decision except costs that do not differ between alternatives.

____ 2. In a decision, variable costs are relevant costs and fixed costs are irrelevant.

____ 3. Sunk costs may be relevant in a decision.

____ 4. Future costs are always relevant in decision-making.

____ 5. Costs that are relevant in one decision are not necessarily relevant in another decision.

____ 6. If a company is able to avoid more in fixed costs than it loses in contribution margin by dropping a product, then it will be better off financially if the product is eliminated.

____ 7. Allocation of common fixed costs to product lines and to other segments of a company helps the manager to see if the product line or segment is profitable.

____ 8. If a product has a negative segment margin, the product should be discontinued.

____ 9. Opportunity cost may be a key factor in a make or buy decision.

____ 10. If there is a constrained resource, a company should emphasize the product that has the highest contribution margin per unit.

____ 11. A joint product should continue to be processed after the split-off point so long as the incremental revenue from such processing exceeds the incremental processing costs.

____ 12. Joint product costs are irrelevant in decisions regarding what to do with joint products after the split-off point.

Multiple Choice

Choose the best answer or response by placing the identifying letter in the space provided.

____ 1. All of the following costs are relevant in a make or buy decision except: a) the opportunity cost of space; b) costs that are avoidable by buying rather than making; c) variable costs of producing the item; d) costs that are differential between the make and buy alternatives; e) all of the above costs are relevant.

____ 2. One of Simplex Company's products has a contribution margin of $50,000 and fixed costs totaling $60,000. If the product is dropped, $40,000 of the fixed costs will continue unchanged. As a result of dropping the product, the company's net operating income should: a) decrease by $50,000; b) increase by $30,000; c) decrease by $30,000; d) increase by $10,000.

____ 3. Halley Company produces 2,000 parts each year that are used in one of its products. The unit product cost of this part is:

Variable manufacturing cost	$ 7.50
Fixed manufacturing cost	6.00
Unit product cost.........................	$13.50

The part can be purchased from an outside supplier for $10 per unit. If the part is purchased from the outside supplier, two-thirds of the fixed manufacturing costs can be eliminated. The effect on net operating income from purchasing the part would be a: a) $3,000 increase; b) $1,000 decrease; c) $7,000 increase; d) $5,000 decrease.

____ 4. Product A has a contribution margin of $8 per unit, a contribution margin ratio of 50%, and requires 4 machine-hours to produce. Product B has a contribution margin of $12 per unit, a contribution margin ratio of 40%, and requires 5 machine-hours to produce. If the constraint is machine-hours, then the company should emphasize: a) Product A; b) Product B.

_____ 5. Sunderson Products, Inc. has received a special order for 1,000 units of a sport-fighting kite. The customer has offered a price of $9.95 for each kite. The unit costs of the kite, at its normal sales level of 30,000 units per year, are detailed below:

Variable production costs	$5.25
Fixed production costs	$2.35
Variable selling costs	$0.75
Fixed selling and administrative costs	$3.45

There is ample idle capacity to produce the special order without any increase in total fixed costs. The variable selling costs on the special order would be $0.15 per unit instead of $0.75 per unit. The special order would have no impact on the company's other sales. What effect would accepting this special order have on the company's net operating income? a) $1,850 increase; b) $1,850 decrease; c) $4,550 increase; d) $4,550 decrease.

_____ 6. Products A and B are joint products. Product A can be sold for $1,200 at the split-off point, or processed further at a cost of $600 and then sold for $1,700. Product B can be sold for $3,000 at the split-off point, or processed further at a cost of $800 and then sold for $4,000. The company should process further: a) Product A; b) Product B; c) both products; d) neither of the products.

Exercises

13-1.   The most recent income statement for the men's formal wear department of Merrill's Department Store is given below:

Sales		$500,000
Less variable expenses		200,000
Contribution margin		300,000
Less fixed expenses:		
Salaries and wages	$150,000	
Insurance on inventories	10,000	
Depreciation of fixtures	65,000*	
Advertising	100,000	325,000
Net operating income (loss)		$ (25,000)

*Six year remaining useful life, with little or no current resale value.

Due to its poor showing, management is thinking about dropping the men's formal wear department. If the department is dropped, a make-work position will be found for one long-time employee who is due to retire in several years. That employee's salary is $30,000. The fixtures in the department would have no resale value and would be hauled to the county dump.
   Prepare an analysis, using the following form, to determine whether the department should be dropped.

Contribution margin lost if the department is dropped .... $ _____

Less avoidable fixed costs:

_____ .... $ _____

_____ ....   _____

_____ ....   _____   _____

Increase (decrease) in operating income .... $_____

Based on this analysis, should the men's formal wear department be dropped?

Chapter 13

Redo the analysis, using the alternate format shown below:

	Keep Department	Drop Department	Difference: Net Operating Income Increase (Decrease)
Sales	$500,000	$_____	$_____
Less variable expenses	200,000	_____	_____
Contribution margin	300,000	_____	_____
Less fixed expenses:			
Salaries and wages	150,000	_____	_____
Insurance on inventories	10,000	_____	_____
Depreciation of equipment	65,000	_____	_____
Advertising	100,000	_____	_____
Total fixed expenses	325,000	_____	_____
Net operating income (loss)	$ (25,000)	$_____	$_____

13-2.   Watson Company produces two products from a common input. Data relating to the two products are given below:

	Product A	Product B
Sales value at the split-off point	$60,000	$120,000
Allocated joint product costs	$45,000	$90,000
Sales value after further processing	$90,000	$200,000
Cost of further processing	$20,000	$85,000

Determine which of the products should be sold at the split-off point, and which should be processed further before sale. Use the form that appears below.

	Product A	Product B
Sales value after further processing	$_____	$_____
Sales value at the split-off point	_____	_____
Incremental revenue from further processing	_____	_____
Less cost of further processing	_____	_____
Profit (loss) from further processing	$_____	$_____

13-3.   Petre Company is now making a small part that is used in one of its products. The company's accounting department reports the following costs of producing the part internally:

	Per Part
Direct materials	$15
Direct labor	10
Variable manufacturing overhead	2
Fixed manufacturing overhead, traceable	4
Fixed manufacturing overhead, allocated common	5
Unit product cost	$36

A total of 75% of the traceable fixed manufacturing overhead cost consists of depreciation of special equipment, and 25% consists of supervisory salaries. The special equipment has no resale value and does not wear out through use. The supervisory salaries could be avoided if production of the part were discontinued.

An outside supplier has offered to sell the parts to Petre Company for $30 each, based on an order of 5,000 parts per year. Should Petre Company accept this offer, or continue to make the parts internally? Assume that direct labor is a variable cost. Use the following form in your answer:

	Relevant Costs for 5,000 Parts	
	Make	Buy
Outside purchase price		$_____
Cost of making internally:		
_____	$_____	
_____	_____	
_____	_____	
_____	_____	
_____	_____	
Total cost	$_____	$_____

13-4. Kuski Corporation makes two models of its hair dryer at a facility in Lexington. The copper-winding machine has been the constraint in the factory in the past. The capacity of this machine is 9,600 minutes per month. Data concerning these two products appear below:

	Standard	*Premium*
Unit selling price	$14.00	$20.00
Variable cost per unit	$5.00	$8.00
Copper-winding machine time per unit	0.5 minute	0.6 minute
Monthly demand	12,000 units	8,000 units

a. Determine if the copper-winding machine is currently a constraint. In other words, does demand exceed capacity? Use the form below to answer this question

	Standard	*Premium*	*Total*
_____	_____	_____	
_____	_____	_____	
Copper-winding time required to satisfy demand	_____	_____	_____

b. Compute the contribution margin per copper-winding minute for the two products using the following form:

	Standard	*Premium*
Unit selling price	_____	_____
Variable cost per unit	_____	_____
Contribution margin per unit	_____	_____
Copper-winding machine time per unit	_____	_____
Contribution margin per minute	_____	_____

c. Assuming that the copper-winding machine is the company's constraint, how many units of each product should be made in order to maximize net operating income?

Answers to Questions and Exercises

True or False

1. T Costs that differ between alternatives are relevant. Costs that do not differ between alternatives are not relevant.

2. F Fixed costs can be relevant and variable costs can be irrelevant. What is relevant and what is irrelevant depends on the particular decision.

3. F Sunk costs are never relevant since they have already been incurred and thus can't be avoided by choosing one alternative over another.

4. F Future costs are relevant only if they differ between alternatives; future costs that do not differ between alternatives are irrelevant.

5. T For example, a product line manager's salary would be relevant in a decision to drop the product line, but would not be relevant in a decision about how much to spend on advertising.

6. T If the avoidable fixed costs exceed the lost contribution margin, profits would increase if the product line were dropped.

7. F Allocation of common fixed costs to product lines and to other segments of a company can easily result in misleading data and can make a product line appear to be unprofitable when in fact it may be one of a company's best products.

8. F Even if a product line has a negative segment margin, the product's costs must still be analyzed to determine if the product should be dropped. For example, depreciation on special equipment with no resale value would be traceable to the product line, but would not be relevant in a decision to drop the product line.

9. T Opportunity cost can be a key factor in *any* decision involving a constrained resource.

10. F The product with the highest contribution margin per unit of the constrained resource should be emphasized. A product might have a high contribution margin per unit but require a disproportionately large amount of the constrained resource.

11. T Processing further under these conditions will increase profits.

12. T At the split-off point, joint product costs have already been incurred and are not affected by what is done with the joint products from that point forward.

Multiple Choice

1. e These costs are all relevant because they all differ between the alternatives.

2. c The computations are:

Contribution margin lost .... $(50,000)
Less avoidable fixed costs 20,000*
Decrease in operating income .... $(30,000)
*$60,000 – $40,000 = $20,000

3. a The computations are:

	Differential Cost	
	Make	Buy
Variable manuf. costs	$ 7.50	—
Avoidable fixed manufacturing cost	4.00	—
Outside purchase price	—	$10.00
Total relevant cost	$11.50	$10.00

2,000 units × $1.50 = $3,000

4. b The computations are:

	A	B
Contribution margin per unit (a)	$8.00	$12.00
Machine-hours to produce (b)	4.00	5.00
CM per machine-hour (a) ÷ (b)	$2.00	$ 2.40

5. c The computations are:

Incremental revenue ($9.95 × 1,000)	$9,950
Incremental costs:	
Variable production ($5.25 × 1,000)	5,250
Variable selling ($0.15 × 1,000)	150
Increase in operating income	$4,550

6. b   The computations are:

	A	B
Sales value after further processing	$1,700	$4,000
Sales value at split-off	1,200	3,000
Incremental sales value	500	1,000
Incremental processing cost	600	800
Advantage (disadvantage) of further processing	$ (100)	$ 200

Exercises

13-1.

Contribution margin lost if the department is dropped		$(300,000)
Less avoidable fixed costs:		
Salaries and wages ($150,000 - $30,000)	$120,000	
Insurance on inventories	10,000	
Advertising	100,000	230,000
Decrease in overall company net operating income		$ (70,000)

Based on the analysis above, the department should not be dropped. The solution using the alternate format appears below:

	Keep Department	Drop Department	Difference: Income Increase or (Decrease)
Sales	$500,000	$ 0	$(500,000)
Less variable expenses	200,000	0	200,000
Contribution margin	300,000	0	(300,000)
Less fixed expenses:			
Salaries and wages	150,000	30,000	120,000
Insurance on inventories	10,000	0	10,000
Depreciation of fixtures	65,000	65,000*	0
Advertising	100,000	0	100,000
Total fixed expenses	325,000	95,000	230,000
Net operating income (loss)	$(25,000)	$(95,000)	$ (70,000)

* If the department were dropped, the remaining book value of the fixtures would be written off immediately. If the department were not dropped, the remaining book value would be written off over a number of years in the form of depreciation charges. In either case, the entire remaining book value will eventually flow through the income statement as charges in one form or another.

13-2.

	Product A	Product B
Sales value after further processing	$ 90,000	$200,000
Sales value at the split-off point	60,000	120,000
Incremental revenue from further processing	30,000	80,000
Less cost of further processing	20,000	85,000
Profit (loss) from further processing	$ 10,000	$ (5,000)

13-3.

	Relevant Costs for 5,000 Parts	
	Make	*Buy*
Outside purchase price		$150,000
Cost of making internally:		
Direct materials	$ 75,000	
Direct labor	50,000	
Variable manufacturing overhead	10,000	
Fixed manufacturing overhead, traceable	5,000	
Fixed manufacturing overhead, allocated common		
Total	$140,000	$150,000
Difference in favor of making..	$10,000	

The depreciation on the equipment and the common fixed overhead would not be avoidable costs.

13-4.
a.   Demand exceeds capacity for the copper-winding machine, as shown below:

	Standard	*Premium*	*Total*
Monthly demand (a)	12,000 units	8,000 units	
Copper-winding machine time per unit (b)	0.5 min./unit	0.6 min./unit	
Copper-winding time required			
to satisfy demand (a) × (b)	6,000 min.	4,800 min.	10,800 min.

b.

	Standard	*Premium*
Unit selling price	$14.00	$20.00
Variable cost per unit	5.00	8.00
Contribution margin per unit (a)	$ 9.00	$12.00
Copper-winding machine time per unit (b)	0.5 min.	0.6 min.
Contribution margin per minute (a) ÷ (b)	$ 18/min.	$ 20/min.

c.   Since the contribution margin per copper-winding minute is higher for the premium model than for the standard model, the premium model should be emphasized. The optimal plan is to produce all 8,000 units of the premium model and use the remaining capacity to make 9,600 units of the standard model.

Total copper-winding time available	9,600 minutes
Time required to produce 8,000 units of the premium model	4,800 minutes
Time remaining with which to make the standard model (a)	4,800 minutes
Time required to make one unit of the standard model (b)	0.5 minute/unit
Number of units of the standard model produced (a) ÷ (b)	9,600 units

Chapter 14

Capital Budgeting Decisions

Chapter Study Suggestions

✳

You must have a solid understanding of the concept of present value to understand the material in this chapter. If you have not worked with present value before, study Appendix 14A, "The Concept of Present Value," before starting the chapter.

Once you understand present value, you will be ready to tackle the capital budgeting methods in the chapter. The first of these methods is called the net present value method. Follow through each number in Exhibits, 14-1 and 14-4 and trace the present value factors back to the tables given at the end of the chapter.

The second capital budgeting method is called the internal rate of return method. It is illustrated in Example D. This method is similar to the net present value method in that both methods are based on discounting future cash flows.

Two other methods of making capital budgeting decisions are presented in the chapter—the payback method and the simple rate of return method.

CHAPTER HIGHLIGHTS

A. *Capital budgeting* involves planning major outlays on projects that commit the company for some time into the future such as purchasing new equipment, building a new facility, or introducing a new product. Capital budgeting usually involves investment; i.e., committing funds now so as to obtain cash inflows in the future.

1. Capital budgeting decisions fall into two broad categories:

a. *Screening decisions:* Potential projects are categorized as acceptable or unacceptable.

b. *Preference decisions*: After screening out all of the unacceptable projects, more projects may remain than can be funded. Consequently, projects must be ranked in order of preference.

2. The time value of money is a central consideration in capital budgeting. A dollar in the future is worth less than a dollar today for the simple reason that a dollar today can be invested to yield more than a dollar in the future.

a. *Discounted cash flow methods* give full recognition to the time value of money.

b. Two of the methods presented in the chapter discount cash flows—the *net present value method* and the *internal rate of return method*.

B. The net present value method is illustrated in Exhibit 14-1, Exhibit 14-2, and Exhibit 14-4. The basic steps in this method are:

1. Determine the required investment.

2. Determine the future cash inflows and outflows that result from the investment.

3. Use the *present value tables* in Appendix 14C to find the appropriate *present value factors*.

a. The values (or factors) in the present value tables depend on the discount rate and the number of periods.

b. The *discount rate* in present value analysis is the company's required rate of return, which is often the company's cost of capital. The *cost of capital* is the average rate of return the company must pay its long-term creditors and stockholders for the use of their funds. The details of the cost of capital are covered in finance courses.

4. Multiply each cash flow by the appropriate present value factor and then sum the results. The end result (which is net of the initial investment) is called the *net present value* of the project.

5. In a screening decision, the investment is acceptable if the net present value is positive. If the net present value is negative, the investment should be rejected.

C. Discounted cash flow analysis is based on *cash flows*—not accounting net operating income.

1. Typical cash flows associated with an investment are:

a. Outflows include initial investment, installation costs; increased working capital needs; repairs and maintenance; and incremental operating costs.

b. Inflows include incremental revenues; reductions in costs; salvage value; and release of working capital at the end of the project.

2. Depreciation is not a cash flow and therefore is not included in net present value calculations. (However, depreciation can affect taxes, which *is* a cash flow. This aspect of depreciation is covered in Appendix 14D.)

3. Projects frequently require an infusion of cash (i.e., working capital) to finance inventories, receivables, and other working capital items. Typically, at the end of the project this working capital can be recovered. Thus, working capital is counted as a cash outflow at the beginning of a project and as a cash inflow at the end of the project.

4. We usually assume that all cash flows, other than the initial investment, occur at the *end* of a period.

D. The internal rate of return method is another discounted cash flow method used in capital budgeting decisions.

1. The *internal rate of return* is the rate of return promised by an investment project over its useful life; it is the discount rate for which the net present value of a project is zero.

2. When the cash flows are the same every year, the following formula can be used to find the internal rate of return:

$$\frac{\text{Factor of the}}{\text{internal rate of return}} = \frac{\text{Investment required}}{\text{Net annual cash inflows}}$$

3. For example, assume an investment of $3,791 is made in a project that will last five years and has no

salvage value. Also assume that the annual cash inflow from the project will be $1,000.

$$\text{Factor of the internal rate of return} = \frac{\$3,791}{\$1,000} = 3.791$$

The same cash inflow is received at the end of every year beginning with the first year, so use Table 14C-4 in Appendix 14C, which contains the present value factors for annuities. Since this is a project with a five-year life, use the 5-year row in the table. Scanning along the 5-year row, it can be seen that this factor represents a 10% rate of return. Therefore, the internal rate of return is 10%.

4. If the cash inflows are not the same every year, the internal rate of return is found using trial and error or a software application. The internal rate of return is whatever discount rate makes the net present value of the project equal zero.

5. In a screening decision, the internal rate of return is compared to the required rate of return. If the internal rate of return is less than the required rate of return, the project is rejected. If it is greater than or equal to the required rate of return, the project is accepted.

E. The *total-cost* or the *incremental-cost* approach can be used in conjunction with the net present value method to compare projects.

1. Exhibit 14-7 illustrates the total cost approach. Note in Exhibit 14-7 that *all* cash inflows and *all* cash outflows for each alternative are included in the solution.

2. The incremental-cost approach ignores all cash flows that are the same under both alternatives. Exhibit 14-8 illustrates this approach.

3. If done correctly, both the total-cost and incremental-cost approaches will lead to the same decision.

F. Sometimes no revenue or cash inflow is involved in a decision. In this situation, the *least cost* alternative should be selected. Exhibits 14-9 and 14-10 illustrate least-cost decisions.

G. It is often difficult to quantify all the costs and benefits involved in a decision. An investment in automation provides a good example.

1. The reduction in direct labor cost from automation may be easy to quantify. Intangible benefits, such as greater throughput or greater flexibility in operations, are usually very difficult to quantify. It would be a mistake to ignore these intangible benefits simply because they are difficult to quantify.

2. The difficulty can often be resolved by computing how large the intangible benefits would have to be to make the investment attractive. The steps in this approach are:

a. Compute the net present value of the tangible costs and benefits. If the result is positive, the investment is acceptable since the intangible benefits simply make it even more attractive.

b. If the net present value of the tangible costs and benefits is negative, compute the additional net annual cash inflows that would make the net present value positive.

c. If the intangible benefits are likely to be at least as large as the required additional net annual cash inflows computed in (2), accept the project.

H. When more acceptable projects exist than can be funded, the projects must be ranked in order of preference.

1. When using the internal rate of return to rank competing investment projects, the preference rule is: *The higher the internal rate of return, the more desirable the project.*

2. If the net present value method is used to rank competing investment projects, the net present value of one project should not be compared directly to the net present value of another project, unless the investments in the projects are equal.

a. To compare projects that require different investment amounts, the *project profitability index* is computed:

$$\text{Project profitability index} = \frac{\text{Net present value of the project}}{\text{Investment required}}$$

The project profitability index is basically the same idea as the contribution margin per unit of the constrained resource in Chapter 13. In this case, the constrained resource is investment funds.

b. The higher the profitability index, the more desirable the project.

I. The present value method is generally superior to the internal rate of return method, although both are used in practice. The internal rate of return method assumes that any cash flows received during the life of the project can be reinvested at rate of return equal to the internal rate of return. This assumption is questionable if the internal rate of return is high. In contrast, the net present value method assumes that any cash flows received during the life of the project are reinvested at a rate of return equal to the discount rate. Ordinarily, this is a more realistic assumption.

J.   Two other capital budgeting methods are considered in the chapter. These methods do not involve discounting cash flows One of these is the payback method.

   1. The *payback period* is the number of years required for an investment project to recover its cost out of the cash receipts it generates.

      a.   When the cash inflows from the project are the same every year, the following formula can be used to compute the payback period:

$$\text{Payback period} = \frac{\text{Investment required}}{\text{Net annual cash inflows}}$$

      b.   If new equipment is replacing old equipment, the "investment required" should be reduced by any salvage value obtained from the disposal of old equipment. And in this case, in computing the "net annual cash inflows," only the incremental cash inflow provided by the new equipment over the old equipment should be used.

   2. The payback period is not a measure of profitability. Rather it is a measure of how long it takes for a project to recover its investment cost.

   3. The payback method ignores the time value of money and all cash flows that occur once the initial cost has been recovered. Therefore, this method is very crude and should be used only with a great deal of caution. Nevertheless, the payback method can be useful in industries where project lives are very short and uncertain.

K.   The simple rate of return method is another capital budgeting method that does not involve discounted cash flows.

   1. The *simple rate of return* method focuses on accounting net operating income rather than on cash flows:

$$\text{Simple rate of retun} = \frac{\text{Annual incremental revenue} - \text{Annual incremental expenses}}{\text{Initial investment}}$$

If new equipment is replacing old equipment, then the "initial investment" in the new equipment is the cost of the new equipment reduced by any salvage value obtained from the old equipment.

   2. Like the payback method, the simple rate of return method does not consider the time value of money. Therefore, the rate of return computed by this method will not be an accurate guide to the profitability of an investment project.

Appendix 14A: The Concept of Present Value

A.   A dollar received today is more valuable than a dollar received in the future for the simple reason that a dollar received today can be invested—yielding more than a dollar in the future.

B.   Present value analysis recognizes the time value of money.

   1. Present value analysis involves expressing a future cash flow in terms of present dollars. When a future cash flow is expressed in terms of its present value, the process is called *discounting*.

   2. Use Table 14C-3 in Appendix 14C to determine the present value of a single sum to be received in the future. This table contains factors for various rates of interest for various periods, which when multiplied by a future sum, will give the sum's present value.

   3. Use Table 14C-4 in Appendix 14C to determine the present value of an *annuity*, or stream, of cash flows. This table contains factors that, when multiplied by the stream of cash flows, will give the stream's present value. Be careful to note that this annuity table is for a very specific type of annuity in which the first payment occurs at the end of the first year.

Appendix 14B: Inflation and Capital Budgeting

A.   Inflation has an impact on both cash flows and the discount rate.

B.   Under certain conditions, it doesn't make any difference whether you adjust both the cash flows and the discount rate for inflation or whether you do not adjust either. However, you must be consistent. If the cash flows are adjusted for inflation, the discount rate should also reflect inflation.

C.   For the sake of simplicity, we assume in the body of the chapter that inflation is zero.

Appendix 14D: Income Taxes in Capital Budgeting Decisions

A. Income taxes add a significant complication to capital budgeting. Both the costs and benefits of a project should be stated on an after-tax basis.

    1. The true cost of a tax-deductible expenditure is the amount of the payment net of any reduction in income taxes due to the payment. The net after-tax cost for a tax-deductible expenditure can be computed as follows:

$$\text{After-tax cost} = (1\text{-Tax rate}) \times \begin{array}{c}\text{Tax deductible} \\ \text{cash expense}\end{array}$$

    2. Not all cash outflows are tax deductible.

        a. An investment in working capital is not tax deductible; it is not an expense.

        b. The cost of a depreciable asset *is not* tax deductible in the period in which it is purchased. However, depreciation on the asset *is* tax deductible. (See section C below.)

        c. Any gain or loss (i.e., difference between salvage value and book value) on disposal of an asset *is* taxable.

B. As with cash expenditures, taxable cash receipts must be placed on an after-tax basis.

    1. A cash receipt net of its tax effect is known as an *after-tax benefit*. The net after-tax cash inflow from revenue or other taxable cash receipts can be computed as follows:

$$\text{After-tax benefits} = (1\text{-Tax rate}) \times \begin{array}{c}\text{Taxable cash} \\ \text{receipt}\end{array}$$

    2. Not all cash receipts are taxable. For example, the release of working capital at the end of a project is not a taxable cash inflow.

C. Depreciation is not a cash outflow. However, depreciation deductions do affect the amount of taxes that a company will pay.

    1. Depreciation deductions act as a *tax shield*. Depreciation deductions shield revenues from taxation and reduce income taxes.

    2. The formula used to compute the tax savings from the depreciation tax shield is:

$$\begin{array}{c}\text{Tax savings from the} \\ \text{depreciation tax shield}\end{array} = \text{Tax rate} \times \begin{array}{c}\text{Depreciation} \\ \text{deduction}\end{array}$$

D. In the United States, the depreciation rules are complex.

    1. To simplify matters, we assume in the text that for tax purposes the entire original cost of an asset (without any reduction for salvage value) is depreciated using the straight-line method.

    2. If an asset is disposed of after it has been fully depreciated for tax purposes, any proceeds are fully taxable.

E. Exhibit 4D-4 contains a comprehensive example of income taxes and capital budgeting. Follow this example carefully step by step.

    1. All cash flows involving tax-deductible expenses and taxable receipts are placed on an after-tax basis by multiplying the cash flow by one minus the tax rate.

    2. Also notice that the depreciation deductions are multiplied *by the tax rate itself* to determine the tax savings (cash inflow) resulting from the tax shield.

    3. *These two above points should be studied with great care until both are thoroughly understood.*

REVIEW AND SELF-TEST
Questions and Exercises

True or False

Enter a T or an F in the blank to indicate whether the statement is true or false.

_____ 1. Under the net present value method, the present value of all cash inflows associated with an investment project is compared to the present value of all cash outflows, with the difference, or net present value, determining whether or not the project is acceptable.

_____ 2. One key shortcoming of discounted cash flow methods is that they do not provide for the recovery of the original investment.

_____ 3. Cash outlays for noncurrent assets such as machines would be considered in a capital budgeting analysis, but not cash outlays for current assets such as inventory.

_____ 4. The internal rate of return is the discount rate for which a project's net present value is zero.

_____ 5. The internal rate of return method makes more realistic assumptions about the rate of return that is earned on cash generated by an investment than the net present value method.

_____ 6. In present value analysis, as the discount rate increases, the present value of a given future cash inflow also increases.

_____ 7. When comparing two investment alternatives, the total-cost approach provides the same ultimate answer as the incremental-cost approach.

_____ 8. When ranking investment projects, a project with a high net present value should be ranked above a project with a lower net present value.

_____ 9. In preference decision situations, the net present value and internal rate of return methods may yield conflicting rankings of projects.

_____ 10. The payback method does not consider the time value of money.

_____ 11. The present value of a cash inflow to be received in 5 years is greater than the present value of the same sum to be received in 10 years.

_____ 12. (Appendix 14D) The after-tax cost of a tax-deductible item is computed by multiplying the amount of the tax deduction by the tax rate.

_____ 13. (Appendix 14D) Since salvage value is not considered when computing depreciation for tax purposes, any salvage value received on sale of an asset after it has been fully depreciated is taxed as income.

_____ 14. (Appendix 14D) The release of working capital at the end of an investment project is a taxable cash inflow.

Multiple Choice

Choose the best answer or response by placing the identifying letter in the space provided.

The following data relate to questions 1 and 2.

Peters Company is considering a machine to further automate its production line. The machine would cost $30,000, and have a ten-year life with no salvage value. It would save $8,000 per year in labor costs, but would increase power costs by $1,000 annually. The company's discount rate is 12%.

_____ 1. The present value of the net annual cost savings is: a) $39,550; b) $45,200; c) $5,650; d) $70,000.

_____ 2. The net present value of the entire project is: a) $(15,200); b) $5,650; c) $9,550; d) $30,000.

_____ 3. Acme Company is considering investing in a new machine that costs $84,900 and that has a useful life of 12 years with no salvage value. The machine will generate $15,000 annually in net cash inflows. The internal rate of return on the investment is: a) 8%; b) 10%; c) 12%; d) 14 %.

_____ 4. White Company's required rate of return and discount rate is 12%. The company is considering an investment that would yield a cash inflow of $10,000 in five years. What is the most that the company should be willing to invest in this project? a) $36,050; b) $5,670; c) $17,637; d) $2,774.

_____ 5. An investment of $30,000 in working capital would provide cash inflows of $10,000 per year for six years. If the company's discount rate is 18%, and if the working capital is released at the end of the six years, then the project's net present value is: a) $4,980; b) $(4,980); c) $16,080; d) $(12,360).

172

___ 6. A project with a 10-year life has tangible costs and benefits with a $113,000 *negative* net present value. The company's discount rate is 12%. What amount of annual cash inflow would have to be provided by the project's intangible benefits in order for the project to be acceptable? a) $11,300; b) $13,560; c) $18,000; d) $20,000

___ 7. A machine is under consideration that would cost $30,000, save $6,000 per year in cash operating costs, and have an expected life of 15 years with zero salvage value. The payback period on the machine is: a) 2 years; b) 7.5 years; c) 5 years; d) 0.2 years.

___ 8. Refer to the data in question (7) above. The simple rate of return is approximately: a) 20%; b) 13.3%; c) 18%; d) 10%.

___ 9. (Appendix 14D) A project is being considered for which the annual cash operating expenses are $20,000. If the company's tax rate is 30%, what is the after-tax cost of these operating expenses? a) $6,000; b) $14,000; c) $20,000; $60,000.

___ 10. (Appendix 14D) A project is being considered for which the annual cash revenues are $80,000. If the company's tax rate is 30%, what is the after-tax benefit of the revenues? a) $0; b) $24,000; c) $56,000; d) $80,000.

___ 11. (Appendix 14D) A company's depreciation deduction is $50,000 and its tax rate is 30%. The company's savings from the depreciation tax shield is: a) $15,000; b) $35,000; c) $50,000; d) $30,000.

___ 12. (Appendix 14D) A company is studying a project that would require a $200,000 working capital investment. If the company's tax rate is 30%, then the initial investment in working capital should be shown in the capital budgeting analysis as a cash outflow of: a) $200,000; b) $140,000; c) $60,000; d) $0.

___ 12. (Appendix 14D) Refer to the data in question (6) above. The working capital would be released for use elsewhere at the end of the project in four years. The company's discount rate is 10%. What is the approximate present value of the after-tax cash flows associated with the release of the working capital? a) $200,000; b) $95,600; c) $136,600; d) $0.

Exercises

14-1. You have recently won $100,000 in a contest. You have been given the option of receiving $100,000 today or receiving $12,000 at the end of each year for the next 20 years.

a. If you can earn 8% on investments, which of these two options would you select? (Note: The net present value method assumes that any cash flows are reinvested at a rate of return equal to the discount rate. Therefore, to answer this question you can compare the net present values of the cash flows under the two alternatives using 8% as the discount rate.)

Item	Year(s)	Amount of Cash Flows	8% Factor	Present Value of Cash Flows
Receive the annuity	_____	_____	_____	$ _____
Receive the lump sum	_____	_____	_____	_____
Net present value in favor				
of _____ ..				$ _____

b. If you can earn 12% on investments, which of these two options would you select?

Item	Year(s)	Amount of Cash Flows	12% Factor	Present Value of Cash Flows
Receive the annuity	_____	$ _____	_____	$ _____
Receive the lump sum	_____	_____	_____	_____
Net present value in favor				
of _____ ..				$ _____

14-2.   Lynde Company has been offered a contract to provide a key replacement part for the Army's main attack helicopter. The contract would expire in eight years. The projected cash flows that result from the contract are given below:

Cost of new equipment	$300,000
Working capital needed	$100,000
Net annual cash inflows	$85,000
Salvage value of equipment in eight years	$50,000

The company's discount rate is 16%. The working capital would be released for use elsewhere at the end of the project.

Complete the analysis below to determine whether the contract should be accepted. (Ignore income taxes.)

Item	*Year(s)*	*Amount of Cash Flows*	*16% Factor*	*Present Value of Cash Flows*
Cost of new equipment	_____	$_____	_____	$_____
Working capital needed	_____	_____	_____	_____
Net annual cash inflows	_____	_____	_____	_____
Salvage value of equipment	_____	_____	_____	_____
Working capital released	_____	_____	_____	_____
Salvage value of equipment	_____	_____	_____	_____
Net present value				$_____

14-3.   Swift Company is considering the purchase of a new machine that will cost $20,000. The machine will provide revenues of $9,000 per year. Out-of-pocket operating costs will be $6,000 per year. The new machine will have a useful life of 10 years and will have zero salvage value. The company's required rate of return is 12%. (Ignore income taxes.) What is the internal rate of return to the nearest whole percent?

Annual revenue	$_____
Annual operating costs	_____
Net annual cash inflow	$_____

$$\text{Factor of the internal rate of return} = \frac{\text{Investment required}}{\text{Net annual cash inflows}}$$

$$= \frac{\rule{3cm}{0.4pt}}{\rule{3cm}{0.4pt}} = \rule{2cm}{0.4pt}$$

14-4.   Harlan Company would like to purchase a new machine that makes wonderfully smooth fruit sorbet that the company can sell in the premium frozen dessert sections of supermarkets. The machine costs $450,000 and has a useful life of ten years with a salvage value of $50,000. Annual revenues and expenses resulting from the new machine are:

Sales revenue		$300,000
Less operating expenses:		
Advertising	$100,000	
Salaries of operators	70,000	
Maintenance	30,000	
Depreciation	40,000	240,000
Net operating income		$ 60,000

a.   Harlan Company will not invest in new equipment unless it promises a payback period of 4 years or less. Compute the payback period on the sorbet machine.

Computation of the net annual cash inflow:

Net operating income .... $_____

Add: Noncash deduction for depreciation .... _____

Net annual cash inflow .... $_____

Computation of the payback period:

$$\text{Payback period} = \frac{\text{Investment required}}{\text{Net annual cash inflows}}$$

$$= \frac{\qquad}{\qquad} = \underline{\quad} \text{years}$$

b.   Compute the simple rate of return on the investment in the new machine.

$$\frac{\text{Simple rate}}{\text{of retun}} = \frac{\text{Annual incremental revenue} - \text{Annual incremental expenses}}{\text{Initial investment}}$$

$$= \frac{\qquad}{\qquad} = \underline{\quad}$$

14-5.   (Appendix 14D) Marvel Company has $60,000 to invest and is considering two alternatives:

	Investment X	Investment Y
Cost of equipment	$60,000	—
Working capital needed	—	$60,000
Annual cash inflows	$20,000	$20,000
Salvage value	$3,000	—
Life of the project	5 years	5 years

The company's after-tax cost of capital is 12%, and the tax rate is 30%.

Compute the net present value of each investment using the form that appears below. The company uses the straight-line method of depreciation for tax purposes, with zero salvage value assumed.

Items and computations	Year(s)	(1) Amount	(2) Tax Effect	(1) × (2) After-Tax Cash Flow	12% Factor	Present Value
Investment X:						
Cost of equipment	___	___	___	___	___	___
Annual cash inflows	___	___	___	___	___	___
Depreciation deductions	___	___	___	___	___	___
Salvage value	___	___	___	___	___	___
Net present value						___
Investment Y:						
Working capital needed	___	___	___	___	___	___
Annual cash inflows	___	___	___	___	___	___
Working capital released	___	___	___	___	___	___
Net present value						___

Answers to Questions and Exercises

True or False

1. T   Exhibit 14-4 illustrates this point.

2. F   Discounted cash flow methods do provide for recovery of original investment, as illustrated in Exhibit 14-3.

3. F   All cash flows should be included in a capital budgeting analysis.

4. T   This statement is true by definition; the principle is illustrated in Exhibit 14-5.

5. F   The opposite is true.

6. F   The opposite is true—the higher the discount rate, the lower is the present value of a given future cash inflow.

7. T   The total-cost approach and the incremental-cost approach are just different ways of obtaining the same result.

8. F   Net present value shouldn't be used to rank projects when investment funds are limited, since one project may have a higher net present value than another simply because it is larger. The project profitability index should be used to compare projects.

9. T   See the example in the text in the section "Comparing the Preference Rules."

10. T   A major defect of the payback method is that dollars are given the same weight regardless of when they are received.

11. T   When discounting, the shorter the time period, the greater the present value.

12. F   The after-tax cost of a tax deductible cash expense is determined by multiplying it by *one minus* the tax rate.

13. T   The salvage value is fully taxable as income since the taxpayer will already have fully depreciated the asset.

14. F   The release of working capital is a return of the taxpayer's original investment (which itself is not a tax deduction) and thus would not be taxable as income.

Multiple Choice

1. a   The computations are:

Savings in labor costs..................	$ 8,000
Less increased power costs	1,000
Net cost savings	$ 7,000
Present value factor for 12% for 10 years (Table 14C-4)	× 5.650
Present value of cost savings	$39,550

2. c   The computations are:

Investment in the machine............	$(30,000)
Present value of cost savings	39,550
Net present value	$ 9,550

3. d   The computations are:

$$\frac{\text{Factor of the internal rate of return}}{} = \frac{\text{Investment required}}{\text{Net annual cash inflows}}$$

$$= \frac{\$84,900}{\$15,000} = 5.660$$

Looking at the 12-year row in the annuity Table 14C-4, a factor of 5.660 equals a return of 14%.

4. b   The computations are:

Return in 5 years	$10,000
Factor for 12% for 5 years (Table 14C-3).........................	× 0.567
Present value	$ 5,670

This is the maximum amount the company is willing to invest. If it were to invest more than $5,670, the net present value of the investment would be negative.

5. c   The computations are:

	Year(s)	Amount	18% Factor	Present Value
Working capital investment	Now	$(30,000)	1.000	$(30,000)
Cash inflow	1-6	10,000	3.498	34,980
Working capital released	6	30,000	0.370	11,100
Net present value				$ 16,080

6. d   The computation is:

$$\frac{\text{Net present value, } \$113,000}{\text{Present value factor, 5.650}} = \$20,000$$

Chapter 14

7. c   The computation is:

$$\text{Payback period} = \frac{\text{Investment required}}{\text{Net annual cash inflows}}$$

$$= \frac{\$30,000}{\$6,000 \text{ per year}} = 5 \text{ years}$$

8. b   The "incremental revenue" is the cost savings of $6,000 per year and the "incremental expense" is the annual depreciation charge of $2,000 = $30,000 ÷ 15 years.

$$\text{Simple rate of return} = \frac{\text{Annual incremental revenues} - \text{Annual incremental expenses}}{\text{Initial investment}}$$

$$= \frac{\$6,000-\$2,000}{\$30,000} = 13.1\%$$

9. b $(1 - 0.30) \times \$20,000 = \$14,000$

10. c $(1 - 0.30) \times \$80,000 = \$56,000$

11. a $0.30 \times \$50,000 = \$15,000$

12. a   Working capital represents an investment, not an expense, so there is no effect on taxes.

13. c   The release of working capital does not affect taxes. Therefore, the entire $200,000 represents an after-tax cash flow. The present value factor for four periods at 10% per period is 0.683, so the present value of the $200,000 is 0.683 × $200,000 or $136,600.

Exercises

14-1. a. The annuity is preferable if the discount rate is 8%:

Item	Year(s)	Amount of Cash Flows	8% Factor	Present Value of Cash Flows
Receive the annuity	1-20	$ 12,000	9.818	$117,816
Receive the lump sum	Now	100,000	1.000	100,000
Net present value in favor of the annuity				$ 17,816

b. The lump sum is preferable if the discount rate is 12%:

Item	Year(s)	Amount of Cash Flows	12% Factor	Present Value of Cash Flows
Receive the annuity	1-20	$ 12,000	7.469	$ 89,628
Receive the lump sum	Now	100,000	1.000	100,000
Net present value in favor of the lump sum				$ 10,372

14-2.

Item	Year(s)	Amount of Cash Flows	16% Factor	Present Value of Cash Flows
Cost of new equipment	Now	($300,000)	1.000	($300,000)
Working capital needed	Now	(100,000)	1.000	(100,000)
Net annual cash receipts	1-8	85,000	4.344	369,240
Salvage value of equipment	8	50,000	0.305	15,250
Working capital released	8	100,000	0.305	30,500
Net present value				$ 14,990

Yes, the contract should be accepted. The net present value is positive, which means that the contract will provide more than the company's 16% required rate of return.

14-3.

Annual revenue	$9,000
Annual operating costs	6,000
Incremental cash inflow	$3,000

$$\frac{\text{Factor of the}}{\text{internal rate of return}} = \frac{\text{Investment required}}{\text{Net annual cash inflows}}$$

$$= \frac{\$20,000}{\$3,000} = 6.667$$

The 6.667 factor falls between the 8% and 9% rates of return in Table 14C-4 and is closest to 8%, therefore the internal rate of return is about 8%.

14-4. a. The net annual cash inflow would be:

Net operating income	$ 60,000
Add: Noncash deduction for depreciation	40,000
Net annual cash inflow	$100,000

The payback period would be:

$$\text{Payback period} = \frac{\text{Investment required}}{\text{Net annual cash inflows}} = \frac{\$450,000}{\$100,000 \text{ per year}} = 4.5 \text{ years}$$

The machine would not be purchased since it will not provide the 4-year payback period required by the company.

b. The simple rate of return would be:

$$\text{Simple rate of return} = \frac{\text{Annual incremental revenues - Annual incremental expenses}}{\text{Initial investment}}$$

$$= \frac{\$300,000 - \$240,000}{\$450,000} = 13.3\%$$

14-5.

Items and computations	Year(s)	(1) Amount	(2) Tax Effect	After-Tax Cash Flow	(1) × (2) 12% Factor	Present Value
Investment X:						
Cost of equipment..	Now	$(60,000)	—	$(60,000)	1.000	$(60,000)
Annual cash inflows......................................	1-5	20,000	1 – 0.30	14,000	3.605	50,470
Depreciation deductions	1-5	12,000	0.30	3,600	3.605	12,978
Salvage value	5	3,000	1 – 0.30	2,100	0.567	1,191
Net present value						$ 4,639
Investment Y:						
Working capital needed	Now	$(60,000)	—	$(60,000)	1.000	$(60,000)
Annual cash inflows	1-5	20,000	1 – 0.30	14,000	3.605	50,470
Working capital released	5	60,000	—	60,000	0.567	34,020
Net present value						$ 24,490

Chapter 15

Service Department Costing:
An Activity Approach

Chapter Study Suggestions

✳

Exhibits 15-2, 15-4, and 15-7 are the key exhibits in this chapter. Exhibit 15-2 illustrates the direct method of allocating service department costs to operating departments and Exhibit 15-4 illustrates the step method. Follow the computations in the exhibits step-by-step, and note the difference in the way the two methods handle the cost data.

Exhibit 15-7 expands on Exhibits 15-2 and 15-4 by showing how breaking costs down into their variable and fixed components can make the allocations more meaningful. Spend the bulk of your study time on the sections titled, "Allocating costs by behavior," and "A summary of cost allocation guidelines." Exhibit 15-7 shows how the ideas in these two sections are implemented in an extended allocation problem. This is a very important exhibit, since it is the basis for many of the longer, more difficult homework problems.

CHAPTER HIGHLIGHTS

A. The two broad classes of departments within an organization are operating departments and service departments.

1. *Operating departments* are those departments or units where the central purposes of the organization are carried out. Examples of operating departments include the surgery department in a hospital, the shoe department in a department store, and production departments in a manufacturing company.

2. *Service departments* do not engage directly in operating activities. Rather, they provide service or assistance to other departments. Examples of service departments include the cafeteria in a hospital, the billing department in a department store, and the purchasing department in a factory.

3. The costs of service departments are typically allocated to operating departments. These allocated costs are then added to the overhead costs of the operating departments and included in predetermined overhead rates.

B. Three major methods are used to allocate service department costs—the direct method, the step method, and the reciprocal method. The methods differ mainly in how they treat services that service departments provide to each other. These services are called *interdepartmental services* or *reciprocal services*.

C. The *direct method* is the simplest, but the least accurate, of the three methods. When the direct method is used, reciprocal services are ignored and service department costs are allocated directly to operating departments. For example, a hospital's custodial staff cleans administrative offices as well as operating rooms and hospital wards. However, in the direct method none of the custodial costs are allocated to the administrative department. Instead, all the custodial costs are allocated *directly* to the operating departments.

D. The *step method* is slightly more complex than the direct method, but it is also more accurate.

1. In the step method, service department costs are allocated in a specific order. Usually, service departments are ranked in terms of the amount of service they provide to other service departments, with the service department that provides the greatest service to the other service departments allocated first.

2. The costs of the first service department are allocated to all the other departments, both service and operating departments. After the first service department's costs have been allocated, it is ignored in subsequent allocations. Then the costs of the next service department are allocated to the *remaining* service departments as well as to the operating departments. However, any services provided by the second service department to the first service department are ignored. No costs are allocated back to the first service department.

3. The allocation proceeds in this manner, stepping through all the service departments. In each step, a service department's costs are allocated to the remaining service departments as well as to the operating departments. After a service department's costs have been allocated, the service department is ignored.

4. By following this procedure, the step method takes into account some of the reciprocal services, but not all of them.

E. Under both the direct and step methods, the service department whose cost is being allocated is never included in the allocation base. For example, when allocating the costs of a cafeteria on the basis of meals served, the meals served to cafeteria workers are ignored.

F. The *reciprocal method* is the most complex and the most accurate method of the three methods for allocating service department costs. The reciprocal method takes all of the reciprocal services fully into account. However, the reciprocal method is seldom used in practice—probably because of its mathematical complexity. This method is covered in more advanced textbooks.

G. Service department costs should be separated into fixed and variable elements and allocated separately to other departments. This procedure provides data that are more useful for planning and controlling operations.

1. The variable costs of providing services should be charged to other departments using as an allocation base whatever causes the variable cost to vary. For example, if maintenance costs increase and decrease in proportion to machine-hours, then machine-hours should be used as the allocation base for maintenance costs.

a. At the beginning of the period, charges to departments for the variable costs of a service department should be computed by multiplying the *budgeted* rate for the service by the *budgeted* use of the service. These allocations, or charges, are used for planning and for computing departmental predetermined overhead rates.

b.   At the end of the period, charges to the departments for the variable costs of a service department should be computed by multiplying the *budgeted* rate (*not actual* rate) for the service by *actual* activity. These charges are used for performance evaluation. If actual rates were used, other departments would implicitly be held responsible for inefficiencies in the service department.

2.   The fixed costs of service departments are incurred in order to have the *capacity* to provide service during a period. This capacity may or may not be fully utilized. The fixed costs of service departments should be allocated to consuming departments in proportion to the capacity they require, not the capacity they use. Thus, the fixed costs should be allocated in *predetermined, lump-sum* amounts.

a.   When allocating fixed costs, the *budgeted* (not actual) costs should be allocated on the basis of either *long-run average* activity or *peak period* requirements (not budgeted or actual activity). The reason for this is that the level of the fixed costs is deter-

mined by management's planning for the long run average or for peak period activity. Management wants to make sure that there is enough capacity to handle peak period or long run average needs.

b.   Once set, lump-sum allocations of fixed costs will not change between the beginning and the end of the period.

c.   A company should not allocate fixed costs with a variable allocation base such as sales dollars. If a variable allocation base is used, the amount of fixed cost allocated to a department will be affected by what happens in other departments. A decrease in activity in other departments will result in an increase in the amount of the fixed cost allocated to the department.

3.   Any difference between the actual service department costs and the costs charged to the operating departments at the end of the period should be retained in the service department as a spending variance. It would be the responsibility of the manager of the service department.

REVIEW AND SELF-TEST
Questions and Exercises

True or False

Enter a T or an F in the blank to indicate whether the statement is true or false.

_____ 1. The direct method of allocating service department costs fully accounts for all reciprocal services among service departments.

_____ 2. When allocating a service department's costs under the direct method, one should never include the service department being allocated in the allocation base. (e.g., The meals served to cafeteria workers should not be included in the allocation base for the cafeteria.)

_____ 3. When allocating a service department's costs under the step method, one *should* include the service department being allocated in the allocation base.

_____ 4. The direct method of cost allocation is simpler than the step method, in that services provided between service departments are ignored.

_____ 5. The reciprocal method is generally considered to be more accurate than the step method of service department allocation.

_____ 6. When the direct method is used, the order in which service departments are allocated makes a difference.

_____ 7. In the step method, the allocation sequence typically begins with the service department that provides the greatest amount of service to other departments.

_____ 8. Variable costs of service departments should be allocated to operating departments in predetermined, lump-sum amounts.

_____ 9. Budgeted costs, rather than actual costs, should always be allocated from service departments to operating departments.

_____ 10. Sales dollars is a good allocation base because sales dollars are easy to work with and reflect a department's "ability to pay."

Multiple Choice

Choose the best answer or response by placing the identifying letter in the space provided.

The following data are used in multiple choice questions 1 through 6:

Oscar Company has two service departments, Personnel and Custodial, and two operating departments, A and B. Budgeted data for the current year appear below:

	Service Departments		Operating Departments	
	Personnel	Custodial	A	B
Overhead costs ...	$800	$600	$2,000	$5,000
Employees	2	18	30	50
Space occupied (000s of square feet)......	20	10	40	80

Personnel costs are allocated on the basis of employees. Custodial costs are allocated on the basis of space occupied. The company makes no distinction between fixed and variable costs in its service department allocations.

_____ 1. If the direct method of service department allocation is used, how much Personnel Department cost would be allocated to Operating Department A? a) $240; b) $300; c) $0; d) $800.

_____ 2. If the direct method of service department allocation is used, how much Personnel Department cost would be allocated back to the Personnel Department? a) $16; b) $800; c) $0; d) $200.

_____ 3. If the direct method of service department allocation is used, what would be the total overhead cost in Operating Department B after the allocations have been completed? a) $5,900; b) $900; c) $5,000; d) $6,400.

_____ 4. If the step method of service department allocation is used and Personnel Department costs are allocated first, how much Personnel Department cost would be allocated to the Custodial Department? a) $146.94; b) $0; c) $144; d) $200.

_____ 5. If the step method of service department allocation is used and Personnel Department costs are allocated first, how much Custodial Department cost would be allocated to the Personnel Department? a) $80; b) $0; c) $99.59; d) $150.

_____ 6. If the step method of service department allocation is used and Personnel Department costs are allocated first, how much Custodial Department cost would be allocated to Operating Department A? a) $0; b) $150; c) $248.94; d) $171.43.

The following data are used in multiple choice questions 7 through 11:

Data for Wasatch Company's two operating departments follow:

	Budgeted Machine Hours	Peak Period Requirement
Operating Department #1	15,000	40%
Operating Department #2	25,000	60
Total machine-hours	40,000	100%

The Wasatch Company has a Repair Department that serves these two operating departments. The variable repair costs are budgeted at $0.20 per machine-hour. Fixed costs are budgeted at $12,000 per year. Fixed Repair Department costs are allocated to operat-ing departments on the basis of peak period requirements.

At the end of the year, the actual machine-hours worked by the operating departments were 16,000 hours for Department #1 and 24,000 hours for Department #2. The actual Repair Department costs were $8,600 variable and $13,000 fixed.

_____ 7. The amount of variable repair cost allocated to Department #1 at the beginning of the year should be: a) $3,000; b) $5,000; c) $4,800; d) $7,200.

_____ 8. The amount of fixed repair cost allocated to Department #2 at the beginning of the year should be: a) $3,000; b) $5,000; c) $4,800; d) $7,200.

_____ 9. The amount of variable repair cost allocated to Department #1 at the end of the year should be: a) $4,800; b) $5,200; c) $3,200; d) $7,200.

_____ 10. The amount of fixed repair cost allocated to Department #2 at the end of the year should be: a) $4,800; b) $7,800; c) $3,200; d) $7,200.

_____ 11. The amount of actual repair costs not allocated to the operating departments and retained in the Repair Department at the end of the year as a spending variance should be: a) $600; b) $1,600; c) $1,000; d) $1,400.

Chapter 15

Exercises

15-1.   Piney Company has three service departments and two operating departments. Cost and other data relating to these departments follow:

	Service Departments			Operating Departments	
	Janitorial	*Cafeteria*	*Engineering*	*Assembly*	*Finishing*
Overhead costs	$60,000	$42,600	$75,000	$230,000	$300,000
Square feet	1,500	2,000	1,000	4,000	3,000
Number of employees ...	15	12	50	200	400

The company allocates Janitorial costs on the basis of square feet. The Cafeteria and Engineering costs are allocated on the basis of the number of employees. The company makes no distinction between variable and fixed service department costs in its allocations of service department costs.

Allocate service department costs to the operating departments using the step method. The company allocates service department costs in the following order: Janitorial, Cafeteria, then Engineering.

	Service Departments			Operating Departments	
	Janitorial	*Cafeteria*	*Engineering*	*Assembly*	*Finishing*
Overhead costs	$ 60,000	$ 42,600	$ 75,000	$ 230,000	$ 300,000
Allocations:					
Janitorial	_____	_____	_____	_____	_____
Cafeteria		_____	_____	_____	_____
Engineering			_____	_____	_____
Total	$_____	$_____	$_____	$_____	$_____

15-2.   Refer to the data in Exercise 15-1 above. Allocate the service department costs to the operating departments using the direct method.

	Service Departments			Operating Departments	
	Janitorial	*Cafeteria*	*Engineering*	*Assembly*	*Finishing*
Overhead costs	$ 60,000	$ 42,600	$ 75,000	$ 230,000	$ 300,000
Allocations:					
Janitorial	_____			_____	_____
Cafeteria		_____		_____	_____
Engineering			_____	_____	_____
Total	$_____	$_____	$_____	$_____	$_____

186

15-3.   The municipal motor pool provides cars on loan to city employees who must travel on official business. The city has three departments that use this service—Public Safety, General Administration, and Sanitation. Data concerning these departments' annual use of the motor pool (in thousands of miles driven) appear below:

	Public Safety	General Administration	Sanitation
Budgeted use (thousands of miles)	600	800	200
Actual use (thousands of miles)	500	900	250
Peak period requirements	35%	50%	15%

The motor pool's budgeted annual fixed costs are $330,000. Peak period requirements determine the level of the fixed costs. Budgeted variable costs are $80 per thousand miles driven.

a.   How much of the motor pool's budgeted costs should be allocated to Public Safety at the beginning of the year for planning purposes?

b.   Suppose the motor pool's actual costs for the year were $345,000 for fixed costs and $138,000 for variable costs. How much of this actual cost should be allocated to Public Safety at the end of the year for performance evaluation purposes?

Answers to Questions and Exercises

True or False

1. F   The direct method entirely ignores reciprocal services among service departments.

2. T   If the service department being allocated is included in the allocation base, then some of the cost will be allocated back to the service department.

3. F   See the answer to (2) above.

4. T   See Exhibit 15-2.

5. T   The reciprocal method fully accounts for all reciprocal services among service departments.

6. F   The order of allocation doesn't make any difference in the direct method. The order of allocation does, however, make a difference in the step method.

7. T   This statement describes the procedure followed using the step method.

8. F   Fixed costs—not variable costs—should be allocated in predetermined, lump-sums.

9. T   Budgeted, rather than actual, costs should be allocated. The service departments should be held responsible for their own cost control. Allocated actual costs to other departments implicitly holds those other departments responsible for the effectiveness of the service department's cost control efforts.

10. F   Sales dollars is a poor allocation base. All other things equal, a department whose sales increases will be allocated more service department costs. In effect, successful departments are penalized by being allocated more cost.

Multiple Choice

1. b   Allocation base = 30 + 50 = 80
       Allocation: (30/80) × $800 = $300

2. c   Even though the Personnel Department has two employees, none of its costs are charged to itself in the direct method or in the step method.

3. a
Original overhead cost in Operating Department B	$5,000
Allocated Personnel Dept. cost: (50/80) × $800	500
Allocated Custodial Dept. cost: (80/120) × $600	400
Total	$5,900

4. a   Allocation base = 18 + 30 + 50 = 98
       Allocation: (18/98) × $800 = $146.94

5. b   In the step method, once a service department's costs have been allocated, the department is ignored in subsequent allocations.

6. c   This problem requires two steps:

Original Custodial cost	$600.00
Allocated from Personnel*	146.94
Custodial cost to be allocated	$746.94

   *See the answer to question (4) above.

   Allocation base = 40 + 80 = 120
   Allocation: (40/120) × $746.94 = $248.98

7. a   15,000 hours × $0.20 per hour = $3,000.

8. d   60% × $12,000 = $7,200.

9. c   16,000 hours × $0.20 per hour = $3,200. The budgeted rate is still used.

10. d   Fixed costs should be allocated in predetermined, lump-sum amounts and the allocation at the end of the year should be the same as at the beginning of the year.

11. b   The computations are:

Actual costs ($8,600 + $13,000)		$21,600
Allocated costs:		
Variable*	$8,000	
Fixed**	12,000	20,000
Unallocated		$ 1,600

   *(16,000 hrs. + 24,000 hrs.) × $0.20 = $8,000
   ** The budgeted amount

Exercises

15-1.

	Service Departments			Operating Departments	
	Janitorial	*Cafeteria*	*Engineering*	*Assembly*	*Finishing*
Overhead costs	$60,000	$42,600	$75,000	$230,000	$300,000
Allocations:					
Janitorial [1]	(60,000)	12,000	6,000	24,000	18,000
Cafeteria [2]		(54,600)	4,200	16,800	33,600
Engineering [3]			(85,200)	28,400	56,800
Total	$ 0	$ 0	$ 0	$299,200	$408,400

$$^1\ \frac{\text{Janitorial cost}}{\text{Total square feet}} = \frac{\$60,000}{10,000\ \text{square feet}} = \$6 \text{ per square foot}$$

$$^2\ \frac{\text{Cafeteria cost}}{\text{Number of employees}} = \frac{\$54,600}{650\ \text{employees}} = \$84 \text{ per employee}$$

$$^3\ \frac{\text{Engineering cost}}{\text{Number of employees}} = \frac{\$85,200}{600\ \text{employees}} = \$142 \text{ per employee}$$

15-2.

	Service Departments			Operating Departments	
	Janitorial	*Cafeteria*	*Engineering*	*Assembly*	*Finishing*
Overhead costs	$60,000	$42,600	$75,000	$230,000	$300,000
Allocation:					
Janitorial [1]	(60,000)			34,286	25,714
Cafeteria [2]		(42,600)		14,200	28,400
Engineering [3]			(75,000)	25,000	50,000
Total	$ 0	$ 0	$ 0	$303,486	$404,114

$$^1\ \frac{\text{Janitorial cost}}{\text{Total square feet}} = \frac{\$60,000}{7,000\ \text{square feet}} = \$8.57 \text{ per square foot}$$

$$^2\ \frac{\text{Cafeteria cost}}{\text{Number of employees}} = \frac{\$42,600}{600\ \text{employees}} = \$71 \text{ per employee}$$

$$^3\ \frac{\text{Engineering cost}}{\text{Number of employees}} = \frac{\$75,000}{600\ \text{employees}} = \$125 \text{ per employee}$$

15-3. a. Variable cost allocation:

        Budgeted rate × Budgeted activity

            $80 per thousand miles × 600 thousand miles .... $ 48,000

        Fixed cost allocation:

        Budgeted fixed cost × Percentage of peak period needs

            $330,000 × 35% 115,500

        Total $163,500

    b. Variable cost allocation:

        Budgeted rate × Actual activity

            $80 per thousand miles × 500 thousand miles .... $ 40,000

        Fixed cost allocation:

        Budgeted fixed cost × Percentage of peak period needs

            $330,000 × 35% 115,500

        Total $155,500

Note that the fixed cost allocation is the same at the end of the period as it was at the beginning of the period.

Chapter 16

"How Well Am I Doing?"— Statement of Cash Flows

Chapter Study Suggestions

✳

This chapter explains how to prepare a statement of cash flows. The statement of cash flows is constructed by examining changes in balance sheet accounts. The chapter contains three key exhibits. The first, Exhibit 16-2, classifies changes in balance sheet accounts as sources and uses of cash. The second key exhibit is Exhibit 16-7, which provides guidelines for classifying transactions as operating, investing, and financing activities. Once transactions have been classified as sources or uses and as operating, investing, or financing activities, a statement of cash flows can be easily constructed. However, you must keep track of many details. Therefore, we recommend a systematic approach based on a worksheet such as the one in Exhibit 16-10.

CHAPTER HIGHLIGHTS

A.   The purpose of the statement of cash flows is to highlight the major activities that have provided and used cash during the period.

B.   The term *cash* on the statement of cash flows is broadly defined to include both cash and cash equivalents. Cash equivalents consist of short-term, highly liquid investments such as Treasury bills, commercial paper, and money market funds that are made solely for the purpose of generating a return on temporarily idle cash.

C.   A period's net cash flow is equal to the change in the cash account during the period. Exhibit 16-1 shows that the change in cash during a period can be expressed in terms of the changes in all of the noncash balance sheet accounts. The statement of cash flows is based on this fact. The statement is basically a listing of changes in the noncash balance sheet accounts.

D.   Changes in noncash account balances can be classified as *sources* and *uses*. On the statement of cash flows, sources increase cash flow and uses reduce cash flow.

  1.   The following are classified as sources:

   a.   Net income.

   b.   Decreases in noncash assets.

   c.   Increases in liabilities.

   d.   Increases in capital stock accounts.

  2.   The following are classified as uses:

   a.   Increases in noncash assets.

   b.   Decreases in liabilities.

   c.   Decreases in capital stock accounts.

   d.   Dividends paid to stockholders.

  3.   The sources and uses usually make intuitive sense. For example, an increase in inventory (a noncash asset) implicitly requires cash and is considered to be a use.

E.   The FASB requires that the statement of cash flows be divided into three sections. These sections relate to *operating activities, investing activities, and financing activities.*

  1.   As a general rule, operating activities directly or indirectly affect net income. These activities include:

   a.   Net income (or net loss).

   b.   Changes in current assets.

   c.   Changes in noncurrent assets that affect net income, such as depreciation and amortization.

   d.   Changes in current liabilities (except for debts to lenders and dividends).

   e.   Changes in noncurrent liabilities that affect net income, such as interest on debt.

  2.   Investing activities consist of changes in noncurrent assets that are not included in net income.

  3.   Financing activities consist of transactions that involve borrowing from creditors (other than the payment of interest), and transactions that involve the owners of the company. Specific financing activities include:

   a.   Changes in current liabilities that are debts to lenders rather than obligations to suppliers, employees, or government.

   b.   Changes in noncurrent liabilities that are not included in net income.

   c.   Changes in capital stock accounts.

   d.   Dividends paid to the company's stockholders.

F.   Companies sometimes acquire assets or dispose of liabilities through *direct exchange transactions*.

  1.   Examples of direct exchange transactions include issuing capital stock in exchange for property and equipment and converting long-term debt into common stock.

  2.   Direct exchanges that affect only non-current balance sheet accounts are not reported on the statement of cash flows. Instead, they are disclosed in a separate schedule.

G.   In some cases, the net change in an account is shown on the statement of cash flows. In other cases, the increases and decreases are disclosed separately. The treatment depends on whether the change appears in the operating activities section or in the investing and financing activities sections.

  1.   For both financing and investing activities, items on the statement of cash flows must be presented in gross amounts rather than in net amounts. For example, if a company buys $100,000 of new equipment and sells $30,000 of used equipment, both amounts must be disclosed rather than the net effect of a $70,000 increase in the equipment account.

2. For operating activities, only the net change in an account is shown on the statement of cash flows.

H. The net result of the cash inflows and outflows arising from operating activities is referred to as the *net cash provided by operating activities*. This figure can be computed using the *direct method* or the *indirect method*.

1. Under the direct method, the income statement is reconstructed on a cash basis from top to bottom. This method is covered in Appendix 16A.

2. Under the indirect method, the net cash provided by operations is computed by starting with net income and adjusting it to a cash basis. The steps to follow in this adjustment process are shown in Exhibit 16-8.

3. The direct and indirect methods yield exactly the same amount for the net cash provided by operating activities.

I. Carefully study Exhibit 16-10, which illustrates the mechanics of putting together a worksheet. Make sure you understand each of the entries on this worksheet. Once this worksheet has been completed, the statement of cash flows can be easily constructed.

J. Carefully study Exhibit 16-12, which illustrates the format of the statement of cash flows. Trace each of the entries from the worksheet in Exhibit 16-10 to the statement of cash flows in Exhibit 16-12.

Appendix 16A: The Direct Method

A. The direct method differs from the indirect method only in the operating activities section of the statement of cash flows. The investing and financing activities sections of the statement are identical for the direct and indirect methods.

B. In the indirect method, the income statement is reconstructed from the top down by converting it to a cash basis.

1. To adjust revenue to a cash basis:

    •   Subtract (add) any increase (decrease) in accounts receivable.

2. To adjust cost of goods sold to a cash basis:

    •   Add (subtract) any increase (decrease) in inventory.

    •   Subtract (add) any increase (decrease) in accounts payable.

3. To adjust operating expenses to a cash basis:

    •   Add (subtract) any increase (decrease) in prepaid expenses.

    •   Subtract (add) any increase (decrease) in accrued liabilities.

    •   Subtract the period's depreciation and amortization charges.

4. To adjust income tax expense to a cash basis:

    •   Subtract (add) any increase (decrease) in taxes payable.

    •   Subtract (add) any increase (decrease) in deferred taxes.

Chapter 16

REVIEW AND SELF-TEST
Questions and Exercises

True or False

Enter a T or an F in the blank to indicate whether the statement is true or false.

___ 1. Dividends received on stock held as an investment are included in the operating activities section of the statement of cash flows.

___ 2. Interest paid on amounts borrowed is included in the financing activities section of the statement of cash flows.

___ 3. Lending money to another entity (such as to a subsidiary) is classified as a financing activity.

___ 4. Paying cash dividends to the company's stockholders is classified as a financing activity.

___ 5. Transactions involving all forms of debt, including accounts payable, short-term borrowing, and long-term borrowing, are classified as financing activities on the statement of cash flows.

___ 6. For both financing and investing activities, items on the statement of cash flows should be presented gross rather than net.

___ 7. The direct and indirect methods can yield different figures for the net cash provided by operating activities.

___ 8. Only changes in noncurrent accounts are analyzed for a statement of cash flows.

___ 9. If a company is profitable, the net cash flow must be positive.

___ 10. (Appendix 16A) The income statement is reconstructed on a cash basis from top to bottom under the direct method of computing the net cash provided by operating activities.

___ 11. (Appendix 16A) In computing the net cash provided by operating activities, depreciation is added to net income under the indirect method, but it is deducted from operating expenses under the direct method.

Multiple Choice

Choose the best answer or response by placing the identifying letter in the space provided.

___ 1. For purposes of constructing a statement of cash flows, an increase in inventory would be classified as: a) a source and an operating activity; b) a use and an operating activity; c) a source and an investing activity; d) a use and an investing activity.

___ 2. An increase in accounts payable would be classified as: a) a source and an operating activity; b) a use and an operating activity; c) a source and a financing activity; d) a use and a financing activity.

___ 3. An increase in bonds payable would be classified as: a) a source and an investing activity; b) a use and an investing activity; c) a source and a financing activity; d) a use and a financing activity.

___ 4. An increase in long-term investments would be classified as: a) a source and an investing activity; b) a use and an investing activity; c) a source and a financing activity; d) a use and a financing activity.

___ 5. Cash dividends paid to the company's stockholders would be classified as: a) a source and an operating activity; b) a use and an operating activity; c) a source and a financing activity; d) a use and a financing activity.

___ 6. An increase in the company's common stock account would be classified as: a) a source and an investing activity; b) a use and an investing activity; c) a source and a financing activity; d) a use and a financing activity.

Exercises

16-1. Ingall Company's comparative balance sheet and income statement for the most recent year follow:

INGALL COMPANY
Comparative Balance Sheet
(dollars in millions)

	Ending Balance	Beginning Balance
Assets		
Cash	$ 14	$ 10
Accounts receivable	21	15
Inventory	50	43
Prepaid expenses	2	6
Plant and equipment	190	140
Less accumulated depreciation	(65)	(54)
Long-term investments	70	90
Total assets	$282	$250
Liabilities and Stockholders' Equity		
Accounts payable	$ 26	$ 25
Accrued liabilities	10	12
Taxes payable	13	18
Bonds payable	50	40
Deferred income taxes	36	31
Common stock	80	70
Retained earnings	67	54
Total liabilities and stockholders' equity	$282	$250

INGALL COMPANY
Income Statement
(dollars in millions)

Sales	$230
Less cost of goods sold	120
Gross margin	110
Less operating expenses	70
Net operating income	40
Gain on sale of long-term investments	5
Income before taxes	45
Less income taxes	14
Net income	$ 31

Notes: Dividends of $18 million were declared and paid during the year. The gain on sale of long-term investments was from the sale of investments for $25 million in cash. These investments had an original cost of $20 million. There were no retirements or disposals of plant or equipment during the year.

Using the blank form on the following page, prepare a worksheet like Exhibit 16-10 for Ingall Company.

INGALL COMPANY
Statement of Cash Flows Worksheet

	Change	Source or use?	Cash Flow Effect	Adjust- ments	Adjusted Effect	Classi- fication
Assets (except cash and cash equivalents)						
Current assets:						
Accounts receivable						
Inventory						
Prepaid expenses						
Noncurrent assets:						
Plant and equipment						
Long-term investments						
Liabilities, Contra-Assets, and Stockholders' Equity						
Contra-assets:						
Accumulated depreciation						
Current liabilities:						
Accounts payable						
Accrued liabilities						
Taxes payable						
Noncurrent liabilities:						
Bonds payable						
Deferred income taxes						
Stockholders' equity:						
Common stock						
Retained earnings						
Net income						
Dividends						
Additional Entries						
Proceeds from sale of long-term investments						
Gain on sale of long-term investments ..						
Total (net cash flow)						

16-2. Determine Ingall Company's net cash provided by operating activities using the indirect method.

Net income		$_____
Adjustments to convert net income to a cash basis:		
Depreciation charges	_____	
_____ in accounts receivable	_____	
_____ in inventory	_____	
_____ in prepaid expenses	_____	
_____ in accounts payable	_____	
_____ in accrued liabilities	_____	
_____ in taxes payable	_____	
_____ in deferred taxes	_____	
Gain on sale of long-term investments	_____	_____
Net cash flow provided by (used in) operations		$_____

16-3. (Appendix 16A) Using the direct method, determine Ingall Company's net cash provided by operating activities.

Sales	$ 230	
Adjustments to convert sales to a cash basis:		
_____ in accounts receivable	_____	$ _____
Cost of goods sold	120	
Adjustments to convert cost of goods sold to a cash basis:		
_____ in inventory	_____	
_____ in accounts payable	_____	_____
Operating expenses	70	
Adjustments to convert operating expenses to a cash basis:		
_____ in prepaid expenses	_____	
_____ in accrued liabilities	_____	
Depreciation charges	_____	_____
Income taxes	14	
Adjustments to convert income taxes to a cash basis:		
_____ in taxes payable	_____	
_____ in deferred taxes	_____	_____
Net cash provided by (used in) operating activities		$_____

16-4. Prepare a statement of cash flows for Ingall Company using the form below.

INGALL COMPANY
Statement of Cash Flows

Operating activities

Net cash provided by (used in) operating activities .... $_____

Investing activities

_____................. $_____

_____.................   _____

Net cash provided by (used in) investing activities ....   _____

Financing activities

_____.................   _____

_____.................   _____

_____.................   _____

Net cash provided by (used in) financing activities ....   _____

Net increase (decrease) in cash ....   _____

Cash balance, beginning ....   _____

Cash balance, ending .... $_____

Answers to Questions and Exercises

True or False

1. T Dividends received enter into the determination of net income and therefore are included in operating rather than investing activities.

2. F Interest paid on amounts borrowed is included in operating activities since interest enters into net income.

3. F Lending money to another entity is classified as an investing activity.

4. T Dividends do not affect net income and therefore are not considered to be an operating activity.

5. F Transactions involving accounts payable are included among operating activities—not financing activities.

6. T Only transactions involving operating activities are presented in net amounts.

7. F The direct and indirect methods will always yield exactly the same figure for the net cash provided by operating activities.

8. F Changes in all noncash accounts, current as well as noncurrent, are analyzed when preparing a statement of cash flows.

9. F The net cash flow may be negative even if a company is profitable. For example, a profitable company may make a major investment using cash reserves it has accumulated in the past.

10. T See Exhibit 16A-1 for an example.

11. T Subtracting depreciation from an expense is equivalent to adding it to net income.

Multiple Choice

1. b Inventory is a current asset. Increases in current assets are classified as uses. Changes in current assets are considered to be the result of operating activities.

2. a Accounts payable is a current liability. Increases in current liabilities are classified as sources. Changes in current liabilities are considered to be the result of operating activities.

3. c Bonds payable is a noncurrent liability. An increase in a noncurrent liability is considered to be a source. A change in a noncurrent liability is considered to be a financing activity unless it enters into net income.

4. b Long-term investments is a noncurrent asset account. An increase in a noncurrent asset is considered to be a use. A change in a noncurrent asset is considered to be an investing activity unless it directly enters into the determination of net income.

5. d Dividends are considered to be a use. They are classified as a financing activity since they do not enter into the determination of net income.

6. c An increase in the common stock account is considered to be a source and a financing activity.

Exercises

16-1. The completed worksheet for Ingall Company appears below:

	Change	Source or use?	Cash Flow Effect	Adjust- ments	Adjusted Effect	Classi- fication*
Assets (except cash and cash equivalents)						
Current assets:						
Accounts receivable	+6	Use	-6		-6	Operating
Inventory	+7	Use	-7		-7	Operating
Prepaid expenses	-4	Source	+4		+4	Operating
Noncurrent assets:						
Plant and equipment	+50	Use	-50		-50	Investing
Long-term investments	-20	Source	+20	-20	0	Investing
Liabilities, Contra-Assets, and Stockholders' Equity						
Contra-assets:						
Accumulated depreciation	+11	Source	+11		+11	Operating
Current liabilities:						
Accounts payable	+1	Source	+1		+1	Operating
Accrued liabilities	-2	Use	-2		-2	Operating
Taxes payable	-5	Use	-5		-5	Operating
Noncurrent liabilities:						
Bonds payable	+10	Source	+10		+10	Financing
Deferred income taxes	+5	Source	+5		+5	Operating
Stockholders' equity:						
Common stock	+10	Source	+10		+10	Financing
Retained earnings						
Net income	+31	Source	+31		+31	Operating
Dividends	-18	Use	-18		-18	Financing
Additional Entries						
Proceeds from sale of						
long-term investments				+25	+25	Investing
Gain on sale of long-term						
investments			___	-5	-5	Operating
Total (net cash flow)			+4	0	+4	

Note: The most difficult part of this worksheet is the adjustment for the sale of the long-term investments. Basically, the adjustment moves the gain on the sale from the operating activities section to the investing section. It would be wise to pay particular attention to this entry and how it affects the statement of cash flows.

16-2.   The operating activities section of the statement of cash flows constructed using the indirect method appears below:

Net income		$31
Adjustments to convert net income to a cash basis:		
Depreciation charges	$11	
Increase in accounts receivable	(6)	
Increase in inventory	(7)	
Decrease in prepaid expenses	4	
Increase in accounts payable	1	
Decrease in accrued liabilities	(2)	
Decrease in taxes payable	(5)	
Increase in deferred taxes	5	
Gain on sale of long-term investments	(5)	(4)
Net cash flow provided by operations		$27

Note that the gain on sale of long-term investments is deducted from net income. This removes the gain from the operating activities section of the statement of cash flows. The gain will show up implicitly in the investing activities section of the statement of cash flows. See the solution to 16-4 below.

16-3.   The direct method can be used to arrive at the same answer as in 16-2 above.

Sales	$230	
Adjustments to convert sales to a cash basis:		
Increase in accounts receivable	(6)	$224
Cost of goods sold	120	
Adjustments to convert cost of goods sold to a cash basis:		
Increase in inventory	7	
Increase in accounts payable	(1)	126
Operating expenses	70	
Adjustments to convert operating expenses to a cash basis:		
Decrease in prepaid expenses	(4)	
Decrease in accrued liabilities	2	
Depreciation charges	(11)	57
Income taxes	14	
Adjustments to convert income taxes to a cash basis:		
Decrease in taxes payable	5	
Increase in deferred taxes	(5)	14
Net cash provided by operating activities		$ 27

16-4.

INGALL COMPANY
Statement of Cash Flows

Operating activities
Net cash provided by operating activities .... $ 27

Investing activities
    Proceeds from sale of long-term investments $25
    Increase in plant and equipment .... (50)
Net cash used for investing activities .... (25)

Financing activities
    Increase in bonds payable 10
    Increase in common stock 10
    Dividends .... (18)
Net cash provided by financing activities 2

Net increase in cash 4
Cash balance, beginning 10
Cash balance, ending $14

Chapter 17

"How Well Am I Doing?"— Financial Statement Analysis

Chapter Study Suggestions

✳

The chapter is divided into two parts. The first part discusses the preparation and use of statements in comparative and common-size form. This part of the chapter is easy and involves nothing more complicated than computing percentages. Your study in this part should be focused on Exhibits 17-1, 17-2, and 17-4 in the text. These exhibits show how statements in comparative and common-size form are prepared.

The second part of the chapter deals with ratio analysis. Altogether, seventeen ratios are presented in this part of the chapter. You should memorize the formula for each ratio since it is likely that you will be expected to know these formulas on exams. This may at first seem like an overwhelming task, but most of the ratios are intuitive and easy to compute. You should also learn how to interpret each ratio. Exhibit 17-7 in the text provides a compact summary of the ratios.

CHAPTER HIGHLIGHTS

A. Financial statement analysis is concerned with assessing the financial condition of a company.

   1. To be most useful, comparisons should be made from one year to another, as well as with other companies within the same industry.

   2. The analyst must be careful not to rely just on financial statement analysis in making a judgment about a company.

     a. The ratios should be viewed as a starting point for analysis rather than as an end in themselves. They indicate what should be pursued in greater depth.

     b. One problem is that companies may use different accounting methods such as LIFO or FIFO and these differences in accounting methods may make comparisons difficult.

     c. Another problem is that the ratios are based on accounting data that really only show what has happened in the past, which may not be a reliable guide to what is going to happen in the future.

B. Three common analytical techniques for financial statement analysis are: 1) dollar and percentage changes on statements (horizontal analysis); 2) common-size statements (vertical analysis); and 3) ratios.

   1. In horizontal analysis two or more yearly statements are placed side by side and changes between years are analyzed. These comparisons are made both in terms of dollars and percentage changes from year to year.

     a. Showing changes in dollar form helps to identify the most significant changes.

     b. Showing changes in percentage form helps to identify the most unusual changes.

     c. Trend percentages are often computed. Each item, such as sales or net income, is stated as a percentage of the same item in a base year.

   2. In a common-size statement, amounts on the balance sheet are stated as a percentage of total assets and amounts on the income statement are stated as a percentage of sales. Showing the balance sheet and the income statement in common-size form helps show the relative importance of the various items and makes it easier to compare companies. Preparation of common-size statements is known as vertical analysis.

   3. The *gross margin percentage* is a particularly important item on the common-size income statement. It is defined as follows:

$$\text{Gross margin percentage} = \frac{\text{Gross margin}}{\text{Sales}}$$

The gross margin percentage is a rough measure of the overall profitability of a company's products. In manufacturing companies, the gross margin percentage should increase as sales increase since fixed manufacturing costs are spread across more units.

   4. In addition to horizontal and vertical analysis, stockholders, short-term creditors, and long-term creditors use a variety of ratios to help them evaluate companies. Ratios that are designed to meet the needs of these three different groups are discussed in sections C, D, and E below.

C. Several ratios provide measures of how well the company is doing from the stockholders' perspective.

   1. *Earnings per share* is an important measure of the annual earnings available for common stockholders. The formula is:

$$\frac{\text{Earnings}}{\text{per share}} = \frac{\text{Net income-Preferred dividends}}{\text{Average number of common shares outstanding}}$$

Preferred dividends are subtracted from net income since they are not an expense on the income statement but reduce the earnings that can be distributed to common stockholders.

   2. The *price-earnings ratio* shows the relation between the market price of a share of stock and the stock's current earnings per share. The price-earnings ratio is computed as follows:

$$\text{Price-earnings ratio} = \frac{\text{Market price per share}}{\text{Earnings per share}}$$

Price-earnings ratios tend to be similar for companies in the same industry. One of the biggest factors affecting the price-earnings ratio is future earnings growth. If investors believe one company is likely to have higher future earnings growth than another, they will bid up the price of the stock with a higher expected future earnings growth and hence it will have a high price-earnings ratio.

   3. The *dividend payout ratio* gauges the proportion of current earnings being paid out as dividends. The formula is:

$$\text{Dividend payout ratio} = \frac{\text{Dividends per share}}{\text{Earnings per share}}$$

A company with a high dividend payout ratio is paying out most of its earnings to stockholders as dividends rather than reinvesting the earnings in the company.

4. The d*ividend yield ratio* measures the cash yield on the common stockholder's investment. The ratio is computed as follows:

$$\text{Dividend yield ratio} = \frac{\text{Dividends per share}}{\text{Market price per share}}$$

Investors hope to profit from both dividends and increases in the market value of the stock they own. The dividend yield measures only the contribution of the dividends. Note that the current market price per share is used in this ratio and not the price the investor originally paid for the shares.

5. The *return on total assets* is a measure of how effectively a company has used its assets. The formula is:

$$\text{Return on total assets} = \frac{\text{Net income} + \left[\begin{array}{c}\text{Interest expense} \times \\ (1\text{-Tax rate})\end{array}\right]}{\text{Average total assets}}$$

a. Note that interest expense is placed on an after-tax basis by multiplying it by one minus the tax rate before being added back to net income.

b. Interest expense is added back to net income to show earnings *before* any distributions have been made to creditors and stockholders. This adjustment results in a total return on assets that measures operating performance independently of how the assets were financed.

6. The *return on common stockholders' equity* measures a company's ability to generate income. The formula is:

$$\text{Return on common stockholders' equity} = \frac{\text{Net income} - \text{Preferred dividends}}{\text{Average common stockholders' equity}}$$

As with earnings per share, preferred dividends are subtracted from net income since preferred dividends reduce the earnings available to common stockholders. The return on common stockholders' equity is often higher than the return on total assets because of financial leverage.

a. *Financial leverage* involves purchasing assets with funds obtained from creditors or from preferred stockholders. If the assets in which the funds are invested earn a greater return than the rate of return required by the suppliers of the funds, then financial leverage is *positive*. Financial leverage is *negative* if

the assets earn a return that is less than the rate of return required by creditors.

b. Sources of leverage include long-term debt, preferred stock, and current liabilities.

7. The *book value per share* measures the common stockholders' equity on a per share basis. The formula is:

$$\frac{\text{Book value}}{\text{per share}} = \frac{\text{Common stockholders' equity}}{\begin{array}{c}\text{Number of common} \\ \text{shares outstanding}\end{array}}$$

a. Note that the denominator in this ratio is the number of common shares outstanding at the end of the year—not the average number of shares outstanding over the year as in the earnings per share calculation.

b. Book value per share is usually less than market value per share. Market value reflects investors' expectations concerning future earnings and dividends. By contrast, book value measures financial effects of already completed transactions. Because of this orientation toward the past, book value is of limited usefulness.

D. Short-term creditors are concerned with being paid on time and are far more concerned with a company's financial assets and cash flows than with its accounting net income.

1. *Working capital* measures the excess of current assets over current liabilities.

$$\text{Working capital} = \frac{\text{Current}}{\text{assets}} - \frac{\text{Current}}{\text{liabilities}}$$

Negative working capital signals that current assets are insufficient to cover current liabilities.

2. The *current ratio* is also a widely used measure of short-term debt-paying ability. The formula is:

$$\text{Current ratio} = \frac{\text{Current assets}}{\text{Current liabilities}}$$

The current ratio, as well as working capital, should be interpreted with care. The *composition* of the assets and liabilities is very important. A high current ratio does not necessarily mean that the company is easily able to pay its current liabilities. For example, most of the current assets may be inventory that is difficult to sell quickly.

3. The *acid-test* or *quick ratio* is designed to measure how well a company can meet its short-term obligations using only its *most liquid* current assets. The formula is:

Chapter 17

$$\text{Acid-test ratio} = \frac{\text{Cash} + \text{Marketable securities} + \text{Current receivables}}{\text{Current liabilities}}$$

Current receivables includes accounts receivable and short-term notes receivable. The current assets in this ratio do not include inventories or prepaid assets since they may be difficult to convert into cash.

4. The *accounts receivable turnover* ratio measures the relation between sales on account and accounts receivable. The formula is:

$$\text{Accounts receivable turnover} = \frac{\text{Sales on account}}{\text{Average accounts receivable balance}}$$

The higher this ratio, the quicker accounts receivable are collected. This is easier to see if the accounts receivable turnover is divided into 365 days. This gives the *average collection period*, which is computed as follows:

$$\text{Average collection period} = \frac{365 \text{ days}}{\text{Accounts receivable turnover}}$$

As its name implies, the average collection period indicates the average number of days required to collect credit sales. Ordinarily a short average collection period is desirable.

5. The *inventory turnover* ratio relates cost of goods sold to the average inventory balance using the following formula:

$$\text{Inventory turnover} = \frac{\text{Cost of goods sold}}{\text{Average inventory balance}}$$

The higher this ratio, the quicker inventory is sold. The *average sale period* measures how many days on average it takes to sell inventory. The formula is:

$$\text{Average sale period} = \frac{365 \text{ days}}{\text{Inventory turnover}}$$

The average sale period can differ dramatically from one industry to another. For example, the average sale period is much shorter in a florist shop than in a jewelry shop. Florists have to sell their inventory quickly or it will perish.

E. Long-term creditors are concerned with both the near-term and the long-term ability of a company to repay its debts.

1. The *times interest earned ratio* gauges the ability of a company to pay the interest it owes. The formula is:

$$\text{Times interest earned} = \frac{\text{Earnings before interest expense and income taxes}}{\text{Interest expense}}$$

Generally, the higher the times interest earned, the greater the ability of the company to make interest payments.

2. The *debt-to-equity ratio* relates debt to equity using the following formula:

$$\text{Debt-to-equity ratio} = \frac{\text{Total liabilities}}{\text{Stockholders' equity}}$$

The lower this ratio, the greater the excess of assets over liabilities. Therefore creditors generally prefer a low debt-to-equity ratio since this provides a large cushion of protection.

REVIEW AND SELF-TEST
Questions and Exercises

True or False

Enter a T or an F in the blank to indicate whether the statement is true or false.

____ 1. Horizontal analysis uses dollar and percentage changes from year to year to highlight trends.

____ 2. Common-size statements focus on companies of similar size and operations.

____ 3. The current ratio is current assets less current liabilities.

____ 4. Trend percentages in financial statements would be an example of vertical analysis.

____ 5. A common-size statement shows items in percentage form, with each item stated as a percentage of a total of which that item is a part.

____ 6. Earnings per share is computed by deducting preferred dividends from net income and dividing the result by the number of common shares outstanding.

____ 7. If earnings remain unchanged and the price-earnings ratio goes up, then the market price of the stock must have gone down.

____ 8. Dividing the market price of a share of stock by the dividends per share gives the price-earnings ratio.

____ 9. Book value per share is not a good predictor of future earnings potential.

____ 10. The acid test ratio excludes inventories from current assets.

____ 11. When computing the return on total assets, after-tax interest expense is subtracted from net income.

____ 12. Inventory turnover is computed by dividing sales by average inventory.

____ 13. If a company's return on total assets is substantially higher than its cost of borrowing, then the common stockholders would normally want the company to have a high debt-to-equity ratio.

Multiple Choice

Choose the best answer or response by placing the identifying letter in the space provided.

____ 1. Artway Corporation's net income last year was $200,000. It paid dividends of $50,000 to the owners of the company's preferred stock. A total of 10,000 shares of common stock were outstanding throughout the year. What was the company's earnings per share for the year? a) $20; b) $5; c) $15; d) $25.

____ 2. Carston Corporation's earnings per share is $3.50 and its market price per share is $28. There are 1 million shares of common stock outstanding. What is the company's price-earnings ratio? a) 43.75; b) 4.375; c) 80.0; d) 8.0.

____ 3. Refer to the data for Carston Corporation in question 2 above. Assume in addition that the company pays an annual dividend of $2.17 per share. What is the company's dividend payout ratio? a) 62%; b) 7.75%; c) 217%; d) 8.9%.

____ 4. Refer again to the data for Carston Corporation in questions 2 and 3 above. What is the company's dividend yield ratio? a) 62%; b) 7.75%; c) 217%; d) 8.9%.

____ 5. Darsden Corporation's net income last year was $800,000; its average assets were $4,000,000; its interest expense was $200,000; and its tax rate was 30%. What was the company's return on total assets? a) 23.5%; b) 25%; c) 16.5%; d) 30%.

____ 6. Kristal Corporation's net income last year was $600,000. The company paid preferred dividends of $200,000 to the owners of its preferred stock. The average common stockholders' equity was $5,000,000. What was the company's return on common stockholders' equity? a) 12%; b) 4%; c) 10%; d) 8%.

____ 7. Harrison Corporation's common stockholders' equity is $24 million. There are 6 million shares of common stock and 2 million shares of preferred stock outstanding. What is the company's book value per share? a) $3.00; b) $4.00; c) $6.00; d) $2.40.

____ 8. J.J. Corporation's current assets are $6 million and its current liabilities are $2 million. What is the company's working capital? a) $6 million; b) $2 million; c) $4 million; d) $8 million.

____ 9. Refer to the data for J.J. Corporation in question 8 above. What is the company's current ratio? a) 3.0 to 1; b) 2.0 to 1; c) 0.33 to 1; d) 0.50 to 1.

____ 10. Refer to the data for J.J. Corporation in question 8 above. Assume in addition that the company has $1 million in cash and marketable securities and $1.2 million in current receivables. What is the company's acid-test ratio? a) 0.8; b) 1.0; c) 1.2 ; d) 1.1.

____ 11. Proctor Corporation had $25 million of credit sales last year and its average accounts receivable balance was $5 million. What was the company's average collection period? a) 73 days; b) 5 days; c) 20 days; d) 84 days.

____ 12. Larimart Corporation's cost of goods sold last year was $750,000 and its average inventory balance was $300,000. What was the company's average days to sell inventory? a) 2.5 days; b) 5 days; c) 146 days; d) 912.5 days.

____ 13. Bresser Corporation's earnings before taxes last year was $42,000 and its interest expense was $6,000. What was the company's times interest earned? a) 12.5; b) 1.25; c) 80; d) 8.0.

____ 14. Nupper Corporation's total liabilities are $320,000 and its stockholders' equity is $400,000. What is the company's debt-to-equity ratio? a) 0.2; b) 1.25; c) 0.8; d) 5.

____ 15. The acid-test ratio: a) can be expected to be less than the current ratio; b) can be expected to be greater than the current ratio; c) could be either greater or less than the current ratio; d) none of these.

Exercises

17-1. The financial statements of Amfac, Inc., are given below for the just completed year (This Year) and for the previous year (Last Year):

AMFAC, INC.
Balance Sheet
December 31

Assets

	This Year	Last Year
Cash	$ 8,000	$ 10,000
Accounts receivable, net	36,000	34,000
Inventory	40,000	32,000
Prepaid expenses	2,000	1,000
Plant and equipment, net	214,000	173,000
Total Assets	$300,000	$250,000

Liabilities & Equities

	This Year	Last Year
Current liabilities	$ 40,000	$ 30,000
Long-term liabilities	60,000	40,000
Preferred stock	50,000	50,000
Common stock	30,000	30,000
Retained earnings	120,000	100,000
Total liabilities and equity	$300,000	$250,000

AMFAC, INC.
Income Statement
For the Year Ended December 31

	This Year
Sales (all on account)	$450 000
Cost of goods sold	270,000
Gross margin	180,000
Operating expenses	129,000
Net operating income	51,000
Interest expense	6,000
Net income before taxes	45,000
Income taxes (30%)	13,500
Net Income	$ 31,500

Preferred dividends were $4,000 this year.

Compute the following ratios for this year:

a.   Current ratio.

b.   Acid-test ratio.

c.   Debt-to-equity ratio.

d.   Average collection period.

e.   Inventory turnover.

f.   Times interest earned.

g.   Return on total assets.

h.   Return on common stockholders' equity.

i.   Is financial leverage positive or negative? Explain.

_____

_____

_____

_____

17-2. Cartwright Company has reported the following data relating to sales and accounts receivable in its most recent annual report

	Year 5	Year 4	Year 3	Year 2	Year 1
Sales	$700,000	$675,000	$650,000	$575,000	$500,000
Accounts receivable	$72,000	$60,000	$52,000	$46,000	$40,000

Express the data above in trend percentages. Use Year 1 as the base year.

	Year 5	Year 4	Year 3	Year 2	Year 1
Sales	_____	_____	_____	_____	_____
Accounts receivable	_____	_____	_____	_____	_____

Comment on the significant information revealed by your trend percentages:

_____

_____

_____

_____

17-3.   Consider the following comparative income statements of Eldredge Company, a jewelry design and manufacturing company:

ELDREDGE COMPANY
Income Statements
For the Years Ended December 31

	This Year	Last Year
Sales	$600,000	$500,000
Cost of goods sold	420,000	331,000
Gross margin	180,000	169,000
Operating expenses:		
Selling expenses	87,000	72,500
Administrative expenses	46,800	51,000
Total operating expenses	133,800	123,500
Net operating income	46,200	45,500
Interest expense	1,200	1,500
Net income before taxes	45,000	44,000
Income taxes	13,500	13,200
Net Income	$ 31,500	$ 30,800

a.   Express the income statements for both years in common-size percentages. Round percentages to one decimal point.

	This Year	Last Year
Sales	_____	_____
Cost of goods sold	_____	_____
Gross margin	_____	_____
Operating expenses:		
Selling expenses	_____	_____
Administrative expenses	_____	_____
Total operating expenses	_____	_____
Net operating income	_____	_____
Interest expense	_____	_____
Net income before taxes	_____	_____
Income taxes	_____	_____
Net Income	_____	_____

b.   Comment briefly on the changes between the two years.

_____

_____

_____

_____

Answers to Questions and Exercises

True or False

1. T This is true by definition.

2. F A common-size statement shows items in percentage form. Each item is stated as a percentage of some total of which that item is a part.

3. F The current ratio is current assets *divided* by current liabilities.

4. F Trend percentages would be an example of horizontal analysis.

5. T This point is discussed in connection with question 2 above.

6. T True by definition.

7. F The opposite is true. If the price-earnings ratio goes up, then the stock is selling for a higher market price per dollar of earnings.

8. F Dividing the market price of a share of stock by the earnings per share gives the price-earnings ratio.

9. T Book value per share is the balance sheet carrying value of completed transactions—it tells little about the future.

10. T Inventories are excluded because they may be difficult to quickly convert to cash.

11. F When computing the total return on assets, the after-tax interest expense is *added back* to net income to remove its effect.

12. F Inventory turnover is computed by dividing cost of goods sold by average inventory.

13. T If a company's return on total assets is higher than its cost of borrowing, then financial leverage is positive. Common stockholders would want the company to use this positive financial leverage to their advantage by having a high amount of debt in the company.

Multiple Choice

1. c The computations are:

$$\text{Earnings per share} = \frac{\text{Net income-Preferred dividends}}{\text{Average number of common shares outstanding}}$$

$$\frac{\$200,000-\$50,000}{10,000} = \$15$$

2. d The computations are:

$$\text{Price-earnings ratio} = \frac{\text{Market price per share}}{\text{Earnings per share}}$$

$$\frac{\$28.00}{\$3.50} = 8.0$$

3. a The computations are:

$$\text{Dividend payout ratio} = \frac{\text{Dividends per share}}{\text{Earnings per share}}$$

$$\frac{\$2.17}{\$3.50} = 62.0\%$$

4. b The computations are:

$$\text{Dividend yield ratio} = \frac{\text{Dividends per share}}{\text{Market price per share}}$$

$$\frac{\$2.17}{\$28.00} = 7.75\%$$

5. a The computations are:

$$\text{Return on total assets} = \frac{\text{Net income} + \left[\text{Interest expense} \times (1\text{-Tax rate}) \right]}{\text{Average total assets}}$$

$$\frac{\$800,000 + \left[\$200,000 \times (1\text{-}0.30) \right]}{\$4,000,000} = 23.5\%$$

Chapter 17

6. d   The computations are:

$$\text{Return on common stockholers' equity} = \frac{\text{Net income} - \text{Preferred dividends}}{\text{Average common stockholders' equity}}$$

$$= \frac{\$600,000 - \$200,000}{\$5,000,000} = 8\%$$

7. b   The computations are:

$$\text{Book value per share} = \frac{\text{Common stockholders' equity}}{\text{Number of common shares outstanding}}$$

$$= \frac{\$24,000,000}{6,000,000 \text{ shares}} = \$4.00 \text{ per share}$$

8. c   The computations are:

$$\text{Working capital} = \text{Current assets} - \text{Current liabilities}$$
$$= \$6,000 - \$2,000 = \$4,000,000$$

9. a   The computations are:

$$\text{Current ratio} = \frac{\text{Current assets}}{\text{Current liabilities}}$$

$$= \frac{\$6,000,000}{\$2,000,000} = 3.0$$

10. d   The computations are:

$$\text{Acid-test ratio} = \frac{\text{Cash} + \text{Marketable securities} + \text{Current receivables}}{\text{Current liabilities}}$$

$$= \frac{\$1,000,000 + \$1,200,000}{\$2,000,000} = 1.1$$

11. a   The computations are:

$$\text{Accounts receivable turnover} = \frac{\text{Sales on account}}{\text{Average accounts receivable balance}}$$

$$= \frac{\$25,000,000}{\$5,000,000} = 5.0$$

$$\text{Average collection period} = \frac{365 \text{ days}}{\text{Accounts receivable turnover}}$$

$$= \frac{365 \text{ days}}{5.0} = 73 \text{ days}$$

12. c   The computations are:

$$\text{Inventory turnover} = \frac{\text{Cost of goods sold}}{\text{Average inventory balance}}$$

$$= \frac{\$750,000}{\$300,000} = 2.5$$

$$\text{Average sale period} = \frac{365 \text{ days}}{\text{Inventory turnover}}$$

$$= \frac{365 \text{ days}}{2.5} = 146 \text{ days}$$

13. d   The computations are:

$$\text{Times interest earned} = \frac{\text{Earnings before interest expense and income taxes}}{\text{Interest expense}}$$

$$= \frac{\$42,000 + \$6,000}{\$6,000} = 8.0$$

14. c   The computations are:

$$\text{Debt-to-equity ratio} = \frac{\text{Total liabilities}}{\text{Stockholders' equity}}$$

$$= \frac{\$320,000}{\$400,000} = 0.8$$

15. a   The acid-test ratio will always be less than the current ratio because it contains fewer assets in the numerator but the same amount of liabilities in the denominator.

Exercises

17-1.

a. $\text{Current ratio} = \dfrac{\text{Current assets}}{\text{Current liabilities}} = \dfrac{\$8,000+\$36,000+\$40,000+\$2,000}{\$40,000} = 2.15$

b. $\dfrac{\text{Acid-test}}{\text{ratio}} = \dfrac{\text{Cash + Marketable securities} + \text{Current receivables}}{\text{Current liabilities}} = \dfrac{\$8,000+\$36,000}{\$40,000} = 1.10$

c. $\dfrac{\text{Debt-to-equity}}{\text{ratio}} = \dfrac{\text{Total liabilities}}{\text{Stockholders' equity}} = \dfrac{\$40,000+\$60,000}{\$50,000+\$30,000+\$120,000} = 0.50$

d. $\dfrac{\text{Accounts receivable}}{\text{turnover}} = \dfrac{\text{Sales on account}}{\text{Average accounts receivable balance}} = \dfrac{\$450,000}{(\$36,000+\$34,000)/2} = 12.9 \text{ (rounded)}$

$\dfrac{\text{Average collection}}{\text{period}} = \dfrac{365 \text{ days}}{\text{Accounts receivable turnover}} = \dfrac{365 \text{ days}}{12.9} = 28 \text{ days (rounded)}$

e. $\dfrac{\text{Inventory}}{\text{turnover}} = \dfrac{\text{Cost of goods sold}}{\text{Average inventory balance}} = \dfrac{\$270,000}{(\$40,000+\$32,000)/2} = 7.5$

f. $\dfrac{\text{Times interest}}{\text{earned}} = \dfrac{\text{Earnings before interest expense and income taxes}}{\text{Interest expense}} = \dfrac{\$51,000}{\$6,000} = 8.5$

g. $\dfrac{\text{Return on}}{\text{total assets}} = \dfrac{\text{Net income} + \left[\begin{array}{c}\text{Interest expense} \times \\ (1\text{-Tax rate})\end{array}\right]}{\text{Average total assets}} = \dfrac{\$31,500+\left[\begin{array}{c}\$6,000 \times \\ (1\text{-}0.30)\end{array}\right]}{(\$300,000+\$250,000)/2} = 13.0\% \text{ (rounded)}$

h.

	End of Year	Beginning of Year
Total stockholders' equity	$200,000	$180,000
Less preferred stock	50,000	50,000
Common stockholders' equity	$150,000	$130,000

$\dfrac{\text{Return on common}}{\text{stockholers' equity}} = \dfrac{\text{Net income} - \text{Preferred dividends}}{\text{Average common stockholders' equity}} = \dfrac{\$31,500\text{-}\$4,000}{(\$150,000+\$130,000)/2} = 19.6\% \text{ (rounded)}$

i. Financial leverage is positive, since the return on the common stockholders' equity is greater than the return on total assets.

17-2.

	Year 5	Year 4	Year 3	Year 2	Year 1
Sales	140%	135%	130%	115%	100%
Accounts receivable	180%	150%	130%	115%	100%

Sales grew by about 15% per year through Year 3, and then dropped off to about a 5% growth rate for the next two years. The accounts receivable grew at about a 15% rate through Year 3, but then rather than dropping off to about a 5% rate, the accounts receivable grew at an even faster rate through Year 5. This suggests that the company may be granting credit too liberally and is having difficulty collecting.

17-3.

a.

ELDREDGE COMPANY
Common-Size Comparative Income Statements
For the Years Ended December 31

	This Year	Last Year
Sales	100.0	100.0
Cost of goods sold	70.0	66.2
Gross margin	30.0	33.8
Operating expenses:		
Selling expenses	14.5	14.5
Administrative expenses	7.8	10.2
Total operating expenses	22.3	24.7
Net operating income	7.7	9.1
Interest expense	0.2	0.3
Net income before taxes	7.5	8.8
Income taxes	2.2	2.6
Net Income	5.3	6.2

b. Cost of goods sold and administrative expenses were the two primary areas affecting the percentage decrease in net income. Cost of goods sold increased from 66.2% of sales in to 70.0% of sales—an increase of 3.8 percentage points. On the other hand, administrative expenses dropped from 10.2% of sales to only 7.8% of sales—a decrease of 2.4 percentage points. The net effect was a decrease in net income as a percentage of sales, which fell from 6.2% of sales to only 5.3% of sales. The increase in the cost of goods sold as a percentage of sales is puzzling since sales increased. Ordinarily, cost of goods sold as a percentage of sales should decrease as sales increase because fixed production costs are spread across more units.

Appendix A

Pricing Products and Services

Study Suggestions

This appendix covers three approaches to pricing—the economists' approach, the absorption costing approach, and target costing. You should memorize the five highlighted equations in the text. These equations describe how these pricing rules work.

APPENDIX HIGHLIGHTS

A. Some companies have little control over the prices they charge, whereas others have significant latitude in their pricing.

    1. Small companies in highly competitive industries that produce standard products typically have little control over the prices they charge. For example, prices for agricultural commodities like corn, wheat, and soybeans are set by the interplay of worldwide supply and demand. Individual farmers have no control over the prices of these commodities.

    2. A company that sells a product that is different from the products offered by other companies or that supplies a big chunk of the market typically has some control over its price.

B. *Cost-plus pricing* is the most common approach to setting prices. Under this approach, a markup is added to a cost base to arrive at the selling price. The formula is:

$$\text{Selling price} = \text{Cost} + (\text{Markup\%} \times \text{Cost})$$

What is the cost base? How is the markup percentage determined?

    1. In *the economists' approach*, the cost base is variable cost and the markup percentage is determined by how sensitive unit sales are to changes in price.

    2. In the *absorption costing approach*, the cost base is the product's absorption costing unit product cost and the markup percentage is a function of a number of factors.

C. The economists' approach recognizes that pricing involves a delicate trade-off. The higher the price, the higher the revenue per unit sold, but the lower the number of units sold. The markup over cost should depend on how sensitive customers are to price. If customers are not particularly sensitive to price, the markup can be high. If they are very sensitive to price, the markup over cost should be low.

    1. The *price elasticity of demand*, ε_d, measures the sensitivity of unit sales to a change in price. The formula in the text for price elasticity is:

$$\varepsilon_d = \frac{\ln(1 + \% \text{ change in quantity sold})}{\ln(1 + \% \text{ change in price})}$$

    a. The natural log, $\ln()$, can be computed using the LN or ln$x$ key on your calculator.

    b. For example, suppose that a 5% increase in price would result in an 8% drop in unit sales.

$$\varepsilon_d = \frac{\ln(1 + (-0.08))}{\ln(1 + (+0.05))} = \frac{\ln(0.92)}{\ln(1.05)} = \frac{-0.08338}{0.04879} = -1.71$$

    c. The price elasticity of demand is negative and less than -1. (The reasons for this are technical.) The greater the absolute value of ε_d, the greater the elasticity of demand. For example, suppose a 5% increase in price results in a 10% drop in unit sales rather than an 8% drop:

$$\varepsilon_d = \frac{\ln(1 + (-0.10))}{\ln(1 + (+0.05))} = \frac{\ln(0.90)}{\ln(1.05)} = \frac{-0.10536}{0.04879} = -2.16$$

    d. As in the above example, when customers are more sensitive to price (i.e., there is a greater reaction to a price change), the absolute value of the price elasticity of demand is greater.

    e. The above formula may be different from the formula you learned if you took an economics class. While the simpler formula found in most introductory economics texts has its uses, it is not of much help in setting prices.

    2. If the price elasticity of demand is constant for a product and the cost of making and selling the product is a combination of variable and fixed costs, the price that would maximize the company's profit is given by the following formula:

$$\text{Profit-maximizing price} = \left(\frac{\varepsilon_d}{1 + \varepsilon_d}\right) \begin{matrix}\text{Variable cost}\\\text{per unit}\end{matrix}$$

    a. Suppose the variable cost per unit is \$1 and the price elasticity of demand is -1.71. The profit-maximizing price is computed as follows:

$$\text{Profit-maximizing price} = \left(\frac{-1.71}{1 + (-1.71)}\right)\$1$$
$$= 2.41 \times \$1 = \$2.41$$

In this case the markup over variable cost is 141%.

    b. Or suppose the variable cost per unit is \$1 and the price elasticity of demand is -2.16. The profit-maximizing price is computed as follows:

$$\text{Profit-maximizing price} = \left(\frac{-2.16}{1 + (-2.16)}\right)\$1$$
$$= 1.86 \times \$1 = \$1.86$$

In this case the markup over variable cost is 86%.

    c. Note that in the case where customers are more sensitive to price (i.e., unit sales drop by 10%

rather than by 8%), the price elasticity of demand is greater and the price and the markup are lower. For example, markups on luxury items are generally higher than on mass-market merchandise because consumers of luxury items are less sensitive to price than other consumers.

     d. The computed profit-maximizing price should be used with caution since it assumes that the price elasticity of demand is constant. It should be interpreted as a signal of the direction the price should move in rather than as a precisely accurate estimate of the price at which profits are maximized.

D. The absorption costing approach to cost-plus pricing attempts to set a price without taking into account consumer demand. In this approach, a product's absorption costing unit product cost is used as the cost base. Selling, general, and administrative (SG&A) expenses are not included in the cost base, but rather are provided for through the markup.

     1. For example, suppose a product's unit product cost is $50 and the markup is 40%:

Unit product cost	$50
Markup—40%	20
Selling price...	$70

     2. The markup percentage may simply be a thumb-rule or it may be computed using the following formula:

$$\text{Markup \% on absorption cost} = \frac{\left(\text{Required ROI} \times \text{Investment}\right) + \text{SG\&A expenses}}{\text{Unit sales} \times \text{Unit product cost}}$$

For example, suppose that the company's required return on investment is 15%; the company has $100,000 invested in the product; selling, general, and administrative expenses associated with the product are $25,000; anticipated unit sales are 10,000 units; and the unit product cost is $20. Then the markup would be computed as follows:

$$\text{Markup \% on absorption cost} = \frac{\left(0.15 \times \$100,000\right) + \$25,000}{10,000 \text{ units} \times \$20 \text{ per unit}} = 20\%$$

     3. *The target ROI will be attained only if the anticipated unit sales volume is attained.* There is absolutely no guarantee that the company will earn its desired profit or even breakeven simply because it uses the absorption costing approach formulas to set prices.

E. Some companies use target costing for new products.

     1. Under the target costing approach, managers estimate how much the new product can be sold for and then deduct the desired profit per unit to arrive at the target cost figure. The formula is:

$$\text{Target cost} = \text{Anticipated selling price} - \text{Desired profit}$$

The product development team is given the responsibility to produce and market the product for no more than this target cost.

     2. The target costing approach is radically different from the traditional cost-plus approach in which the product is first designed, then costs are determined, and then finally the price is computed with a markup based on desired profits. Unfortunately, the traditional cost-plus approach may result in prices that customers are not willing to pay.

REVIEW AND SELF-TEST
Questions and Exercises

True or False

Enter a T or an F in the blank to indicate whether the statement is true or false.

____ 1. The price elasticity of demand measures how sensitive cost is to changes in demand that occur because of changes in prices.

____ 2. If the price elasticity of demand for a product is -2.00 rather than -1.50, then a given percentage price increase will result in a larger percentage decrease in the quantity sold.

____ 3. The more elastic the demand for a product, the higher the markup over variable cost should be.

____ 4. Since the profit-maximizing price does not include any allowance for fixed costs, the price may have to be increased to ensure that the fixed costs are covered.

____ 5. If a company has a 20% desired rate of return on investment, then it should add a 20% markup to its products under the absorption costing approach to cost-plus pricing.

____ 6. Both the markup and the cost base under absorption costing approach to cost-plus pricing depend on the anticipated unit sales. (Assume that all units produced are sold.)

____ 7. The absorption costing approach to cost-plus pricing may not maximize profits, but at least it ensures that the company will not lose any money on a product and will earn its required rate of return.

____ 8. Under target costing, the selling price is first estimated and then a target for the product's cost is established.

Multiple Choice

Choose the best answer or response by placing the identifying letter in the space provided.

____ 1. Every 5% decrease in price leads to a 7% increase in units sold for a particular product. The product's price elasticity of demand is: a) -1.60; b) 1.60; c) -1.32; d) 1.32.

____ 2. What is the profit-maximizing price for a product whose price elasticity of demand is -2.30 and whose unit variable cost is $10? a) $23.00; b) $17.69; c) $13.00; d) $33.00.

____ 3. Lerner, Inc. has provided the following data for one of its products:

Direct materials	$8
Direct labor	$7
Variable manufacturing overhead	$2
Variable SG&A expenses	$3

The company produces and sells 15,000 units of this product each year. Fixed manufacturing overhead cost is $15,000 per year and fixed SG&A expense is $30,000 per year. If the company uses the absorption costing approach to cost-plus pricing and desires a 50% markup, the selling price per unit would be: a) $34.50; b) $31.50; c) $27.00; d) $23.00.

____ 4. Justin Corp. estimates that an investment of $800,000 would be needed to produce and sell 20,000 units of a new product each year. At this level of activity, the unit product cost would be $100. Selling, general, and administrative expenses would be $500,000 per year. If a 25% return on investment is desired, then the markup for the new product under the absorption costing approach to cost-plus pricing would be: a) 35%; b) 25%; c) 62.5%; d) 100%.

____ 5. Vintage RR, Inc. is considering a new line of model railroad engines. To compete effectively, the engines would be priced at $45. The company expects to be able to sell 2,000 engines a year at this price. The company requires a return on investment of 20%. The new product line would require an investment of $150,000. The target cost per engine would be: a) $30; b) $45; c) $15; d) $60.

Exercises

A-1.   Karling Furniture recently raised the selling price of its colonial desk from $495 to $529. As a consequence, unit sales fell from 300 units to 270 units per period.

a.   Estimate the price elasticity of demand of the colonial desk.

% change in price = $\dfrac{\quad-\quad}{\underline{\qquad}}$ = $\underline{\qquad}$

% change in quantity sold = $\dfrac{\quad-\quad}{\underline{\qquad}}$ = $\underline{\qquad}$

$$\varepsilon_d = \frac{\ln(1+\% \text{ change in quantity sold})}{\ln(1+\% \text{ change in price})} = \frac{\ln(1+\underline{\quad})}{\ln(1+\underline{\quad})} = \frac{\ln(\underline{\quad})}{\ln(\underline{\quad})} = \frac{\underline{\quad}}{\underline{\quad}} = \underline{\qquad}$$

b.   If the variable cost of producing and selling the desk is $280, what effect did raising the price of the desk have on the company's net operating income?

c.   Estimate the profit-maximizing price for the desk.

$$\text{Profit-maximizing price} = \left(\frac{\varepsilon_d}{1+\varepsilon_d}\right) \frac{\text{Variable cost}}{\text{per unit}}$$

$$= \left(\frac{\underline{\quad}}{1+(\underline{\quad})}\right)\underline{\quad} = \underline{\quad} \times \underline{\quad} = \underline{\quad}$$

Pricing Appendix

A-2. Costs relating to a product made by Mackey Company are given below:

Direct materials	$10
Direct labor	$12
Variable manufacturing overhead	$1
Fixed manufacturing overhead ($210,000 total)	$7
Variable SG&A expenses	$2
Fixed SG&A expenses ($90,000 total)	$3

Assume that the company uses the absorption costing approach to cost-plus pricing and a 50% markup. Compute the selling price for the above product.

_____ $ _____

_____   _____

_____   _____

_____   _____

Unit product cost ....   _____

Markup—50% ....   _____

Selling price .... $ _____

A-3. Speckart Company's required return on investment is 25%. An investment of $800,000 will be needed to produce and market 30,000 units of a particular product each year. The unit product cost will be $50 at this level of activity, and the SG&A expense will total $400,000 per year. Compute the markup percentage for the product, assuming that the company uses the absorption costing approach to cost-plus pricing.

$$\text{Markup \% on absorption cost} = \frac{\left(\begin{array}{c}\text{Required ROI} \\ \times \text{Investment}\end{array}\right) + \begin{array}{c}\text{SG\&A} \\ \text{expenses}\end{array}}{\text{Unit sales} \times \text{Unit product cost}}$$

$$\text{Markup \% on absorption cost} = \frac{(\underline{\quad} \times \underline{\quad\quad}) + \underline{\quad\quad}}{\underline{\quad\quad} \times \underline{\quad}} = \frac{\underline{\quad\quad\quad}}{\underline{\quad\quad\quad}} = \underline{\quad}\%$$

222

Answers to Questions and Exercises

True or False

1. F The price elasticity of demand has nothing to do with cost.

2. T The larger the absolute value of the price elasticity of demand, the larger the percentage change in units sold for a given percentage change in price.

3. F The opposite is true. The more elastic the demand for a product, the lower the markup over variable cost should be. Elastic demand indicates that customers are very sensitive to price and even a small increase in price will have a large impact on the number of units sold.

4. F If the formula for the profit-maximizing price really provides the price that maximizes the company's profit, increasing the price would result in a decline in the company's profit. If fixed costs are not covered at the profit-maximizing price, the product should be dropped. Raising its price won't help.

5. F The markup is determined in a more complicated manner than simply marking up cost by the desired ROI.

6. T Unit sales appears in the denominator of the formula for the markup. The cost base also depends on the unit sales since the unit product cost under absorption costing is an average cost that depends on the number of units produced.

7. F There is no assurance that the company will break even using the absorption costing approach. If customers do not buy as many units as anticipated, the company may lose money.

8. T Target costing is used to establish allowable costs, not selling prices.

Multiple Choice

1. c

$$\varepsilon_d = \frac{\ln(1+(+0.07))}{\ln(1+(-0.05))} = \frac{\ln(1.07)}{\ln(0.95)} = \frac{0.06766}{-0.05129} = -1.32$$

2. b

$$\text{Profit-maximizing price} = \left(\frac{-2.30}{1+(-2.30)}\right)\$10$$
$$= 1.769 \times \$10$$
$$= \$17.69$$

3. c

Direct materials	$ 8
Direct labor	7
Variable manufacturing overhead	2
Fixed manufacturing overhead ($15,000 ÷ 15,000 units)	1
Unit product cost	18
Markup—50%	9
Selling price	$27

4. a

$$\text{Markup \% on absorption cost} = \frac{(0.25 \times \$800,000) + \$500,000}{20,000 \times \$100}$$
$$= 35\%$$

5. a

Projected sales ($45 × 2,000)	$90,000
Less desired profit (20% × $150,000)	30,000
Target cost for 2,000 units	$60,000

$$\text{Target cost} = \$60,000 \div 2,000 \text{ units}$$
$$= \$30 \text{ per unit}$$

Pricing Appendix

Exercises

A-1. a.

$$\% \text{ change in price} = \frac{\$529\text{-}\$495}{\$495} = +6.87\%$$

$$\% \text{ change in quantity sold} = \frac{270\text{-}300}{300} = -10.00\%$$

$$\varepsilon_d = \frac{\ln(1+\% \text{ change in quantity sold})}{\ln(1+\% \text{ change in price})} = \frac{\ln(1+(-0.1000))}{\ln(1+(+0.0687))} = \frac{\ln(0.9000)}{\ln(1.0687)} = \frac{-0.10536}{0.06644} = -1.59$$

b. The impact of the increase in price on net operating income can be computed as follows:

	Selling Price of $495 300	Selling Price of $529 270
Unit sales		
Sales	$148,500	$142,830
Variable expenses	84,000	75,600
Contribution margin	$ 64,500	$ 67,230

Assuming that the change in price and quantity sold had no effect on fixed costs, the result of increasing the price was an increase in net operating income of $2,730 ($67,230 – $64,500).

c. $$\text{Profit-maximizing price} = \left(\frac{\varepsilon_d}{1+\varepsilon_d}\right)\begin{matrix}\text{Variable cost}\\\text{per unit}\end{matrix} = \left(\frac{-1.59}{1+(-1.59)}\right)\$280 = 2.70 \times \$280 = \$756$$

Since this price is a lot higher than the price that is currently being charged, it would be prudent to raise the price slowly, checking to make sure that profits really do increase after each increase in price.

A-2.

Direct materials	$10
Direct labor	12
Variable manufacturing overhead	1
Fixed manufacturing overhead	7
Unit product cost	30
Markup—50%	15
Selling price	$45

A-3. $$\text{Markup \% on absorption cost} = \frac{(0.25 \times \$800,000) + \$400,000}{30,000 \times \$50} = \frac{\$600,000}{\$1,500,000} = 40\%$$

Appendix B

Profitability Analysis

Study Suggestions

This appendix builds on material in earlier chapters—specifically, the sections on *Segment Reporting and Profitability Analysis* in Chapter 12, *Utilization of a Constrained Resource* in Chapter 13, and *Preference Decisions—The Ranking of Investment Projects* in Chapter 14. Review these sections before reading the Profitability Analysis Appendix. Once you understand the material in those sections, you should have little difficulty mastering the Profitability Analysis Appendix.

APPENDIX HIGHLIGHTS

A. *Absolute versus Relative Profitability.*

    1. A business segment such as a product, customer, sales channel, or store is said to be *absolutely* profitable if eliminating that business segment would, without making any other change, increase the total profit of the overall organization.

    2. Even if all business segments are absolutely profitable, managers may still be interested in determining which are the *most* profitable. A business segment is *relatively* more profitable than another if cutting back on the first segment allows expansion of the second segment, with the consequence that the overall profit of the organization increases. Relative profitability is of concern only when some constraint forces the organization to make trade-offs among segments. In the absence of such a constraint, all segments that are absolutely profitable should be pursued.

B. The absolute profitability of a business segment is assessed by subtracting the incremental (avoidable) costs of the segment from its incremental revenues. See the section *Segment Reporting and Profitability Analysis* in Chapter 12 for more details.

C. The relative profitability of business segments is assessed using the profitability index, which is defined as follows:

$$\text{Profitability index} = \frac{\text{Incremental profit from the segment}}{\text{Amount of the constrained resource required by the segment}}$$

    1. The incremental profit from a segment is the difference between the incremental revenues from the segment and its incremental (avoidable) costs. The incremental profit from a segment is its absolute profitability.

    2. We have encountered the relative profitability concept before in the section *Preference Decisions—The Ranking of Investment Projects* in Chapter 14. In that chapter, the segments were long-term projects, the constraint was the total amount of funds available for investment in the projects, and the incremental profit from the segment (i.e., project) was its net present value:

$$\text{Project profitability index} = \frac{\text{Net present value of the project}}{\text{Investment required by the project}}$$

    3. The profitability index is used to decide how to best use a constrained resource. First identify all of the business segments that require the use of the constrained resource. Compute the profitability index for each of them. Then rank the segments in order of the profitability index. Starting at the top of the list with the most profitable segment, move down the list until all of the constrained resource is consumed. All segments above that point in the list are accepted and all segments below that point in the list are rejected.

D. *Volume trade-off decisions* occur when: (1) a constraint forces volume trade-offs among products—producing more of one product results in producing less of another—and (2) fixed costs are not affected by the decision.

    1. In a volume trade-off decision, the profitability index becomes:

$$\text{Profitability index in a volume trade-off decision} = \frac{\text{Unit contribution margin}}{\text{Amount of the constrained resource required by one unit of the product}}$$

    2. We encountered volume trade-off decisions in the section *Utilization of a Constrained Resource* in Chapter 13.

E. An *opportunity cost* is incurred whenever a constrained resource is used. If a constrained resource is used to produce one product, it cannot be used to produce another. The opportunity cost of making a product is the amount of contribution margin given up by not making the other product.

    1. The *marginal product* is the product whose production would be cut back or expanded if more or less of the constrained resource were available.

    2. The opportunity cost of using the constrained resource is the profitability index of the marginal product. In other words, the opportunity cost of using the constrained resource is the contribution margin per unit of the constrained resource for the product whose volume is cut back.

    3. The price of a new product should cover its variable cost plus any opportunity cost. Its opportunity cost is equal to the profitability index of the marginal product multiplied by the amount of the constrained resource that each unit of the new product would require.

REVIEW AND SELF-TEST
Questions and Exercises

True or False

Enter a T or an F in the blank to indicate whether the statement is true or false.

____ 1. If a company has a constrained resource, then there is no point in determining the absolute profitability of its segments.

____ 2. If one product's absolute profitability is higher than another product's, then it is relatively profitable as well.

____ 3. Relative profitability is determined by dividing a segment's margin, net of fully allocated fixed common costs, by its sales.

____ 4. In a volume trade-off situation, the opportunity cost of using a constrained resource is equal to the profitability index of the marginal product.

____ 5. The price of a new product should cover both its variable cost and its opportunity cost.

____ 6. The opportunity cost of using N units of the constrained resource is equal N times the profitability index of the marginal product.

Multiple Choice

Choose the best answer or response by placing the identifying letter in the space provided.

____ 1. If a segment's incremental revenue is $120,000, its incremental cost is $90,000, and it uses 60 hours of the constrained resource, what is its profitability index? (a) $30,000; (b) $2,000 per hour; (c) $500 per hour; (d) 0.25.

____ 2. If a product's selling price is $25, its variable cost is $16, and it uses 2 ounces of the constrained resource, what is its profitability index in a volume trade-off decision? (a) $9; (b) $4.50 per ounce; (c) $12.50 per ounce; (d) 0.36.

____ 3. Two products at Prime Products Corporation use the constrained resource—a high-cost milling machine. Data concerning those products follow:

	Alpha	Beta
Unit contribution margin	$12	$18
Constrained resource required per unit.......	1 minute	2 minutes
Monthly demand	6,000 units	4,000 units

A total of 10,000 minutes on the milling machine are available next month. In order to maximize the company's profit for the month, how many units of product Beta should be produced? (a) 4,000 units; (b) 2,000 units; (c) 2,800 units; (d) 0 units.

____ 4. Refer to the data in question 3 above. In addition to products Alpha and Beta, Prime Products Corporation is considering introducing a new product, Charlie, whose variable cost would be $10 and that would require 3 minutes on the milling machine. The selling price for this new product should be at least: (a) $37; (b) $10; (c) $19; (d) $27.

Profitability Analysis Appendix

Exercises

B-1.   Advanced Concepts, an advertising agency, is considering a number of potential jobs for the forthcoming month. The constrained resource in the agency is the managing partner's time. During the month, 150 hours of the managing director's time are available to work on jobs. Data concerning the potential jobs appear below:

Segment	Incremental Profit	Amount of Constrained Resource Required
Job 1	$9,575	25 hours
Job 2	$9,854	26 hours
Job 3	$6,528	17 hours
Job 4	$4,392	12 hours
Job 5	$11,594	34 hours
Job 6	$9,870	35 hours
Job 7	$7,704	24 hours
Job 8	$3,895	19 hours
Job 9	$13,500	36 hours
Job 10	$5,772	26 hours

a.   Compute the profitability index for each job.

Segment	Incremental Profit (A)	Amount of Constrained Resource Required (B)	Profitability Index (A) ÷ (B)
Job 1	$9,575	25 hours	$_____ per hour
Job 2	$9,854	26 hours	$_____ per hour
Job 3	$6,528	17 hours	$_____ per hour
Job 4	$4,392	12 hours	$_____ per hour
Job 5	$11,594	34 hours	$_____ per hour
Job 6	$9,870	35 hours	$_____ per hour
Job 7	$7,704	24 hours	$_____ per hour
Job 8	$3,895	19 hours	$_____ per hour
Job 9	$13,500	36 hours	$_____ per hour
Job 10	$5,772	26 hours	$_____ per hour

b.   Sort the jobs according to the profitability index and decide which jobs to accept.

Segment	Profitability Index	Amount of Constrained Resource Required	Cumulative Amount of Constrained Resource Required
Job ____	$_____ per hour	____ hours	_____ hours
Job ____	$_____ per hour	____ hours	_____ hours
Job ____	$_____ per hour	____ hours	_____ hours
Job ____	$_____ per hour	____ hours	_____ hours
Job ____	$_____ per hour	____ hours	_____ hours
Job ____	$_____ per hour	____ hours	_____ hours
Job ____	$_____ per hour	____ hours	_____ hours
Job ____	$_____ per hour	____ hours	_____ hours
Job ____	$_____ per hour	____ hours	_____ hours
Job ____	$_____ per hour	____ hours	_____ hours

c.   Determine the total incremental profit for the jobs that you have accepted.

Segment	Incremental Profit
Job ____	$_____
Job ____	_____
Job ____	_____
Job ____	_____
Job ____	_____
Job ____	_____
Total.............	$_____

B-2. Forward Products Corporation has two products that require the use of the company's bottleneck—a specialized welding machine that is available for 70,000 minutes per year. Data concerning those two products appear below:

	Vrimax	*Kirval*
Selling price	$184.00 per unit	$198.00 per unit
Variable cost	$110.40 per unit	$138.60 per unit
Amount of the constrained resource required...........	8 minutes per unit	6 minutes per unit
Annual demand	7,700 units	2,800 units

a. Is there enough capacity on the bottleneck to satisfy demand?

	Vrimax	*Kirval*	*Total*
Amount of the constrained resource required..	8 minutes per unit	6 minutes per unit	
Annual demand	7,700 units	2,800 units	
Total constrained resource required ...	_____ minutes	_____ minutes	_____ minutes

b. Compute the profitability index for each product to determine which is the more profitable.

	Vrimax	*Kirval*
Selling price	$184.00 per unit	$198.00 per unit
Variable cost	110.40 per unit	138.60 per unit
Unit contribution margin....................	$_____ per unit	$_____ per unit
Amount of the constrained resource required by one unit.........................	8 minutes per unit	6 minutes per unit
Profitability index..............................	$_____ per minute	$_____ per minute

c. How much of each product should be produced?

Total constrained resource available..	70,000
Less constrained resource required to produce _____ units of _____	_____
Remaining constrained resource available...	_____
Less constrained resource required to produce _____ units of _____	_____
Remaining constrained resource available...	_____

d. If you plan above is adopted, what would be the total contribution margin for the year?

	Vrimax	*Kirval*	*Total*
Unit contribution margin...............	_____	_____	
Volume	_____	_____	
Contribution margin......................	_____	_____	_____

Answers to Questions and Exercises

True or False

1. F   If a company has a constrained resource, it is even more important than it would otherwise be to determine if any segments are absolutely unprofitable. Dropping an unprofitable segment would not only avoid an unnecessary loss, it would free up some of the constrained resource to be used elsewhere.

2. F   The relative profitability of two products depends on two factors, not one. In addition to their absolute profitability, relative profitability depends on the amount of the constrained resource each uses.

3. F   A segment's relative profitability is determined by dividing its incremental profit by the amount of the constrained resource it requires.

4. T   Opportunity cost is determined by what is given up by taking an action. In a volume trade-off decision, if the constrained resource is used to produce more of one product, less must be produced of another product.

5. T   If the selling price of a new product does not cover both its variable cost and its opportunity cost, the company would be better off producing more of the marginal product.

6. T   The opportunity cost of using one unit of the constrained resource is equal to the profitability index of the marginal product. The opportunity cost of using N units of the constrained resource is equal to N times the profitability index of the marginal product.

Multiple Choice

1. c

Incremental revenue................	$120,000
Incremental cost......................	90,000
Incremental profit (a).............	$ 30,000
Constrained resource used (b).	60 hours
Profitability index (a) ÷ (b)....	$500 per hour

2. b

Selling price...........................	$25
Variable cost...........................	16
Unit variable cost (a)..............	$ 9
Constrained resource used (b).	2 ounces
Profitability index (a) ÷ (b)....	$4.50 per ounce

3. b   All 6,000 units of Alpha demanded by the market should be produced because it is the more profitable product. (See the computation of the profitability index below.) This would require 6,000 minutes of the milling machine time. The remaining 4,000 minutes should be used to produce 2,000 units of product Beta.

	Alpha	*Beta*
Unit contribution margin......................	$12	$18
Constrained resource required per unit	1 minute	2 minutes
Profitability index	$12 per minute	$9 per minute

4. a   The selling price of the new product should at least cover its variable cost plus opportunity cost. The opportunity cost of using the constrained resource is $9 per minute—the profitability index of the marginal product, Beta, from the previous question. Therefore, the selling price should at least cover the variable cost of $10 plus the opportunity cost of $9 per minute × 3 minutes, or $37.

Exercises

B-1.   a.   The profitability index would be computed as follows:

Segment	Incremental Profit (A)	Amount of Constrained Resource Required (B)	Profitability Index (A) ÷ (B)
Job 1	$9,575	25 hours	$383 per hour
Job 2	$9,854	26 hours	$379 per hour
Job 3	$6,528	17 hours	$384 per hour
Job 4	$4,392	12 hours	$366 per hour
Job 5	$11,594	34 hours	$341 per hour
Job 6	$9,870	35 hours	$282 per hour
Job 7	$7,704	24 hours	$321 per hour
Job 8	$3,895	19 hours	$205 per hour
Job 9	$13,500	36 hours	$375 per hour
Job 10	$5,772	26 hours	$222 per hour

b.   The jobs should be ranked on the basis of the profitability index.

Segment	Profitability Index	Amount of Constrained Resource Required	Cumulative Amount of Constrained Resource Required
Job 3	$384 per hour	17 hours	17 hours
Job 1	$383 per hour	25 hours	42 hours
Job 2	$379 per hour	26 hours	68 hours
Job 9	$375 per hour	36 hours	104 hours
Job 4	$366 per hour	12 hours	116 hours
Job 5	$341 per hour	34 hours	150 hours
Job 7	$321 per hour	24 hours	174 hours
Job 6	$282 per hour	35 hours	209 hours
Job 10	$222 per hour	26 hours	235 hours
Job 8	$205 per hour	19 hours	254 hours

The jobs that would generate the most profit for the 150 available hours are Job 3, Job 1, Job 2, Job 9, Job 4, and Job 5.

c.   The total incremental profit from the accepted jobs would be $55,443.

Segment	Incremental Profit
Job 3	$ 6,528
Job 1	9,575
Job 2	9,854
Job 9	13,500
Job 4	4,392
Job 5	11,594
Total	$55,443

B-2.   a.   The total amount of the constrained resource needed to meet annual demand is computed as follows:

	Vrimax	*Kirval*	*Total*
Amount of the constrained resource required (a)	8 minutes per unit	6 minutes per unit	
Annual demand (b).............................	7,700 units	2,800 units	
Total constrained resource required (a) × (b)	61,600 minutes	16,800 minutes	78,400 minutes

Since only 70,000 minutes are available, the company will be unable to meet demand.

b.   The products should be ranked on the basis of the profitability index.

	Vrimax	*Kirval*
Selling price	$184.00 per unit	$198.00 per unit
Variable cost	110.40 per unit	138.60 per unit
Unit contribution margin (a)...............	$ 73.60 per unit	$ 59.40 per unit
Amount of the constrained resource required by one unit (b)	8 minutes per unit	6 minutes per unit
Profitability index (a) ÷ (b)	$9.20 per minute	$9.90 per minute

Kirval is more profitable than Vrimax.

c.   The optimal plan would be to produce all 2,800 units of Kirval demanded by the market and use any remaining minutes on the constrained resource to produce Vrimax.

Total constrained resource available...	70,000
Less constrained resource required to produce 2,800 units of Kirval.........	16,800
Remaining constrained resource available..	53,200
Less constrained resource required by 6,650 units of Vrimax	53,200
Remaining constrained resource available..	0

d.   By following the above plan, the company would have a total contribution margin of $655,760.

	Vrimax	*Kirval*	*Total*
Unit contribution margin (a)	$73.60	$59.40	
Volume (b).....................................	6,650	2,800	
Contribution margin (a) × (b)	$489,440	$166,320	$655,760